Tim Williams
(207) 737-2298 Foriegn
Relations/

Politics

TAMING
AMERICAN
POWER

TAMING AMERICAN POWER

The Global Response
to U.S. Primacy

STEPHEN M. WALT

HARVARD UNIVERSITY

W. W. NORTON & COMPANY   NEW YORK · LONDON

Excerpts from Stephen M. Walt, "Keeping the World 'Off Balance': Self Restraint and U.S. Foreign Policy" in *America Unrivaled: The Future of the Balance of Power*, edited by John G. Ikenberry, used by permission of the publisher, Cornell University Press. Copyright © 2002 by Cornell University.

Manufacturing by The Courier Companies, Inc.
Book design by Chris Welch
Production manager: Amanda Morrison

Library of Congress Cataloging-in-Publication Data

Walt, Stephen M., 1955–
Taming American power : the global response to U.S. primacy /
Stephen M. Walt.— 1st ed.
p. cm.
Includes bibliographical references and index.
ISBN 0-393-05203-6 (hardcover)
1. United States—Foreign relations—2001– 2. Balance of power. 3. International
relations. 4. World politics—21st century. I. Title.
JZ1480.W35 2005
327.73—dc22

2005011136

W. W. Norton & Company, Inc., 500 Fifth Avenue, New York, N.Y. 10110
www.wwnorton.com

W. W. Norton & Company Ltd., Castle House, 75/76 Wells Street, London W1T 3QT

1 2 3 4 5 6 7 8 9 0

For Gabriel and Katherine

CONTENTS

I dread our own power and our own ambition; I dread our being too much dreaded. . . . We may say that we shall not abuse this astonishing and hitherto unheard-of power. But every other nation will think we shall abuse it. It is impossible but that, sooner or later, this state of things must produce a combination against us which may end in our ruin.

—Edmund Burke

PREFACE

Describing the United States as the mightiest state since Rome has become a cliché, but like most clichés, it also captures an essential feature of reality. The United States enjoys a position of power unseen for centuries, and citizens around the world are intensely aware of that fact. For Americans, this dominant position is both a source of pride and an opportunity: it gives the United States a large margin of security and some capacity to mold the world according to U.S. interests and values. Within the United States, therefore, the debate about U.S. primacy is mostly about the best way to use its vast power.

By contrast, the rest of the world sees U.S. primacy as increasingly troubling. Not only is our position a direct threat to states whose interests and values clash with ours, but even our fellow-democracies now worry about the concentration of power in Washington's hands. Over the past several years, they have also become increasingly alarmed by the ways that U.S. leaders have chosen to use that power. While Americans debate how they should use their power, the rest of the world is preoccupied with what it can do to *tame* American power. Some states want to contain or reduce it, others seek to harness and exploit it, but American power is a feature of the international landscape that no state can easily ignore.

This book examines the global response to U.S. primacy. It explores the different ways that the United States has used its power and explains why the rest of the world fears, resents, and sometimes hates America's current global role. It describes the different strategies that states have devised for dealing with American power and argues that these strategies are often surprisingly effective. The United States may be far stronger than any other country—or even any likely coalition of rival powers—but other states have many ways to thwart, harass, undermine, deter, annoy, and generally interfere with U.S. efforts to promote its own interests.

Any attempt to devise an effective foreign policy for the United States must take into account the strategies of both friends and foes. Once we understand how other states are trying to tame American power, it becomes easier to devise a foreign policy that will minimize opposition and maximize global support. In particular, the global response to U.S. primacy suggests that the United States should return to a more restrained policy of "offshore balancing" and devote more attention to persuading others that its policies are legitimate and broadly beneficial.

Though great power like ours can be isolating, the United States cannot and should not withdraw from active engagement in world affairs. To reap the full benefits of its position of primacy, and to avoid repeating the horrors of the past hundred years, the United States must learn to conduct its foreign policy with greater wisdom and restraint. This book explains why these adjustments are necessary and outlines what a more mature foreign policy would be.

Stephen M. Walt
Cambridge, Massachusetts

THE PROBLEM OF
AMERICAN POWER

What should the United States do with its power? U.S. leaders have wrestled with this question since the founding of the country, and especially since America's rise to Great Power status.[1] At times, the answer has seemed obvious—for example, "containing" the Soviet Union was the clear objective during the Cold War—but periods of transition have invariably produced broader debates about the purposes to which U.S. power should be put. The debate over America's role in the world began anew when the Soviet Union collapsed and the United States stood alone at the pinnacle of world power, and a host of pundits, scholars, and former policymakers quickly began to offer advice on what the United States should do with this unprecedented opportunity.[2]

Should America seize this "unipolar moment" to export the ideals of freedom and democracy, use its economic and military power to deny dictators access to weapons of mass destruction, and take active measures to prevent the emergence of a future "peer competitor?"[3] Should the United States strive for global hegemony or should it be content to lead a multilateral coalition of stable or aspiring democracies?[4] Should U.S. leaders concentrate on building more robust international institutions, strengthening the authority of international law, helping relieve global poverty, and preventing gross violations of human rights?[5] Does it still make sense for the United States to keep large military forces deployed around the world in order to dampen regional competition and keep the danger of major war at a minimum?[6] Or could the United States return to its earlier position as an "offshore balancer," ready to deploy its power if its vital interests were threatened but no longer maintaining a large overseas military presence?[7]

These are all important questions, and it is hardly surprising that Americans have been actively debating the strategic options that now lie before them. Consensus has proven elusive, however, because the range of options is quite broad and because there has been no single threat or target to concentrate the national mind. Even the terrorist attacks on September 11, 2001, did not produce unanimity; although there was broad agreement on the importance of going after al Qaeda, the 2004 presidential campaign showed there is still no national consensus on how terrorism should be fought, or how the United States should use its unmatched power to advance either its own interests or the broader welfare of humankind. No one can deny the importance of American power, but how it will be used in the future remains contested.

But what does one do *about* American power? That is the question the rest of the world has faced, and never more acutely than in the past decade. With so much power concentrated in the hands of one state—a state whose citizens have long seen themselves as uniquely virtuous and destined to lead the rest of the world—how should other states respond? Is U.S. primacy a source of global stability and an opportunity to extend universal values of freedom, democracy, and human rights? Will primacy facilitate the expansion of global markets and a corresponding increase in global wealth and welfare? Or is America's dominant position something that other states should resist, so that their own interests are not disregarded or trampled upon by the overwhelming power of the United States?

Imagine, for a moment, that you are president of France. You are the leader of a proud nation that was once the strongest country in the world, and that has been an important cultural force for over four centuries. The ideological roots of French democracy are similar—but not identical—to those of the United States, and your citizens find some aspects of American society troubling. American foreign policy often strikes you as naïve and overweening, and your vision of the ideal world order—a vision you share with most of your predecessors—is one where no single state enjoys a dominant position.[8] What, then, do you do about the United States?

Suppose, instead, that you were prime minister of India. You govern the world's most populous democracy, but your country's relationship with the United States has often been prickly. India is the most powerful state in South Asia, but relations with neighboring Pakistan remain bitter and potentially explosive—especially now that both states have nuclear weapons—and you face a number of other security problems both inside your country and in the surrounding region. The rising power of China threatens to leave India in a position of permanent inferiority, yet America's current predominance—and its ability to act unilaterally when it wishes—is also disquieting. Is there some way to take advantage of this situation in order to advance India's national interests?

What if you were President Vladimir Putin of Russia? You have inherited the shattered core of the former Soviet Union, and thus occupy the unenviable position of leading a society that the United States defeated during the long Cold War. Russians may be better off with competitive markets and some semblance of a democratic system, but they have paid a large price to get there, and it is humiliating to be in this position after decades as one of the world's two superpowers. Russia still retains remnants of its role as a superpower—such as an aging nuclear arsenal—but it is a pale shadow of the former Soviet empire and no match for the United States. So how do you keep the United States from imposing its will—as it did when it helped Germany reunify and incorporated your former allies into NATO—and how do you improve your own position in a world dominated by the looming shadow of American power?

Or imagine being Tony Blair, or one of his successors. Britain no longer has an empire, but history, culture, and the assiduous deference of every prime minister since Winston Churchill has given you a "special relationship" with the American colossus. So how can you use American power to magnify your own position on the world stage, and to help you accomplish your own foreign-policy goals?

Consider a more daunting challenge. Suppose you were Kim Jong Il of North Korea. You are the unchallenged leader of one of the world's oddest countries, an ideological relic trapped in totalitarian poverty. Your country's entire gross national product is less than 4 percent of the sum that the United States spends on its military alone, and your population faces recurrent fuel shortages and the possibility of famine every year. Your own armed forces are technologically backward and no longer a match for the forces of your more success-ful cousins to the south. Bill Clinton called you a "rogue state," George W. Bush said you were part of an "axis of evil," and even your longtime allies in the People's Republic of China are increas-ingly ambivalent. Given the vast gulf between the power that you control and the capabilities that any U.S. president can wield, what can you possibly do to stay in power, maintain some freedom of action, and perhaps even improve your position?

Or what if you were Ariel Sharon? More than fifty years have passed since the founding of the state of Israel. Aided by the energy and determination of Israel's citizens, and by large amounts of eco-nomic and military aid from the United States, Israel has defeated its various neighbors in a series of wars, expanded the territory under its control, and is now the dominant military power in the region. Yet these successes have not brought tranquility, because you still face the stubborn resistance of three million Palestinian Arabs living either in Israel proper or in the occupied territories of the West Bank and

Gaza. Israel has signed peace treaties with Egypt and Jordan, but relations remain frosty at best. Despite its many achievements, Israel remains dependent on U.S. largesse and diplomatic protection. During the Cold War, this support could be justified by the claim that Israel was a "strategic asset." But the Cold War is over, and critics now argue that Israel's policies are a growing liability in the effort to defeat al Qaeda. Under these difficult circumstances, how do you ensure that the United States remains firmly on your side?

How do you deal with American power? As all of these examples illustrate, that question is a—if not the—central issue for leaders in every corner of the globe. The problem of U.S. power is not the only challenge they face, but it is an issue they cannot ignore. Given the vast concentration of power in American hands, what U.S. leaders decide to do—and what they choose not to do—will inevitably have far-reaching effects on the fates of other leaders and other societies. Whether they like it or not, developing a strategy for dealing with American power has become an essential element of statecraft for every country in the world.

The question is one that Americans should care about as well. When a handful of foreign terrorists can kill nearly three thousand Americans on a sunny September morning, it is hard to argue that we need not worry about how other people are reacting to U.S. power. Although the United States enjoys a position of primacy that is unique in modern history, it nonetheless shares the planet with nearly two hundred other states. What these other states (and, in some cases, nonstate actors) do will inevitably affect America's ability to achieve its own foreign-policy goals. The United States cannot negotiate new trade agreements to boost the U.S. economy without cooperation from others. It cannot halt the spread of nuclear technology or control the dissemination of loose nuclear material without active and sustained support from many other countries. It cannot go to war without access to foreign military facilities—access that other countries can always withhold—and its military actions will not receive the mantle of legitimacy unless other states, and especially the current members of the United Nations Security Council, give their approval. And if it does go to war on its own (or with largely symbolic "coalitions of the willing"), then U.S. soldiers will do most of the fighting and dying and U.S. taxpayers will have to foot the bill. Even an unrivaled superpower like the United States cannot defeat the shadowy forces of global terrorism without active, enthusiastic, 24/7 cooperation from foreign intelligence services and law enforcement agencies. U.S. primacy gives it many advantages, but what others do will still determine whether U.S. foreign policy succeeds or fails.

In short, if others agree with U.S. goals and endorse the means it has chosen to pursue them, then success is more likely and will require less effort. On the other hand, if other states oppose U.S. goals or are simply concerned about keeping American power in check, then U.S. leaders will find it harder to accomplish even worthy objectives. The more we know about the ways that others view U.S. power, and the more we understand about the strategies they are using to deal with it, the better equipped we will be to fashion a foreign policy that will maximize global support and minimize opposition.

That is the central task of this book: to explore the global response to American power. The central question is not "What should the United States do with its power?"; it is "What can other states do *about* U.S. power?" As we shall see, their responses are not always negative. Many states see U.S. power as a positive force in the world and are primarily interested in ensuring that it is used in ways that advance their own particular interests. Nonetheless, even close U.S. allies sometimes worry about the legitimacy, moral acceptability, and wisdom of U.S. policy, and they have tried to develop ways to minimize its negative consequences. At the same time, other states have more serious objections to America's position in the world and the policies it pursues, and they employ a variety of strategies to thwart U.S. aims and to further their own interests in the face of American power.

How to Think about U.S. Primacy

In writing this book, my aim is to explain why other states are uncomfortable with U.S. primacy and to describe how they are responding to it. I have not sought to construct a single theory to explain the various responses, and I have resisted the temptation to shoehorn the behavior of other states into a single theoretical tradition. Instead, I have borrowed freely from the existing theoretical approaches to international politics (including some of my own work), but in a deliberately eclectic fashion. From the realist tradition, I take the basic insight that states in anarchy are acutely sensitive to the balance of power and generally uncomfortable whenever one state—no matter how virtuous or benevolent—becomes significantly stronger than the others.[9] From liberalism, I take the notion that different social groups within states may exert independent influences on foreign policy, and that foreign powers may consciously try to manipulate another state's internal politics in order to influence its international conduct.[10] From the "constructivist" approach to world politics, I borrow the important idea that states respond not just to the physical power that the United States possesses, and not just to the policies that the United States pursues, but also to the ways that U.S. power is described and understood, and the meanings that are attached to its use.[11] It matters, in other words, if prevailing global discourse portrays the United States as a "benevolent hegemon," an "indispensable power," a "rogue superpower," or a "unilateralist empire." Similarly, is U.S. power being used in a manner that is consistent with a widely shared body of norms and collective understandings, or is it simply a case of "the strong doing what they can"?

I have also plundered other bodies of scholarship in search of additional ideas. Within the field of international relations, for example, there is a small but useful literature on "weak states" that analyzes the strategies of minor powers in a world dominated by Great Powers.[12] Within sociology and anthropology, there are a number of prominent works analyzing the different strategies found in highly skewed social orders (e.g., prisons, concentration camps, slave societies, feudal orders, etc.), where the stronger actors have seemingly total control over the weaker parties.[13] Although these works were neither inspired by nor directed at problems of international politics, they offer intriguing hints about the strategies that weaker states may adopt when a single country stands alone at the pinnacle of world power.

In a prison, concentration camp, slave plantation, or feudal estate, for example, the governing authorities have nearly absolute control over the weaker parties. There is no question who is stronger, even though the weaker members are often far more numerous, and their condition of material weakness is usually reinforced by an ideology justifying sharp status distinctions (e.g., slaves or peasants are routinely portrayed as innately inferior and thus deserving of their condition). The dominant group enjoys enormous autonomy and can usually force the weaker parties to do whatever they want. When the supporting ideology is fully embraced, moreover, the weaker parties may regard this situation as appropriate and just.

Yet total control is rarely possible, even when power is highly concentrated. Wardens and prison guards cannot monitor every single action that the inmates might take; they must therefore choose which infractions to watch for and which to let slip. They can establish a system of rewards and punishments to deter violations, but prisoners invariably find ways to evade the rules, and it is rarely worth the effort to try to root out every possible violation. Indeed, as the workings of any black market reveal, the more restrictions you impose, the greater the potential rewards for successfully evading them. Inmates are never wholly without resources, and they can bargain for additional privileges by agreeing to do other things for the people in charge.[14] In short, even when one group has a near-monopoly on power, the weaker parties can still find ways to get some of what they want and to resist the order that the authorities are trying to impose.

In the same way, factory workers can resist pressure from above by shirking, by "dragging their feet," or by adopting "work-to-rule" tactics.[15] Foremen and supervisors are often forced to acquiesce in the face of these strategies, because they need to keep the plant running efficiently in order to keep their own positions. Weaker parties can also use the ruling group's own moral principles and legitimating ideology to constrain the ruler's power. For example, if a feudal lord's status as a member of the "nobility" is justified in part by his alleged moral superiority (as implied by his assuming responsibility for the welfare of his tenants), then tenants can invoke that principle in order to obtain better treatment. Their demands can be ignored or denied, of course, but an aristocrat whose position rests in part on the principle of *noblesse oblige* could not ignore such requests completely.[16]

The same logic appears in more "normal" social settings, such as a typical nuclear family. Parents are physically stronger than their younger children, and they control the available financial resources. Yet even the harshest parent never gets complete and instant obedience. A child can refuse to go to bed and, once put there by force, can resist going to sleep. Even a toddler can usually find many ways to limit the effective authority of his or her parents, in order to do less of what the parents want and more of what the child wants. They can cry, stall, do something amusing, or merely wait until the parent's attention is diverted. Parents frequently succumb to these tactics, especially when seated in a public waiting room or when dinner guests are arriving downstairs. They are still far stronger in some absolute sense, but it is often more effective to give in a little, instead of using the full power at one's disposal, especially when using it could easily make things worse.

But what does this have to do with world politics? I do not mean to suggest that the United States is a "slaveholder on a global scale" or the international equivalent of a feudal lord or prison warden. (There may be some writers and political activists who endorse such a view, but I am not one of them.) Nor is the United States the "parent" and the rest of the world its "children." Analogies between these situations where power is asymmetrically distributed and the current condition of U.S. primacy are admittedly imperfect and must therefore be used with caution. True hierarchical orders rest on asymmetries of power and powerful legitimating ideologies, and most of them are enforced by the authority of the state and its own monopoly on legitimate violence. In world politics, by contrast, all sovereign states are of equal formal status (even though the power they control varies enormously), and no country can make a binding and legitimate claim to formal authority over other countries. Indeed, the doctrine of national self-determination argues exactly the opposite: no country—no matter how powerful—is legitimately authorized to give binding orders to another government, save in specific sets of circumstances that are defined and regulated by international law.[17] States do make demands on one another, of course, but whether the demands are met is determined largely by the balance of power and interest and not on the basis of formal obligation.

These caveats notwithstanding, the literature on highly skewed social orders encourages us to think more broadly about how the power of the United States appears to others. It also directs our attention to the different and often subtle strategies that weaker states can employ to constrain, manipulate, resist, exploit, evade, undermine, and in general deal with the reality of U.S. power.

Is it possible to stand up to the United States? Can weaker states balance U.S. power by joining forces with others—as traditional balance-of-power theory would predict—or is America too far ahead to be checked? Can they mobilize their own resources in ways that will make it too expensive for the United States to press them? Or can they "just say no," in the hope that the United States will not retaliate? Can weak states extract concessions by threatening to pursue some action that the United States opposes but cannot easily prevent? When will such tactics work? Is it possible to bind U.S. power within existing international institutions—and if so, when and how? Can other states mobilize broader global resistance by casting doubt on the legitimacy of U.S. leadership and the moral character of U.S. policy?

Will other states choose to align with the American colossus, so as to avoid facing its "focused enmity"?[18] If a state does align with the United States, can its leaders establish strong personal bonds with their American counterparts, and thereby gain benefits or concessions that are not available to others? Can other states manipulate U.S. domestic politics in order to ensure that U.S. power is used to their benefit?

In the chapters that follow, I show that the answer to each of these questions is "yes." Although the United States is far and away the most powerful country in the world—and arguably the most powerful country in modern history—other states have many options for dealing with U.S. power. Most of these strategies do not seek to alter the global balance of power (at least not anytime soon), and they do not threaten the U.S. homeland directly. But they do affect America's ability to achieve its foreign-policy goals, and thus its ability to fashion a more desirable world.

THE REMAINDER OF the book is organized as follows. Chapter 1 describes the dominant global position of the United States and summarizes the various ways that the United States has used its power since the end of the Cold War. I argue that the United States is in a position of power that is historically unprecedented, and that it has used its power to mold a world that would be compatible with U.S. interests and values. The United States has not acted as a "status quo" power: rather, it has used its position of primacy to increase its influence, to enhance its position vis-à-vis potential rivals, and to deal with specific security threats.

Chapter 2 explores the broad gap between America's perception of its own global role and the ways that role is perceived abroad, focusing primarily on the reasons why other states do not always welcome U.S. dominance. Although Americans tend to see the U.S. role in the world in positive and benevolent terms, citizens elsewhere are far more skeptical. Even states that are generally pro-American worry about the concentration of power in U.S. hands, and other states openly oppose it. I argue that other states fear, resent, or hate the United States partly because of "what it is" (i.e., the world's most powerful country), but also because of what it has done in the past and is doing today. I then consider why Americans often fail to recognize the roots of this resentment, and thus fail to understand why the global reaction to U.S. primacy has ranged from ambivalence to resentment to overt opposition.

Chapter 3 considers the various strategies that states can employ if they find it necessary or desirable to oppose U.S. primacy. One option is *balancing*, either by mobilizing internal resources or by allying with others. I explain why efforts to form balancing coalitions have been quite modest, and why states have tended to engage either in "soft balancing" (with others) or internal balancing (on their own), the latter option being pursued largely through various *asymmetric strategies*, including conventional military responses, terrorism, or the acquisition of weapons of mass destruction (WMD).

A second strategy is *balking*, whereby other states either ignore U.S. requests or do the bare minimum to carry them out, thereby hindering U.S. efforts while attempting to avoid an overt clash. Third, states may pursue the strategy of *binding*, which is the use of norms and institutions to constrain U.S. freedom of action. I argue that this tactic will not work on core issues of military security, both because the United States can act independently in many military situations and because it can usually attract enough international support to make military action possible. Binding is a more effective tactic in other areas—such as international economic affairs—however, because the U.S. advantage is not as pronounced and it has less capacity to "go it alone." States can also gain concessions through *blackmail* (i.e., threatening to take some undesirable action unless the United States offers compensation), and I explore the conditions in which this strategy is likely to work. Finally, states (and some non-state actors) can also try to challenge the legitimacy of America's global position and the policies that the United States is currently pursuing. The strategy of *delegitimation* seeks to portray the United States as a morally bankrupt society whose actions abroad are generally selfish, capricious, cruel to others, and not in the best interests of mankind. By encouraging more and more people to question America's global leadership, this strategy seeks to make it harder for the United States to win support, while simultaneously encouraging self-doubt among Americans themselves.

Chapter 4 examines the various strategies that states may follow if they choose to accommodate U.S. power and to cooperate with U.S. foreign policy. One strategy is to *bandwagon* with the United States in order to avoid being pressured or attacked, and I argue that this response has been and will continue to be rare. States may behave prudently in the face of U.S. power, but "winning through intimidation" is not going to work very often. Instead, states that align with the United States will do so either to gain protection against regional rivals (*regional balancing)* or to enhance their own global position by gaining influence in Washington. Foreign leaders may also try a strategy of *bonding*—in effect trying to form close personal ties with U.S. officials and lending their support to specific U.S. policies—in the hopes of gaining additional influence over what the United States does. Foreign governments may also try to manipulate the U.S. domestic political system directly, by *penetrating* the American body politic and giving individual politicians strong incentives to favor closer ties. To show how a strategy of penetration works, I focus in detail on the operations of the Israel lobby, which is far and away the most successful example of a country using the U.S. political system to gain influence over U.S. foreign policy. I also offer briefer studies of the Indian and Armenian lobbies, which show that the Israeli example is far from unique.

The final chapter describes what the United States should do in response. If other states have many options for dealing with U.S. power, then U.S. foreign policy must be molded with their reactions in mind. How can the United States encourage states to see its dominant position as beneficial (or at least bearable), and how can it convince them that its foreign-policy actions deserve broad international support? How can it ensure that it is not exploited by countries that appear to embrace U.S. values and goals but are also trying to manipulate U.S. power for their own purposes and may themselves behave in ways that are contrary to U.S. interests and values? How can the United States make its global position more legitimate in the eyes of others? In brief, I argue that America's current position requires greater knowledge, wisdom, and self-restraint than ever before, and that achieving this level of wisdom will require fundamental changes in the ways Americans approach the world.

This is the true paradox of American primacy: Instead of enabling the United States to act however it wishes, America's dominant position encourages other states to fear our unchecked power and look for ways to constrain it. If we want the rest of the world to welcome U.S. primacy, therefore, we must convince them that American power is not something to be tamed, but rather something that will be used judiciously and for the broader benefit of mankind.

TAMING
AMERICAN
POWER

CHAPTER 1

THE FOREIGN POLICY OF AMERICAN PRIMACY

What a difference two decades can make. In 1980, America was obsessed with its rivalry with the Soviet Union and brought cold-warrior Ronald Reagan to Washington to make sure it didn't fall dangerously behind its communist adversary. Ten years later, with the Soviet Union imploding, the United States found itself without a Great Power rival but quickly began to worry about Japan's seemingly unstoppable economic momentum. These fears evaporated when the Japanese bubble burst, and the sclerotic Japanese political system seemed unable to implement meaningful reforms. While Japan stagnated, the United States enjoyed eight years of robust economic growth, its preeminence in the world more apparent with each passing year. Most of the world's major powers were now U.S. allies, and its principal enemies were a handful of minor "rogue states" and a shadowy terrorist network whose ambitions and abilities were at that point only partly understood. As the new millennium dawned, the United States stood alone at the pinnacle of world power.

Although careful, at first, not to risk too much blood or treasure, America did not simply sit back and savor its privileged position.

Rather, U.S. leaders saw the unchecked power at their disposal as an opportunity to mold the international environment, to enhance the U.S. position even more, and to reap even greater benefits in the future.

How did the United States do this? In broad terms, America's leaders have sought to persuade as many countries as possible to embrace their particular vision of a liberal-capitalist world order. States that welcomed U.S. leadership were rewarded; states that resisted it were ignored or punished. America's overarching objective, reports Richard N. Haass, former head of the State Department's Policy Planning Staff and now president of the Council on Foreign Relations, was to integrate other countries "into arrangements that will sustain a world consistent with U.S. interests and values and thereby promote peace, prosperity, and justice."[1]

These broad objectives were pursued by all three post–Cold War presidents—George H. W. Bush, William Clinton, and George W. Bush—though critical differences exist between the approaches undertaken by the first two and the third. In general, both the main goals of U.S. foreign policy and the strategies used to achieve these goals did not change fundamentally under the first Bush administration and the Clinton administration. Each sought to preserve or increase U.S. power and influence, to prevent the spread of weapons of mass destruction, to further liberalize the world economy, and to promote the core U.S. values of democracy and human rights. Both administrations pursued these goals by working within the preexisting Cold War order—and especially the multilateral institutions created since 1945—while seeking to maximize U.S. influence within these arrangements. Although the absence of a unifying threat and concerns about U.S. power created occasional frictions with other countries—including some long-term U.S. allies—America's standing in most of the world was quite positive as the twentieth century ended.

By contrast, President George W. Bush's approach to foreign policy marked a clear departure from the policies of his predecessors.

Although Bush also sought to enhance U.S. power, oppose the spread of weapons of mass destruction, and promote an open world economy and democratic values, his administration was more skeptical of existing international institutions—including America's Cold War alliances—and far more willing to "go it alone" in foreign affairs. Convinced that other states would follow if U.S. leadership was clear and uncompromising, and emboldened by a surge of domestic and international support following the terrorist attacks on September 11, 2001, Bush chose to use American power—and especially its military power—to eliminate perceived threats and to promote U.S. ideals around the world. Bush's basic goals were not radically different from those of his predecessors, but his willingness to use U.S. muscle to achieve them—and to act alone—was new, and startling. Predictably, this new approach to foreign policy alarmed many other countries and sparked a steady decline in the U.S. image abroad.

The Foundations of American Primacy

The U.S. position in the current world order is best understood as one of *primacy*. The United States is not a global hegemon, because it cannot physically control the entire globe and thus cannot compel other states to do whatever it wants.[2] Indeed, as we shall see throughout this book, even relatively weak states retain considerable freedom of action in the face of U.S. power. Nonetheless, the United States is also something more than just "first among equals." By virtually any measure, the United States enjoys an asymmetry of power unseen since the emergence of the modern state system. Some leading powers in the past had gained an advantage in one dimension or another—for example, in 1850 Great Britain controlled about 70 percent of Europe's wealth while the number-two power, France, controlled only 16 percent—but the United States is the only Great Power in modern history to establish a clear lead in virtually every important dimension of power.[3] The United States has the world's largest economy, an overwhelming military advantage, a dominant position in key international institutions, and far-reaching cultural and ideological influence. Moreover, these advantages are magnified by a favorable geopolitical position.[4] If *primacy* is defined as being "first in order, importance or authority," or holding "first or chief place," then it is an apt description of America's current position.[5]

Economic Dominance

Economic strength is the foundation for national power. The United States has been blessed with the world's largest economy for over a century. The U.S. share of global production ballooned to nearly 50 percent after World War II—reflecting the damage that other countries had suffered during the war—and then gradually declined as the rest of the world recovered. Nevertheless, it has hovered between 25 and 30 percent from 1960 to the present, and the U.S. economy is still roughly 60 percent larger than its nearest rival, Japan.[6] Moreover, the U.S. economy has grown more rapidly than the economies of most of the other major industrial powers since the mid-1990s.

The U.S. economy is also more diverse and self-sufficient than the other major economic powers, making it less vulnerable to unexpected economic shifts. As Thomas Friedman and others have emphasized, American society remains unusually open to immigration and innovation, which makes it more adept at adapting to new conditions.[7] According to MIT's "*Technology Review* Patent Scorecard," American companies were the top innovators in the automotive, aerospace, biotechnology, pharmaceutical, chemical, computer, telecommunications, and semiconductor industries between 1998 and 2002, and trailed Japan (the number-two innovator) only in electronics.[8] Even if these trends were to reverse, it would take several decades before any other country could acquire a gross national product (GNP) equal to America's, let alone a similar combination of size and per capita income.[9]

The size and diversity of the U.S. economy gives it considerable political leverage. Although the United States is more dependent on the outside world than it was a generation ago, it still depends far less on others than they depend on it. In 2000, for example, only three countries had lower ratios of trade to gross domestic product (GDP) than the United States, and only one of them was a major military power.[10] This relatively low level of interdependence insulates the United States from foreign pressure and strengthens America's political clout. Does anyone really wonder why China behaved with such restraint following the forced landing of a U.S. reconnaissance aircraft on Chinese soil in March 2001? The answer is simple: Chinese exports to the United States were a whopping 5 percent of Chinese GDP (19 percent of total Chinese exports) and critical to Chinese economic growth. U.S. exports to China, by contrast, were a mere 0.16 percent of U.S. GDP.[11] Because Beijing could not afford a disruption in economic ties, it agreed to release the crew and return the damaged plane to the United States after offering little more than a token protest over U.S. spying.

A state can be wealthy without being powerful, of course—think of Brunei, Kuwait, or Switzerland—but it is impossible to be a Great Power without a large and diverse economy. In particular, a strong economy enables a state to create and equip a powerful military force. Today, the United States is not only the world's foremost economic power; it is clearly the dominant military power as well.

Military Supremacy

While America's economic advantages are manifold, its military lead is simply overwhelming. Virtually all the major powers (except China) reduced their defense spending when the Cold War ended, and many continue to do so, but the decline in the U.S. military budget was smaller than most of the others. Defense spending turned back up again in the late 1990s and has continued to rise ever since. As a result, U.S. defense expenditures in 2003 were nearly 40 percent of the global total and almost seven times larger than that of the number-two power (China). To put it another way, U.S. defense spending was equal to the amount spent on defense by the next thirteen countries combined. And because many of these countries are close U.S. allies, these figures if anything understate the U.S. advantage.[12] The United States also spends more to keep itself in the vanguard of military technology. The U.S. Department of Defense now spends over $50 billion annually for "research, development, testing, and evaluation," an amount larger than the entire defense budget of Germany, Great Britain, France, Russia, Japan, or China.[13]

The relative efficiency of the U.S. military increases this daunting gap in military investment even more. For all the complaints about "waste, fraud, and abuse" and "no-bid" contracts in the Pentagon, the United States gets more battlefield bang for its defense bucks than other major powers do. For example, the combined defense budgets of America's European allies are roughly two-thirds of the U.S. defense total, but the EU is not yet able to put 60,000 well-equipped troops in the field within sixty days and keep them there for a year. By contrast, the United States deployed more than 500,000 troops in the Persian Gulf for Operations Desert Shield and Desert Storm; mobilized substantial air, ground, and naval forces in Kosovo in 1999 and in Afghanistan in 2001; and then deployed more than 180,000 troops and other personnel to topple Saddam Hussein in 2003.

America's military preeminence is both reflected by and enhanced by its global military presence. As of 2004, the United States had roughly 250,000 soldiers, sailors, and airmen deployed in more than a hundred countries. It has 1,000 or more troops in at least a dozen countries, not counting the forces currently occupying Iraq.[14] Smaller contingents are also active in dozens of countries, and the United States provides military training for personnel from over 130 countries.[15] The United States maintains hundreds of military bases and other facilities around the world, with an estimated replacement value of $118 billion.[16] The United States has the largest and most sophisticated arsenal of strategic nuclear weapons, and it is the only country with a global power projection capability, stealth aircraft, a large arsenal of precision-guided munitions, and integrated surveillance, reconnaissance, and command-and-control capabilities.[17] U.S. military personnel are also far better trained.[18]

U.S. success in its post–Cold War military endeavors thus needs little further explanation. The United States has fought three opponents since 1990: Iraq (twice), Serbia, and the Taliban regime in Afghanistan. Each of these wars was a gross mismatch: total U.S. defense spending was more than fifty times greater than Iraq's, more than two hundred times greater than Serbia's, and more than a thousand times that of the Taliban. The occupation of Iraq reminds us that supremacy on the battlefield does not guarantee effective postwar reconstruction or an unfettered peace, but the United States can still be confident about its ability to defeat any other country in a direct test of military strength.

Given these disparities, the United States could have defeated any of its recent foes without active military assistance from any other country. Indeed, the "coalitions" that the United States has organized and led during this period have been decidedly one-sided affairs. With the partial exception of Great Britain, its various allies have provided token forces largely for symbolic purposes. By 2001, the United States was refusing to let even its closest allies take on meaningful combat roles in Afghanistan (except for postwar peacekeeping), so that it would not have to coordinate its military activities with any other country. Historian Paul Kennedy correctly termed this a "Potemkin alliance," where "the U.S. does 98 percent of the fighting, the British 2 percent, and the Japanese steam around Mauritius."[19] The U.S. Air Force performed the lion's share of the patrol duties over the "no-fly zones" in Iraq (with a modest assist from Great Britain), and the U.S. military has also provided logistical support for peacekeeping operations in Africa, East Timor, and elsewhere. The gap was perhaps most apparent in the invasion of Iraq: the United States supplied over 80 percent of the occupying force and used over

10 percent of its total military manpower. By contrast, the other members of the coalition used less than 1 percent of their personnel.[20]

Clearly, no single state can hope to match the combined U.S. economic and military capabilities, and even a large coalition would find it difficult to amass a comparable portfolio of power. This imbalance does not mean, however, that the United States can simply issue orders to the rest of the world and expect instant obedience, as the recent U.S. experiences in Iraq, Iran, and North Korea remind us, and the strains of its current activities could undermine U.S. superiority over the longer term. For the foreseeable future, however, America's military predominance will be an essential element of its position of primacy.

Institutional Influence

States use international institutions to coordinate and regulate certain joint activities. Peacekeeping, for example, falls under the auspices of the United Nations; international trade is regulated by the World Trade Organization (WTO); and international finance and global development are guided (in part) by the International Monetary Fund (IMF) and the World Bank. Other international organizations deal with global health issues, the environment, and a host of other common concerns. Institutions neither substitute for state power nor exert powerful constraints on Great Power behavior, but they can provide useful mechanisms for overcoming dilemmas of collective action and other obstacles to multilateral cooperation.[21]

The norms and rules that govern these institutions will prevent any single state (or group of states) from controlling them completely, yet the United States plays a unique role in the most important global organizations. In the United Nations, the United States is one of five permanent members in the Security Council, and thus retains veto rights over all matters falling within the council's aegis. Because of its military dominance, the United States can also ignore the Security Council when it wants to, as it did in waging war in

Kosovo in 1999 and in Iraq in 2003. The United States is also the dominant power within the North Atlantic Treaty Organization (NATO). The position of NATO Supreme Allied Commander Europe (SACEUR) is always held by an American officer—who also commands all U.S. forces in the European theater. Further, the United States can at any time reduce its commitment to Europe's security because it is not on the same continent; the Europeans do not have that option. Although "political consultation does exist within the North Atlantic Council," notes Guillaume Parmentier, the former head of external relations at NATO headquarters, "these negotiations are very often no more than a formality. . . . It has almost always been American initiatives that have brought about changes in the Alliance."[22]

More important, the rules governing the operation of many global institutions strengthen the hands of U.S. officials. In addition to its Security Council veto, for example, the United States also contributes the largest share (22 percent) of the UN's annual budget.[23] When the United States withholds some of its assigned share (as it did in the 1990s), the shortfall has a direct effect on what the UN is able to accomplish. When a U.S. president decides that the UN secretary-general is acting contrary to U.S. interests—as Bill Clinton did during the tenure of Boutros Boutros-Ghali—he can orchestrate his or her removal.[24] Similarly, U.S. contributions to IMF and World Bank capital subscriptions entitle it to a voting share on their executive boards sufficient to veto any major policy change. Thus, while the United States does not "control" these institutions, both are highly sensitive to Washington's wishes. As one student of the IMF and the World Bank puts it, "The record of lending from both institutions strongly suggests a pattern of U.S. interests and preferences."[25]

Cultural and Ideological Impact

Another key advantage for the United States is its ability to shape the preferences of others—to make them want what America wants—

through the inherent attractiveness of U.S. culture, ideology, and institutions. This "soft power" remains hard to define or measure, but there is little doubt that the United States casts a long cultural and ideological shadow over the rest of the world.[26] Not only is English increasingly the *lingua franca* of diplomacy, science, and international business, but the American university system is a potent mechanism for socializing foreign elites.[27] There were nearly 600,000 foreign students studying at U.S. universities in 2002–3, for example, roughly double the total from two decades earlier.[28] In addition to becoming familiar with U.S. norms, foreign students in the United States absorb prevailing U.S. attitudes about politics and economics, especially the emphasis on competitive markets, democratic institutions, and the rule of law.[29] As *Die Zeit* editor Josef Joffe puts it, "If there is a global civilization, it is American. Nor is it just McDonald's and Hollywood, it is also Microsoft and Harvard. Wealthy Romans used to send their children to Greek universities; today's Greeks, that is, the Europeans, send their kids to Roman, that is, American, universities."[30] Even in the Arab world, where the United States is presently unpopular, America's educational institutions continue to attract students and continue to serve as an inspirational model.[31] This sort of influence can have unexpected payoffs: for example, Libya's decision to end its prolonged isolation and to abandon its efforts to acquire weapons of mass destruction was due in part to the influence of reform-oriented Prime Minister Shukri Ghanem, who received a PhD in economics from the Fletcher School of Law and Diplomacy in Medford, Massachusetts.[32]

The effects of America's preeminent position in higher education are reinforced by the pervasiveness of U.S. mass media.[33] As of 2004, the top twenty-five highest-grossing films of all time were U.S. productions, even if one omits U.S. ticket sales and looks solely at foreign revenues. American consumer products and brand names are ubiquitous, along with U.S. sports and media figures. When the Cold War ended and was followed by the economic boom of the

1990s, free markets and democratic governance became more appealing worldwide. American primacy, therefore, extends into the cultural realm, though the ultimate impact of this level of penetration is unclear. While American ideas and cultural icons seem to enjoy greater appeal today than in the past, many societies remain wary of "Americanization," and a few are openly hostile to it.

The Blessings of Geography

Economic, military, institutional, and cultural dominance may define U.S. primacy, but its geopolitical situation is the icing on the cake. The United States is the only Great Power in the Western Hemisphere, and it is physically separated from other major powers by two enormous oceanic moats. As Jules Jusseraud, French ambassador to the United States from 1902 to 1925, once observed, America is "blessed among the nations. On the north, she had a weak neighbor; on the south, another weak neighbor; on the east, fish, and the west, fish."[34]

America's geographic separation from the other major powers reduces the threat of direct invasion while mitigating the sense of threat that U.S. power might pose to others, thereby lowering their incentives to join forces against the United States. And because the other major powers lie in close proximity to one another, they are inclined to worry more about each other than they do about the United States. In fact, the United States has long been the perfect ally for many Eurasian states. Its power ensures that its voice is heard and its actions felt, but it lies a comfortable distance away and does not threaten to conquer its allies. Over thirty years ago, Chinese leader Mao Zedong justified the rapprochement between China and the United States by saying, "Didn't our ancestors counsel negotiating with faraway countries while fighting with those that are near?" Ten years ago, a European diplomat told an American scholar that "A European power broker would be a hegemon. We can agree on U.S. leadership, but not on one of our own."[35]

Geography also helps explain why it would be difficult to conjure up an anti-American coalition combining Russia, China, and India. These states share lengthy borders and troubled pasts and still regard each other with considerable suspicion. Although one cannot entirely rule out the possibility of a grand anti-American coalition were the United States to behave too aggressively, it would take a remarkable feat of American diplomatic incompetence to bring it about.

How Has the United States Used Its Power?

The Virtues of Primacy

It may be lonely at the top, but the view is compelling. Having achieved a preeminent global position, U.S. leaders have been eager to preserve and protect it. They understand, as do most Americans, that primacy confers important benefits. Primacy makes other states less likely to threaten the United States or its vital interests, and it gives the United States the power to defend these interests if challenges do arise. By dampening Great Power competition and giving the United States the capacity to shape regional balances of power, primacy also contributes to a more tranquil international environment. That tranquility in turn fosters global prosperity, because investors and traders can operate more widely when the danger of war is remote. Primacy also gives the United States a greater capacity to work for positive ends—the advancement of human rights, the alleviation of poverty and disease, the control of weapons of mass destruction, etc.—although it provides no guarantee of success.

The United States relishes its position of primacy, and no presidential candidate ever campaigns on a pledge to "make America number two." Instead, the central goal of U.S. foreign policy since the end of the Cold War has been to consolidate and, where possible, to enhance its preeminent position. The United States has acted for humanitarian reasons on occasion—as when it intervened in Bosnia and Kosovo, for example—but the main thrust of its policy has been to advance its own interests and increase its relative power.

As we shall see, however, there are important differences between the exercise of primacy by George H. W. Bush and Bill Clinton on the one hand and George W. Bush on the other. All three have worked to improve the U.S. position and to use the power at their disposal to shape the world in the U.S. image, but they have done so in markedly different ways.

Primacy and Security:
Promoting a Favorable Imbalance of Power

Preserving U.S. dominance. International politics is a dangerous business, and having more power is generally preferable to having less. Being the strongest state does not protect the United States from all dangers—September 11, 2001, certainly proved that—but it does give the United States a greater capacity to respond to dangers that do arise. Primacy also deters many challenges to U.S. interests, because potential adversaries know that the United States is strong enough to respond if pressed. Secretary of Defense Donald Rumsfeld captured this benefit of primacy perfectly by saying, "We want to be so powerful and so forward-looking that it is clear to others that they . . . ought not to be doing things that are imposing threats and dangers to us."[36]

American primacy did not just happen, of course. U.S. leaders recognized America's potential strength from the first days of independence, and successive presidents focused on expanding across a continent, preserving national unity, building industrial power, and eventually excluding other Great Powers from the Western Hemisphere—all with an eye toward establishing the United States as the dominant power in its own hemisphere and as a major power on the global stage. Good luck played a role in America's rise to world power, but it was also the conscious objective of U.S. policy.[37]

The same perspective has informed U.S. foreign policy for the past half-century. Indeed, U.S. leaders sought a preponderance of power in America's favor from the very beginning of the Cold War. As the

Policy Planning Staff at the State Department concluded in 1947, "[T]o seek less than preponderant power would be to opt for defeat. Preponderant power must be the object of U.S. policy."[38] Thus, the collapse of the Soviet Union was not just a lucky accident of history; it was the intended result of four decades of sustained U.S. effort. Although "containment" was the official label of Cold War policy, the real U.S. objective was Communism's complete defeat.[39]

When the irreversible erosion of Soviet power eventually forced Mikhail Gorbachev to offer unprecedented concessions in the mid-1980s, the United States didn't respond by offering reciprocal concessions or by trying to keep bipolarity intact. Instead, U.S. leaders increased their demands as Moscow's position grew weaker and eventually negotiated the dissolution of the Warsaw Pact and the reunification of Germany despite strong Soviet misgivings. When Gorbachev complained in 1986 that "U.S. policy is one of extorting more and more concessions," U.S. Secretary of State George Shultz merely replied, "I'm weeping for you."[40] And when the Soviet Union began to come apart in 1990, the United States did not lift a finger to hold it together. Instead, President George H. W. Bush welcomed the disappearance of a longtime rival, believing that "the best arrangement would be diffusion, with many different states, none of which would have the awesome power of the Soviet Union." The result, Bush later recalled, was the United States "standing alone at the height of power . . . with the rarest opportunity to shape the world."[41]

The desire for primacy also explains why the United States did not dismantle its vast military arsenal once the Soviet Union collapsed. Instead, each U.S. administration made it clear that it intended to maintain a clear margin of superiority over the rest of the world. In 1992, George H. W. Bush's administration prepared a draft "Defense Guidance," arguing that the United States "must sufficiently account for the interests of the advanced industrial nations to discourage them from challenging our leadership or seeking to overturn the established political and economic order." The way to accomplish this goal was equally clear: The United States should maintain military capabilities large enough to discourage potential rivals from even trying to compete.[42]

The Clinton administration placed less rhetorical emphasis on U.S. military power, but it also sought to "maintain the best-trained, best-equipped and best-led military force in the world" and to ensure "that U.S. forces continue to have unchallenged superiority in the 21st century."[43] This goal became even clearer under George W. Bush, whose official *National Security Strategy* declared that U.S. military forces will be "strong enough to dissuade potential adversaries from pursuing a military build-up in hopes of surpassing, or equaling, the power of the United States."[44]

The desire for primacy can also be seen in U.S. efforts to limit the spread of weapons of mass destruction (WMD) and especially nuclear weapons, while maintaining a large and sophisticated nuclear arsenal of its own. Because the United States has the world's strongest conventional forces, halting or slowing the spread of WMD is obviously in its own self-interest. If weaker states obtain WMD, they may be able to deter the use of U.S. conventional forces, thereby undercutting U.S. military superiority and eroding U.S. global influence.[45] U.S. leaders also fear that rogue states armed with WMD might behave more aggressively, thereby making regional conflict more likely and threatening U.S. interests directly, or that the spread of WMD would make it easier for terrorists to obtain them.[46]

For all these reasons, the United States has conducted a broad campaign to limit the spread of WMD and to maintain a dominant position at the highest levels of strategic competition. It used its economic and political clout to persuade the former Soviet republics of Kazakhstan, Belarus, and Ukraine to give up the nuclear arsenals they had inherited when the Soviet Union dissolved. The United States subsequently launched a broad array of programs to bring Russia's vast and poorly monitored arsenal under more reliable control.[47] The United States supported the permanent extension of the

Nuclear Non-Proliferation Treaty (NPT) in 1995 and actively tried to discourage countries such as Libya, North Korea, India, and Pakistan from pursuing a nuclear option.[48] The United States has also pressured Russia not to sell a nuclear reactor to Iran and has favored strong measures to persuade Iran to end its clandestine nuclear programs. These efforts have been accompanied by a parallel campaign to deny potential proliferators access to modern ballistic missile technology, which would merely compound the perceived threat from WMD.[49]

The final element in the U.S. quest to preserve its position of primacy is its own strategic weapons program. The United States has made significant cuts in its nuclear arsenal since the end of the Cold War, but it has done this primarily by retiring outmoded or superfluous systems. At the same time, it has continued to modernize its remaining strategic forces while negotiating parallel reductions in Russia's aging arsenal. In addition, the first Bush administration and the Clinton administration continued to fund research and development for missile defenses, and the second Bush administration took the further step of abrogating the 1972 Anti-Ballistic Missile Treaty (despite strong opposition from many U.S. allies) and declared that the United States would begin deploying missile defenses as soon as they could be developed. The second Bush administration also completed a Nuclear Posture Review in 2004 recommending development of a new generation of nuclear weapons, including bunker-busting "mini-nukes."[50]

The underlying purpose of these initiatives, as several analysts have noted, is to preserve U.S. superiority and thus maintain America's overall freedom of action.[51] At a minimum, overwhelming nuclear superiority—including the development of some form of national missile defense—is intended to keep so-called rogue states from deterring the use of U.S. conventional forces by threatening to launch a handful of nuclear weapons at U.S. territory. At a maximum, the combination of highly accurate offensive forces, an increasingly unreliable Russian arsenal, and improved strategic defenses might provide the United States with a genuine "first-strike" capability. Needless to say, countries with smaller nuclear arsenals would be even more vulnerable. Even if U.S. leaders cannot be 100 percent sure that such an attack would succeed, other states may fear this possibility and be more inclined to defer to U.S. wishes. America's strategic ambitions even extend into outer space. As Undersecretary of the Air Force Peter B. Teets told an Air Force Association exposition in September 2004, "the fact is, we need to reach for that goal [of space supremacy]. It is the ultimate high ground."[52]

The bottom line is clear: The United States remains committed to maintaining—and, if possible, enhancing—its position of primacy, at virtually all levels of strategic competition.

Expanded global influence. A similar desire to improve its global position can also be seen in U.S. alliance policy. When the Soviet Union collapsed, U.S. leaders might have concluded that there was no longer a major threat to "contain," and thus less need for a global network of formal military alliances. Indeed, this logic led many Europeans and Asians to worry about a precipitous U.S. withdrawal. Instead of liquidating its existing commitments, however, the United States chose to expand its formal ties in Europe and Asia while retaining its central leadership role.

In Europe, the United States initiated and led a process of expansion that increased NATO from sixteen to twenty-six members by 2004.[53] At the same time, the United States remained wary of developments that might diminish its influence. In particular, U.S. officials sought to prevent other European security institutions from supplanting NATO, because NATO was still seen as the best vehicle for retaining U.S. influence on European security issues. The role of SACEUR remained in U.S. hands, and the United States blocked a French proposal to assign NATO's Southern Command to a European officer in 1996.[54] American officials in all three (Clinton and Bush) administrations remained ambivalent about European efforts to strengthen their own defense capabilities, warning that such efforts would be desirable only if they did not "undermine" the alliance.

Special demands on NATO brought the dominant position of the United States into sharp relief. The United States controlled the negotiations that ended the Bosnian civil war and sent the largest contingent to the stabilization force that arrived to implement the accord. The United States also took the lead role in the negotiations that led to war against Serbia in 1999 and designed the military strategy that eventually brought Serbia's capitulation. America's European allies complained during both episodes, but they could do little to stop the United States from imposing its preferences upon them.[55]

Maintaining a favorable position in Asia has been equally important. Despite fears that the Soviet collapse would lead to a U.S. withdrawal, the United States has maintained a substantial military presence and worked to strengthen its security relations with several regional powers.[56] In addition to renegotiating its security treaty with Japan and maintaining its long-standing alliance with South Korea, the United States also opened diplomatic relations with Vietnam in 1995 and obtained expanded basing rights in Singapore in 1999.

China's economic expansion poses a potential long-term threat to U.S. primacy, and the United States has tried to limit the impact of this trend in two ways. On the one hand, the United States has gone to considerable lengths to encourage China to integrate itself within global institutions such as the World Trade Organization (WTO); on the other hand, it has also sought to deter China from taking aggressive action against Taiwan or against other U.S. allies in the region.[57] Concerns about China's potential have been more evident under George W. Bush, who took office declaring that China was "a competitor, not a strategic partner," and pledging that Beijing would be "unthreatened but not unchecked."[58] This preoccupation with China was partly eclipsed by September 11 and the new focus on terrorism, but Bush still sought to discourage China from becoming a "peer competitor." Accordingly, Bush's 2002 *National Security Strategy* welcomed the emergence of a "strong, peaceful and prosperous China" but warned that if China tried to obtain "advanced military capabilities," it would be following an "outdated path" that "would hamper its pursuit of national greatness."[59] In Asia, as in Europe, the United States wants to remain the dominant power.

The post–Cold War era also saw the United States taking a more active role in shaping the balance of power in the Middle East and Persian Gulf. During the Cold War, the United States sought to defend its core interests—the security of Israel and access to oil—primarily by supporting local allies (Israel, Saudi Arabia, Iran, Jordan, etc.) while avoiding direct military involvement in the region. When serious threats arose—as in the aftermath of the Iranian revolution in 1980—the United States was also willing to give support to local dictatorships such as Saddam Hussein's Iraq.[60] In general, however, the United States maintained a modest military presence in the region, and its forces did not participate in direct combat operations.[61]

This detached approach ended when Iraq invaded Kuwait in August 1990. To prevent Iraq from threatening other oil producers or using Kuwait's oil revenues to amass even more military power, the United States led a multinational coalition to expel Iraq from Kuwait and force Saddam Hussein to dismantle his nuclear, chemical, and biological weapons programs under the watchful eyes of UN weapons inspectors. Once the Gulf War was over, the United States increased its military presence in the region and kept these forces busy.[62] U.S. aircraft patrolled Iraqi airspace continuously after the end of the Gulf War, and U.S. and British aircraft attacked Iraqi facilities repeatedly. The United States also took the lead role in maintaining economic sanctions against the Iraqi government (despite dwindling international support), in order to prevent Iraq from rebuilding the military forces and weapons programs that had been destroyed or dismantled as a result of the Gulf War. At the same time, the United States also sought to prevent Iran from increasing its own military capabilities—through a policy known as "dual containment"—

largely by denying it easy access to advanced weapons technology.[63] What was not fully recognized at the time, unfortunately, was the emergence of an Islamic terrorist group—al Qaeda—partly inspired by opposition to the U.S. presence on "holy" Muslim soil.

Thus, the Gulf War and its aftermath were not just vehicles to restore the status quo ante; rather, the United States saw these events as opportunities to tilt the regional balance in its favor. Under George H. W. Bush and Clinton, however, the United States did so as part of a multilateral effort, and did not try to remove existing regimes from power. As discussed at great length below, George W. Bush's administration took a more ambitious approach to the Middle East and the Gulf, and eventually chose to use U.S. military power to begin a far-reaching transformation of the region.

Primacy and Prosperity

It is sometimes said that interdependence produces peace, but it may be more accurate to say that peace encourages greater interdependence.[64] By fostering a more stable world, therefore, U.S. primacy also encourages global prosperity. Investors are more willing to send capital abroad when the danger of war is remote, and states worry less about being dependent on others when they have little reason to fear that these connections might be severed. When states are relatively secure, they will also be less concerned about how the benefits from cooperation are distributed. By this argument, U.S. primacy creates political conditions conducive to expanding international trade and investment.

U.S. leaders have also sought to foster an international economic order that would enhance U.S. prosperity and advance other U.S. interests. Specifically, the United States has used its power to reduce barriers to trade and investment, and to create and maintain the institutions on which the current international economic order rests. In doing so, it has also sought to persuade other countries to adopt domestic institutions that are compatible with basic U.S. practices.

Accordingly, what we now think of as "globalization" is itself partly an artifact of U.S. primacy.[65]

Trade policy. As the world's largest economy, the United States has a powerful interest in free trade. Reducing artificial barriers to free trade brings lower prices for U.S. consumers and facilitates U.S. exports, thereby raising U.S. living standards and fostering U.S. economic growth. Accordingly, the United States has generally been a proponent of trade liberalization, except in particular sectors with significant domestic political influence (e.g., steel, textiles, certain farm products, etc.) that would be hurt by increased foreign competition.

On balance, the United States has pursued the goal of continued liberalization during the first decade of the unipolar era. Notable achievements include the North American Free Trade Agreement (NAFTA), which was signed by President George H. W. Bush and ratified under President Clinton, and the successful completion of the Uruguay Round in 1994, which established the World Trade Organization. The United States also helped organize and convene other global and regional forums (such as the Asia Pacific Economic Cooperation group (APEC) and the Transatlantic Economic Partnership (TEP) forum), and conducted an ambitious export promotion policy. All three post–Cold War administrations have negotiated bilateral trade agreements with particular countries and have used the threat of retaliatory sanctions to persuade other countries to open their markets to U.S. goods.[66] The results were generally favorable: U.S. exports increased by about 11 percent between 1992 and 1999, and this expansion accounted for roughly 20 percent of U.S. GDP growth during that time.[67]

The liberal theory of free trade tells us that all countries benefit from reducing barriers to trade, and U.S. efforts to create a more liberal international economic order were probably not intended to make the United States richer and others poorer. Yet the agreements that were reached were particularly favorable to U.S. interests. In addition to lowering tariffs on industrial and manufactured goods, for example, the Uruguay Round also included extended trading rules to the service and agriculture sectors, provided new guarantees for intellectual property rights, and reached a partial agreement on "trade-related investment measures," in each case covering an area where the United States had a strong competitive position. It also created a new dispute-resolution system that favors the United States, because the new system depends in part on each state's ability to retaliate and the United States has by far the world's most potent retaliatory capacity. The Uruguay Round also took aim at a number of nontariff barriers to trade, which other countries have relied upon more than the United States has, and the United States also stood to reap disproportionate benefits from agreements on telecommunications, information technology, and financial services, because the United States enjoys a competitive advantage in these sectors.

By contrast, the United States successfully resisted efforts to end agricultural subsidies, and although it did agree to phase out the protectionist Multi-Fiber Agreement, its own tariffs on textiles remained high. Nor did the WTO agreement bar the United States from threatening unilateral sanctions or prevent U.S. trade negotiators from pursuing an array of bilateral and regional arrangements outside the WTO framework.

Furthermore, U.S. negotiators have increasingly insisted that trade agreements also cover areas that were previously regarded as purely domestic issues (e.g., labor standards, environmental protection, intellectual property, government regulations, etc.), and both NAFTA and the WTO incorporated these issues (albeit to varying degrees). As a result, these agreements require signatories to bring a host of domestic institutions and procedures into conformity with specific treaty-defined standards. For example, joining NAFTA forced Mexico to submit its enforcement of labor and environmental standards to international oversight, and China's accession to the WTO required it to commit to major domestic economic reforms and a host of specific rules on tariffs, nontariff barriers, anti-dumping, subsidies, and technology transfers. Moreover, these adjustments have to be made rapidly, which increases the degree of internal disruption. The United States and Western Europe were already in compliance with many of these principles, so adjusting to them was comparatively easy.

Many of these reforms are desirable for their own sake, and entering a bilateral or multilateral agreement is one way for reformist politicians to "lock in" a more market-oriented approach. Yet the fact remains that these institutions were largely "made in America" (and, to a lesser extent, in Europe and Japan), and countries that joined later—such as China—have had to accept a set of rules that they had little role in shaping and that did not reflect their own ideal preferences.[68]

The use of U.S. economic clout was also apparent in what former Bush administration Trade Representative Robert Zoellick termed a strategy of "competitive liberalization." Although the Bush team was committed to advancing the Doha Round of multilateral trade talks, it also pursued an ambitious array of bilateral trade negotiations.[69] These bilateral talks were used to reward governments that were cooperating closely with the United States, and to encourage other states to adopt social and political institutions that the United States favored. The sheer size of the U.S. economy gave it considerable leverage over smaller exporting countries, because other states have to worry about being excluded from the U.S. market if they do not cooperate on U.S. terms.[70] As Zoellick put it, "The strategy is simple: The U.S. is spurring a competition in liberalization. . . . Our FTAs [free trade agreements] are encouraging reformers . . . they establish prototypes for liberalization in areas such as services, e-commerce, intellectual property for knowledge societies, transparency in government regulation, and better enforcement of labor and environmental protections."[71] Thus, the Bush administration's trade strategy sought to maximize U.S. leverage and encourage other states to adopt institutions and practices that are largely "made in America."

International finance. Liberalization on U.S. terms has been the general goal in the realm of international finance as well. Capital mobility has increased dramatically in the past two decades, due to declining communications costs, the spread of market systems, and expanded trade.[72] U.S. leaders have encouraged these trends, however, based on the belief that integrating more countries into global financial markets would encourage more rapid economic growth, but also because U.S. banks and financial-services firms were likely to benefit from the removal of political barriers in the financial sector. Unfortunately, these same trends may also have increased the volatility of the international financial system and helped produce financial crises in Mexico, Brazil, and Russia, as well as the Asian financial crises of 1997.

These events underscored the need for new international arrangements to reduce the costs and risks of financial volatility. The United States has supported these efforts, while emphasizing the importance of domestic institutional reform in countries with corrupt, opaque, or underregulated financial sectors. As with trade, this objective means that other states will have to bring their domestic financial practices more in line with those of the United States and other advanced industrial countries. Toward this end, the Bush administration has called for reform of the major international development banks (e.g., the World Bank), focusing in particular on the need for "greater emphasis on measurable results and activities that increase productivity, including private sector development."[73]

The second Bush administration has sought to pursue the same goals in an even more assertive fashion through its Millennium Challenge Account (MCA) initiative. If funded, the MCA will increase annual U.S. development assistance by $5 billion by 2006 (an increase of roughly 50 percent), with the additional aid targeted at countries "that are pursuing policies and building institutions that adhere to the principles of good governance." "Good governance," however, means conforming to a set of pre-specified benchmarks based on U.S. practices, including strengthening the rule of law, liberalizing economic and political institutions, and generally conducting pro-growth economic policies.[74] Reduced to its essentials, the campaign to reform existing development institutions and the decision to tie U.S. aid to political reform are part of a broader effort to use U.S. economic power to encourage other countries to become more like the United States. These remedies may be wholly desirable from an economic point of view, but they also provide another example of America's seeking to impose its own preferred solutions on others.

Primacy, Democracy, and Human Rights

In addition to shaping the global economy, America's attempt to mold a favorable world order included a continued effort to promote U.S. ideals of democracy and human rights. These are hardly new goals, of course, as U.S. leaders have always claimed to uphold demo-cratic values and have on occasion made good on this pledge.[75] Since 1991, however, the United States has been more visibly committed to spreading democracy and preventing large-scale human-rights abuses. Under President George H. W. Bush, for example, the U.S. Agency for International Development formally adopted the promo-tion of democracy as one of its core objectives, and adherence to democratic principles became an important criterion for admission to key Western institutions. In 1995, the Clinton administration made "enlarging" the sphere of democratic rule a centerpiece of its own national security strategy.[76] President George W. Bush declared in 2002 that "freedom, democracy, and free enterprise" are the world's "single sustainable model for national success," and his second inaugural address focused on the promotion of freedom and democ-racy worldwide.[77] And, as just noted, the United States has also increasingly linked foreign aid and trade concessions to the adoption of democratic norms and institutions.

The United States favors the spread of democracy in part because it believes that other peoples would be better off if they were able to select their own leaders in free and fair elections, and because it believes that this development will be good for the United States as well.[78] In particular, democracies are believed to be less likely to fight each other, more likely to engage in free trade, and more inclined to support the United States in the international arena. As the Clinton administration's 1995 *National Security Strategy* report put it, "The more that democracy and . . . liberalization take hold in the world . . . the safer our nation is likely to be and the more our people are likely to prosper."[79] To this end, the United States and its allies have also made membership in institutions such as NATO conditional on the implementation of democratic reforms—thereby giving aspiring members a greater incentive to establish genuine democratic institutions—and they have provided direct assistance to pro-democracy groups.[80] These efforts can claim some degree of success, insofar as the number of democratic states has increased sharply in the 1990s, and the "level of freedom worldwide" reached its highest recorded level by the end of that decade.[81] Finally, the United States used its armed forces to remove or defeat authoritarian leaders in Haiti (1994), Bosnia (1995), Kosovo (1999), Afghanistan (2002), and Iraq (2003), albeit for both self-interested and humanitarian reasons.

The end of the Cold War facilitated these efforts in several ways. The collapse of the Soviet Union removed the main threat to U.S. national security and made it less necessary to tolerate anticommunist dictatorships. Victory in the Cold War made U.S. ideals and values more appealing to others and bolstered U.S. faith in its own virtues. The defeat of Communism also opened the door to democratic transitions in Eastern Europe and parts of Central Asia, reinforcing a trend that was already underway in Latin America and elsewhere.

For all these reasons, promoting democracy has become a more visible issue on the U.S. foreign-policy agenda. Yet an increased rhetorical commitment to these ideals has not been matched by a similar commitment of time, money, troops, or political capital. In the 1990s, for example, the U.S. government spent roughly $2 billion each year to "promote democracy," a sum equal to one-fifth of the

U.S. military-assistance budget and less than 1 percent of the U.S. defense budget.[82] Presidents George H. W. Bush and Bill Clinton paid scant attention to the lack of democracy in China, Egypt, Saudi Arabia, and much of the Middle East, because these states were either too powerful or strategically vital to pressure on these issues. President George W. Bush has gone further in calling for the spread of democracy in the Arab and Islamic world, but like his predecessors, he has been willing to work with nondemocratic governments in Pakistan, Uzbekistan, China, Saudi Arabia, Egypt, and elsewhere when U.S. interests required.

Consistent with its ideological commitment to individual freedom, the United States has also sought to foster a world where basic human rights were respected and large-scale human-rights abuses (including torture, extrajudicial execution, loss of civil liberties, genocide, etc.) did not occur. The rhetoric was strong, but the will to act remained weak. On the positive side, the first Bush administration did send troops to distribute food in Somalia in 1992, even though the U.S. strategic interests in this region were negligible. The United States also intervened in Haiti in 1994 in order to restore President Jean-Bertrand Aristide to power and took the lead role in fashioning the 1995 Dayton Accords that ended the civil war in Bosnia. The United States also orchestrated NATO's effort to halt Serbian human-rights abuses in Kosovo and provided logistical support for the Australian-led peacekeeping force that entered East Timor in 1999.

On the other hand, no U.S. president has been willing to risk much blood or treasure solely to promote democracy or to advance human rights. The Clinton administration withdrew U.S. forces from Somalia after a single engagement left twenty-two U.S. soldiers dead, and this debacle helped discourage Clinton from intervening to prevent a subsequent genocide in Rwanda.[83] Clinton also learned that pressing China on human-rights issues merely poisoned relations with Beijing and sparked protests from U.S. businesses, and his administration generally downplayed these issues. Despite ample evidence of human-rights violations, the United States intervened in Bosnia with great reluctance and eventually transferred most of the burden of implementing the Dayton Accords to its European allies. The United States used an intensive air campaign to compel Serbia to grant autonomy to Kosovo, but its obvious reluctance to commit ground troops reinforced the perception that America would not risk its own soldiers' lives in order to save the lives of foreigners. U.S. reluctance was further highlighted during the 2000 presidential campaign, when candidate George W. Bush repeatedly criticized the Clinton administration for its "nation-building" efforts and made it clear that he did not think such activities were in the U.S. national interest. The United States has also reacted mildly to Israeli repression on the West Bank and in the Gaza Strip and has done little to halt Russia's brutal treatment of its Chechen minority. Although President Clinton eventually signed the convention to create the International Criminal Court (whose main purpose is to prosecute individuals accused of crimes against humanity), President George W. Bush formally removed the U.S. "signature" and put strong pressure on a number of other countries to reject the treaty. Along with most other major powers, the United States has also been slow to act to halt mass killings in the Darfur region of Sudan.

Although America rarely lives up to its idealistic rhetoric, the belief that the United States should try to promote U.S. ideals abroad has helped reinforce the domestic consensus in favor of an activist foreign policy. Conservative supporters of U.S. primacy can favor using U.S. power to stabilize key regions and to discourage the emergence of "peer competitors," while liberal ideologues can endorse using U.S. power to halt large-scale human-rights abuses and to promote democratic rule. Thus, a broad spectrum of Americans now supports efforts to remake the world in the U.S. image, albeit for somewhat different reasons.

Primacy, Hubris, and September 11

When a country is as strong as the United States now is, its leaders inevitably will be tempted to pursue far-reaching objectives abroad. If they are initially successful, they may succumb to "victory disease," taking on ever-more-ambitious goals in the belief that past successes will be easy to duplicate. The danger of hubris grows apace, because it is hard to identify the limits of one's power in advance. As the late Senator Richard B. Russell (who was hardly an isolationist) warned in 1967, "We should not unilaterally assume the function of policing the world. If it is easy for us to go anywhere and do anything, we will always be going somewhere and doing something."[84]

The hubris born of prior success helps us understand the shifts in U.S. foreign policy after 2000, and especially the U.S. response to the terrorist attacks on September 11. As noted above, Presidents George H. W. Bush and William J. Clinton sought to take advantage of U.S. primacy within the existing geopolitical structures bequeathed by the Cold War. Both were "conservative" administrations insofar as they sought to enhance the U.S. position in the world while preserving the alliances, institutional commitments, and broad multilateralist approach that had won the Cold War. Both administrations also enjoyed a run of easy victories: Iraq was swiftly defeated in the Gulf War, the U.S. and Britain enforced "no-fly zones" there for more than a decade without losing a single plane, NATO's intervention in Bosnia ended a lengthy civil war with few allied casualties, and even the unexpectedly messy war in Kosovo turned out to be a rather low-cost affair. Most important, both administrations managed to use U.S. primacy in ways that minimized global opposition to U.S. power.[85]

Like his predecessors, President George W. Bush also sought to maintain U.S. primacy, enhance U.S. prosperity, and encourage the spread of U.S. values to other countries. But it soon became clear that Bush was less committed to the traditional Cold War structures and more willing to use U.S. power to alter the international status quo.[86] The Bush team was firmly convinced that history was on

America's side, and that U.S. power should be used to reinforce what then-National Security Advisor (now Secretary of State) Condoleezza Rice termed the "powerful secular trends moving the world toward . . . democracy and individual liberty."[87]

Confidence in U.S. power also implied a greater willingness to "go it alone" in foreign affairs, even if this approach led to major disruptions in the existing international order. By September 2001, the Bush administration had formally rejected the Kyoto Protocol on global warming, begun an active campaign to discredit the International Criminal Court, and derailed efforts to negotiate a stronger verification protocol for the Biological Weapons Convention. Bush also opposed a new international effort to restrict the global trade in small arms and reiterated U.S. opposition to the landmines convention. This string of unilateralist gestures led the normally pro-American *Economist* to ask, "Has George Bush ever met a treaty that he liked? . . . It is hard to avoid the suspicion that it is the very idea of multilateral cooperation that Mr. Bush objects to."[88]

The al Qaeda terrorist attacks on September 11 encouraged the Bush administration to take this approach to a new level. Bush became a "war president" overnight, and international terrorism occupied the rhetorical center of U.S. foreign policy. September 11 also reinforced Bush's unilateralist inclinations and his tendency to divide the world into friends and enemies. In declaring war on all terrorists "of global reach," Bush made it clear that other states and political groups had to choose sides. "We will make no distinction between the terrorists who committed these acts and those who harbor them," he said on the evening of September 11, a point he emphasized again in a speech to Congress on September 20. "Every nation, in every region, now has a decision to make," he declared. "Either you are with us, or you are with the terrorists."[89]

September 11 also allowed Bush's advisers to articulate a fundamental revision in U.S. national security strategy, one that reflected their underlying belief that contemporary international norms did not operate to America's advantage. This new approach downplayed the traditional U.S. reliance on deterrence and emphasized the need to "preempt" potential threats before they emerged. Declaring that "the gravest danger to freedom lies at the crossroads of radicalism and technology," the new Bush strategy warned that "the United States can no longer rely solely on a reactive posture as we have in the past." In particular, the new *National Security Strategy* called for "anticipatory action to defend ourselves, even if uncertainty remained as to the time and the place of the enemy's attack." In other words, the United States was now declaring that it would use military force to prevent certain states (or terrorist groups) from acquiring potentially dangerous weaponry. Although the administration called this a strategy of "preemption," they were in fact articulating a rationale for preventive war.[90]

The invasion of Iraq in March 2003 offered the first demonstration of the new "Bush Doctrine" in action. Unfortunately, the decision for war was based on a false reading of the prewar intelligence and inaccurate judgments about the likely consequences of a U.S. invasion. Iraq turned out not to have any weapons of mass destruction, and Saddam Hussein did not have meaningful ties to al Qaeda. Prewar hopes that the United States would be welcomed as liberators and that it would be easy to form a viable post-Saddam government proved equally illusory. The U.S.-led invasion had little trouble defeating Iraq's third-rate army, but the occupation forces soon found themselves confronted by a resilient and deadly insurgency, a collapsed Iraqi economy, and a simmering political rivalry among Iraq's Shi'ite, Sunni, and Kurdish communities. Iraqi resentment at the U.S. presence increased as the occupation dragged on, and President Bush began his second term in a quagmire of his own creation.

Most important of all, the war in Iraq reinforced global concerns about the unchecked nature of U.S. power. The Bush administration's earlier acts of unilateralism had upset a number of key U.S. allies and made it more difficult for Bush to rally support within the

UN Security Council. But the decision to use force against Iraq—in defiance of the Security Council and widespread global opposition—brought the problem of U.S. primacy into sharp relief. The issue was straightforward: how can other states be comfortable and secure when U.S. decisions affect all of their interests, and when the United States is strong enough to act pretty much as it wishes? Saddam Hussein was by all accounts a despicable tyrant, but the war and its aftermath led other countries to question the desirability of one state's declaring that it will wage preventive war whenever it chooses, and on the basis of its own interpretation of evidence. The war in Iraq showed *how* the United States was using its position of primacy, and *why* this approach was deeply alarming to others.

Conclusion

The end of the Cold War left the United States in an extraordinary position—one that many states might envy but none could match. Rather than relaxing at the pinnacle of power, the United States sought to extend its dominant position and to mold a world that would favor U.S. interests even more. Because it was already in remarkably good shape, U.S. efforts under Presidents George H. W. Bush and William J. Clinton were relatively modest and were conducted within the confines of existing multilateral arrangements. From the moment that President George W. Bush took office, but especially after September 11, he sought to take advantage of U.S. primacy and to use it in an unconstrained way, in order to eliminate potential threats, further enhance America's global position, and encourage the spread of American ideals and institutions.

Primacy makes many things possible, and most countries would be happy to trade places with the United States. Yet primacy also brings with it at least one obvious danger. No matter how noble the aims of the United States may be, its position in the world and its activities abroad are likely to alarm, irritate, and at times anger others. As the world's most powerful country, the United States will inevitably face greater suspicion and resentment than it did when it was one of several Great Powers (as it was from 1900 to 1945), or even when it was one of two superpowers (as it was from 1945 to 1989). In a world of independent states, the strongest one is always a potential threat to the rest, if only because they cannot be entirely sure what it is going to do with the power at its command. This tendency may be muted if the United States acts wisely, but what appears to Americans as wisdom does not always play that way overseas. What hangs in the balance, in short, is the way the rest of the world perceives and responds to U.S. primacy. America may be a genuinely benevolent force in today's world, but the rest of the world does not always see it that way. In the next chapter, I examine why this is so.

CHAPTER 2

THE ROOTS OF RESENTMENT

O ne month after the September 11 attacks (and more than a year before the invasion of Iraq), President George W. Bush told a prime-time news conference that he was surprised to learn that there was "vitriolic hatred" of America in other parts of the world. Bush said he was "amazed that there is such misunderstanding of what our country is about, that people would hate us. . . . like most Americans, I just can't believe it. Because I know how good we are." To address the problem, the president concluded, "We've got to do a better job of making our case."[1]

Bush's comments undoubtedly struck a resonant chord with most of his listeners, because Americans tend to see their country as a positive force in the world. According to former President Bill Clinton, for example, the United States is a "beacon of hope to peoples around the world," and "indispensable to the forging of stable political relations."[2] This self-congratulatory view of America's global role is routinely echoed by scholars and pundits alike, thereby reinforcing Americans' sense of their own benevolent global role. According to Harvard University political scientist Samuel P. Huntington, for example, U.S. primacy is central "to the future of freedom, democracy, open economies, and international order in the world."[3] Neo-conservative columnist Charles Krauthammer calls U.S. power "the landmine between barbarism and civilization," and historian Niall Ferguson suggests that "the alternative to a single superpower is not a multilateral utopia, but the anarchic nightmare of a new Dark Age."[4]

Thus, U.S. leaders, scholars, and public intellectuals routinely cast U.S. primacy in a favorable light and justify U.S. involvement overseas by pointing to the benefits it brings to the United States and to others. Not surprisingly, most Americans view U.S. primacy in equally favorable terms. According to the World Values Survey, for example, more than 70 percent of U.S. citizens declare themselves to be "very proud" to be Americans (by comparison, less than half the people in countries such as France, Great Britain, Italy, or the Netherlands say they are "very proud" of their own nationality), and the Pew Global Attitudes Project found that 79 percent of all Americans believe it is good "that American ideas and customs are spreading around the world."[5] Similarly, a 2001 survey of U.S. opinion leaders reported that over half of them believe that the United States is popular because it "does a lot of good around the world," and nearly 80 percent of U.S. citizens believe that the United States does either the "right amount" or "too much" to help solve global problems.[6]

Yet the rest of the world does not see U.S. primacy in quite the same way. On the one hand, people around the world admire American democracy, respect America's scientific and technological achievements, and regard the United States as a "land of opportunity."[7] But on the other hand, the percentage of foreign populations with a "favorable view" of the United States has plummeted since 1999. As Table 1 shows, the invasion of Iraq in 2003 exacerbated these trends, but the decline was already underway before the war.

In other words, there is a broad gap between how Americans perceive the U.S. role in the world and how that role is understood by others. In November/December 2001, for example, 70 percent of a select group of U.S. opinion leaders believed that U.S. foreign policy

TABLE 1

Percent with a "Favorable" Image of the United States

	2000	2002	3/2003	5/2003	3/2004
Canada	71	72	—	63	—
Great Britain	82	75	48	70	58
Italy	76	70	34	60	—
France	62	63	31	43	37
Germany	78	61	25	45	38
Spain	—	—	14	36	—
Poland	86	79	50	—	—
Russia	37	61	28	36	—
Morocco	77	—	—	27	27
Lebanon	35	—	—	27	—
Turkey	52	30	12	15	30
Jordan	25	—	—	1	5
Pakistan	23	10	—	13	21
Egypt	—	6	—	13	—
Brazil	—	52	—	34	—
Indonesia	75	61	—	15	—
South Korea	58	53	—	46	—
Palestinian Authority	—	14	—	1	—
Nigeria	—	77	—	61	—

Sources: "What the World Thinks in 2002," December 4, 2002; "Views of a Changing World, June 2003"; "Mistrust of America in Europe Ever Higher, Muslim Anger Persists," March 16, 2004. All from *Pew Global Attitudes Project*, Pew Research Center for the People and the Press, Washington, DC, available at www.people-press.org.

was "taking the interests of its partners into account" in conducting the war on terrorism. When the same question was asked of a group of opinion leaders from ten other countries, however, only one-third

TABLE 2

How Do You View U.S. Influence in the World?

	Mainly Positive	Mainly Negative	Depends/ Don't Know
Argentina	19 percent	55 percent	26 percent
Germany	27	54	19
Russia	16	63	21
Canada	34	60	6
Mexico	11	57	32
France	38	54	8
Australia	40	52	8
Indonesia	38	51	11
Brazil	42	51	7
Chile	29	50	21
Great Britain	44	50	6
Lebanon	33	49	18
South Korea	52	45	3
China	40	42	18
Italy	49	40	11
South Africa	56	35	9
Japan	24	31	45
India	54	30	16
Poland	52	21	27
Philippines	88	9	3

Source: BBC World Service and Global Poll Research Partners, January 19, 2005.

of their foreign counterparts shared this view.[8] Similarly, two-thirds of Americans believe the "war on terrorism" is a sincere effort to address this threat, but, as Table 3 shows, citizens of other countries are much more likely than Americans to attribute U.S. conduct in the war on terrorism to a variety of selfish motives.[9]

TABLE 3

"Why Do You Think the U.S. Is Conducting the War on Terrorism?"

(Percent answering "yes" to each alternative)

Country	To Control Mideast Oil?	To Dominate the World?	To Target Unfriendly Muslim Governments?	To Protect Israel?
United States	*18*	*13*	*13*	*11*
Great Britain	33	24	21	19
Russia	51	44	25	11
France	58	53	44	23
Germany	60	47	40	30
Pakistan	54	55	51	44
Turkey	64	61	47	45
Morocco	63	60	46	54
Jordan	71	61	53	70

Source: "Mistrust of America in Europe Ever Higher, Muslim Anger Persists," March 16, 2004. *Pew Global Attitudes Project*, Pew Research Center for the People and the Press, Washington, DC, available at www.people-press.org.

Other surveys of mass opinion reveal a similar gulf between how others see the United States and how Americans see themselves. As shown in Table 4, more than 70 percent of Americans believe that U.S. foreign policy takes into account the interests of others either "a great deal" or "a fair amount," but citizens in most other countries are more likely to say that U.S. foreign policy considers the interests of others "not much" or "not at all."[10] Similarly, in 2003, over 60 percent of the U.S. population approved of President George W. Bush's handling of international policy, but only 30 percent of Europeans surveyed agreed.[11] As Table 5 reveals, there is also an entirely pre-

TABLE 4

"Does U.S. Foreign Policy Consider Interests of Others?"

Country	Yes (Great Deal + Fair Amount)		No (Not Much + Not At All)	
	2002	2004	2002	2004
United States	*75 percent*	*70 percent*	*25 percent*	*27 percent*
Great Britain	44	36	55	61
France	21	14	76	84
Germany	32	29	66	69
Pakistan	23	18	62	48
Russia	22	20	71	73
Turkey	9	14	86	79
Jordan	28	16	71	77
Morocco	31	34	63	57

Sources: "What the World Thinks in 2002," and "Mistrust of America in Europe Ever Higher, Muslim Anger Persists." *Pew Global Attitudes Project*, Pew Research Center for the People and the Press, Washington, DC, available at www.people-press.org.

dictable gap between U.S. and European views on the desirability of America's being the world's only superpower.

Nor is this pattern confined to Europe. Bush's overall approval rating in the United States was 61 percent in March 2004, but his scores in other countries were dramatically lower. Indeed, Bush's standing lagged well behind that of Osama bin Laden in Pakistan, Jordan, and Morocco.[12] And in Iraq, 35 percent of the population held a "favorable" or "very favorable" view of bin Laden in August 2003, and 50 percent said they believed the United States would probably "hurt Iraq" over the next five years. By April 2004, in fact, a Gallup/

ITABLE 5

**"In Thinking About International Affairs,
Which Statement Comes Closer to Your Position
About the United States and the European Union?"**

Country	U.S. Should Remain Only Superpower	EU Should Become Superpower
United States	*42 percent*	*37 percent*
Great Britain	22	52
France	5	89
Germany	8	70
Netherlands	9	65
Italy	5	80
Poland	10	63
Portugal	7	80

Source: *Transatlantic Trends*, German Marshall Fund of the United States, June 2003. Survey conducted June 2003.

CNN/*USA Today* poll reported that 59 percent of Iraqis thought U.S. military actions in Iraq were "unjustified," and a survey commissioned by the Coalition Provisional Authority in May 2004 found that 80 percent of Iraqis had "no confidence" in the ability of the U.S.-led coalition to improve the situation in their country.[13]

In short, Americans see their country as a positive force in the world, but the rest of the world is decidedly ambivalent. The United States does have vocal defenders such as British Prime Minister Tony Blair (who has publicly denounced anti-Americanism as a "foolish indulgence"), but it also has more than its share of prominent and equally vocal critics.[14] Indian author Arundhati Roy explained the September 11 attacks by saying, "American foreign policy has created a huge, simmering reservoir of resentment"; novelist John le Carré greeted the war on Iraq by declaring in *The Times* (London), "The

United States has gone mad"; and playwright Harold Pinter judged the United States to be "beyond reason" and likened it to Nazi Germany.[15] Nobel Prize–winning German author Günter Grass warned, "This man Bush is a danger to his own country"; the mayor of London, Ken Livingstone, called Bush "the greatest threat to life on this planet that we've most probably ever seen"; and physicist Stephen Hawking told a London rally that the U.S. invasion of Iraq was a "war crime" based on "lies."[16]

The U.S. image is especially bleak in the Arab and Islamic world. A June 2004 survey of six Arab countries confirmed that these populations hold overwhelmingly negative views of the U.S. role in the world, despite somewhat positive attitudes toward U.S. science and technology, American movies and TV, and even the American people themselves. In particular, fewer than 10 percent of those surveyed in Egypt, Morocco, Saudi Arabia, Jordan, Lebanon, and the United Arab Emirates (UAE) have favorable views of U.S. policy toward the Arabs in general, the Palestinians, the war on terrorism, and Iraq.[17] And when asked to identify their "first thought" when America is mentioned, the most common response in Egypt, the UAE, and Saudi Arabia was "unfair foreign policy."[18]

Such sentiments are not confined to the Arab and Islamic world, however. Indeed, they can now be found in every corner of the globe, including America's long-standing democratic allies. As *The Economist* concluded in February 2003, "There exists a widening gulf of incomprehension between the people of America and the peoples of Europe."[19] In November 2003, in fact, 53 percent of Europeans thought the United States had a "negative role" on "peace in the world," and only 27 percent thought the U.S. role was positive.[20]

What is going on here? If U.S. primacy is a force for good in the world—as U.S. leaders proclaim and Americans overwhelmingly believe—then why don't other countries recognize this? Is it simple envy, the product of irrational hatreds, or a prudent and predictable reaction to the asymmetry of power in Washington's hands?

For some commentators, the problem is "who we are." According to President Bush, "America was targeted for attack because we're the brightest beacon for freedom and opportunity in the world."[21] Or, as he later explained, "The terrorists who attacked our country on September the 11th, 2001 were not protesting our policies. They were protesting our existence. Some say that by fighting the terrorists abroad since September the 11th, we only stir up a hornet's nest. But the terrorists who struck that day were stirred up already. If America were not fighting terrorists in Iraq, and Afghanistan, and elsewhere, what would these thousands of killers do, suddenly begin leading productive lives of service and charity?"[22] From this perspective, opposition to the United States is an inevitable, and thus unavoidable, reaction either to the concentration of power in U.S. hands or the specific political and cultural values that the United States represents. And if that were the whole story, there would be little the United States could do about it.

Other observers blame anti-Americanism primarily on "what we do." It is not just U.S. power or U.S. values, it is also the specific ways that U.S. power is used and the specific ways that U.S. leaders justify America's global role. Thus, the late author Susan Sontag saw September 11 as a direct response (however reprehensible) to America's own actions, asking, "Where is the acknowledgment that this was not a 'cowardly' attack on 'civilization' or 'liberty' or 'the free world' but an attack on the world's self-proclaimed superpower, undertaken as a consequence of specific American alliances and actions?"[23] Of course, if America's actions are largely responsible for the rising tide of resentment, then it might be possible to reduce these tendencies by using U.S. power differently, and by adopting a different approach to dealing with the rest of the world.[24]

Which is it? The answer (unfortunately) is: "Both." American power does worry friends and foes alike, and America's values can be a source of friction as well as admiration. But that is not the most important part of the story. Opposition to the United States is driven primarily by the ways that the United States uses its power, both in the past and at present, and especially when the United States acts in an overweening or hypocritical fashion.

The remainder of this chapter explores these issues in greater detail, focusing on two main themes. I begin by asking why other societies might fear, resent, or hate us for "what we are," and then consider why such attitudes are affected even more by "what we do." I then explain why Americans often fail to understand these tendencies. Why do we often underestimate the degree of foreign resentment, and why do we overlook our own role in generating it?

"They Fear (or Hate or Resent) Us for What We Are"

Fear of American Power

The end of the Cold War altered many key features of world politics, but it did not affect the essential nature of the international system. States still live in a condition of anarchy, where there is no world government to protect them from each other. In particular, each state must try to provide its own security as best it can. As a result, states are prone to worry if one state becomes more powerful than the rest, and especially if it becomes so strong that it can impose its will with impunity.[25] Winston Churchill's summary of British foreign policy captures the logic of this position perfectly: "For four hundred years the foreign policy of England has been to oppose the strongest, most aggressive, most dominating power on the Continent. . . . [W]e always took the harder course, joined with the less strong powers, and thus defeated the Continental military tyrant whoever he was."[26] The same principle has governed U.S. grand strategy since its rise to Great Power status: U.S. leaders have consistently opposed any state that threatened to establish regional hegemony in Europe or Asia, so as to avoid facing a rival power with capabilities comparable to America's own.[27]

From this perspective, it is easy to understand why other states worry about U.S. primacy. They worry because the United States is strong enough to act pretty much as it wishes, and other states cannot be sure that Washington will not use its immense power to threaten their own interests. Back in 2000, for example, the official Russian National Security Concept warned of "attempts to create an international relations structure based on domination by developed Western countries . . . under U.S. leadership and *designed for unilateral solutions (including the use of military force) to key issues in world politics*."[28] More recently, the Bush administration's emphasis on "preemption" was greeted by a chorus of foreign criticism, such as German Foreign Minister Joschka Fischer's comment that "a world order in which the national interests of the strongest power is the criterion for military action simply cannot work."[29]

"But wait," many Americans would respond, "we are a peace-loving country that uses its power to advance the greater good of humankind." Even more than most Great Powers, America's faith in its own rectitude leads both its leaders and its citizens to discount the possibility that others might find U.S. power worrisome or threatening. Neoconservative Richard Perle believes that "U.S. power is always potentially a source for good in the world," and columnist Charles Krauthammer declares that what protects civilization from barbarism "is not parchment but power, and in a unipolar world, American power—wielded, if necessary, unilaterally. If necessary, preemptively."[30] Not to be outdone, *Newsweek* diplomatic correspondent Michael Hirsh concludes that, "for all its fumbling, the role played by the United States is the greatest gift the world has received in many, many centuries, possibly all of recorded history."[31] Or, as George W. Bush remarked during the 2000 presidential campaign, "The United States has a great and guiding goal: to turn this time of American influence into generations of democratic peace."[32] Who could disagree with that? Americans think their noble aims are apparent to all, which means that only evil or aggressive regimes have any reason to fear American power.

There are at least four problems with this defense of U.S. primacy, however. First, as discussed in greater detail below, the U.S. record is not as pure as many Americans believe. The United States has used its power to harm other countries in the past—including states that were not especially evil or aggressive—and other states are well aware of this fact. Pious declarations of American virtue may find a receptive audience at home, but they are unlikely to convince those who have felt the sharp end of U.S. power themselves.

Second, other states worry about U.S. power because they know that conflicts of interest will inevitably arise. Because each state has a different endowment of resources, a unique geographic location, and its own particular history, each inevitably has somewhat different preferences on most issues. Landlocked countries and maritime powers have different views about the Law of the Sea, just as upwind and downwind countries generally have different interests on the issue of acid rain. Wealthy industrial powers want to lower barriers to trade in manufactured goods and services; developing countries want to reduce tariffs on agricultural products and textiles. States with different historical and cultural traditions disagree about human rights. In world politics, conflicts of interest are inescapable. And when they occur, stronger states are more likely to get their way and weaker states are more likely to have to adjust. In short, other countries dislike U.S. primacy for the same reason that Americans prefer it: on balance, weaker states have to adjust their behavior to the preferences of more powerful states. No matter how hard U.S. leaders try to reassure other states about America's benevolent intentions, therefore, other states are going to worry about American power.

Third, even if it were true that the United States had consistently acted for the greater good in the past, other states do not know how the United States will behave in the future. No state can know what another state might choose to do, which means that a large imbalance of power in anyone's favor will always be daunting to others. The United States may have done less harm per unit of power than other major powers have, but the rest of the world cannot be sure that it will remain benevolent, especially when its position of primacy gives it unprecedented freedom of action. As a senior Chinese diplomat put it in 2000, "How can we base our own national security on your assurances of good will?" Or as Oxford historian Timothy Garton Ash noted in April 2002: "The problem with American power is not that it is American. The problem is simply the power. It would be dangerous even for an archangel to wield so much power."[33]

"But the United States is a democracy," some Americans might insist, "and democracies don't fight each other. Tyrants and dictators may have reason to fear us, but our fellow democracies share the same ideals and need not worry about our dominance." The claim that "democracies don't fight each other" may be empirically correct (though it remains controversial among scholars of international relations), but it does not mean that other states have no reason to fear U.S. power. Not every state is a democracy, for one thing, and as John M. Owen and Ido Oren have shown, how the United States deals with other states depends in large part on whether we *perceive* them to be democratic or not.[34] Moreover, even states that can feel confident the United States will not attack them still have reason to worry about the concentration of power in American hands. Britain, France, and Israel did not think the United States was going to attack them during the Suez War of 1956, for example, but U.S. economic and diplomatic pressure still forced them into a humiliating withdrawal from the territories they had conquered.[35] Nor did the United States threaten to use military force when it abandoned the gold standard in 1971 and destroyed the Bretton Woods monetary order, but it did use its superior economic position to force other states to bear the costs of this shift.

"Not so fast," a reader familiar with contemporary social-science theory might counter. "Democratic leaders can also make more credible promises than authoritarian leaders can, because their citizens are more likely to remove them from power if they renege on their commitments." If so, then other states need not worry that the United States will become aggressive in the future, because U.S. leaders cannot renege on prior pledges of restraint without incurring significant domestic political costs.[36] Some scholars also maintain that U.S. primacy is more acceptable to other states because the United States has consciously chosen to "bind" itself within key international institutions (such as NATO), in effect exercising self-restraint in order to reassure others about its benevolent intentions.[37] Both arguments imply that other states need not worry that U.S. power would be used in harmful ways—either because U.S. leaders will remain bound by past promises or because U.S. leaders will recognize that the long-term benefits of multilateral cooperation will outweigh any short-term gains from unilateral action.

These features may diminish concerns about U.S. power somewhat, but they cannot eliminate them. As we saw in the previous chapter, the United States already dominates institutions such as NATO and the World Bank, which makes them at best a weak constraint on its own freedom of action. And as discussed at length in chapter 3, efforts to "bind" the United States within a web of institutional ties have generally failed, save in certain specialized areas where the U.S. advantage is less pronounced. Similarly, the alleged ability of democracies to make more credible commitments did not prevent the United States from abandoning the gold standard in 1971 or abrogating the 1972 Anti-Ballistic Missile Treaty in the fall of 2001, to the consternation of many long-standing allies. Bill Clinton signed the convention establishing the International Criminal Court, but George Bush removed the U.S. "signature" a few months later. Democracies may be less arbitrary or fickle than their authoritarian counterparts, but they can still change their minds. After all, isn't that why they hold elections?

There is a final reason why no state can be entirely comfortable with the concentration of power in the hands of the United States. Even if the United States were consistently trying to act for the general good of mankind, its policies can still do considerable damage inadvertently. Assurances about America's benevolent intentions may be of little value if actions undertaken for noble reasons end up hurting others by accident. After all, the United States did not *intend* to destabilize Cambodia in the early 1970s, but its intervention there helped pave the way for the Khmer Rouge and thus contributed indirectly to a massive genocide. The United States surely did not intend its support for the Afghan *mujaheddin* to lead to creation of a global network of Islamic terrorists, but that is in fact what happened. The Bush administration was obviously not trying to get al Qaeda to attack the Madrid subway system when it courted Spanish support for the war in Iraq, but that was still one of the unintended effects of its policies.

Less dramatically, U.S. legislators are not actively seeking to stifle third-world development or put foreigners out of work when they erect protectionist tariffs against foreign textiles or extend agricultural subsidies to American farmers; they are simply trying to protect jobs in their home districts and enhance their own prospects for reelection. But the effect on developing countries is no different than if they had acted with deliberate malice.

Looking ahead, if U.S. efforts to transform the Middle East end up destabilizing key oil producers and driving up world oil prices, then every oil-importing country would suffer, even though the United States did not mean to harm them. If the United States were to launch a preventive war against North Korea, or attempt a surgical strike against its nuclear production facilities, this action could trigger a destructive war on the Korean Peninsula and do massive damage to South Korea and possibly Japan. But these results would not have been our intention, merely a tragic side effect.

The point should be clear. The conduct of foreign policy is rife with unintended consequences, and the bigger you are and the more freedom of action you enjoy, the more damage you can cause even if you don't mean to do it.[38] The late Canadian Prime Minister Pierre

Trudeau captured the problem perfectly some years ago, when he remarked that living next to the United States was "like sleeping with an elephant. No matter how friendly and even-tempered the beast, . . . one is affected by every twitch and grunt."[39] This problem may be especially acute for neighboring states like Canada, but America's dominant position means that its "twitches and grunts" are now felt in every corner of the globe. Even if other countries were convinced that the United States was in fact uniquely virtuous and acting only for the greater good, they would still have good reasons to worry about how America was going to use its power. At the very least, the rest of the world would be foolish to assume that the United States would never act in ways that could harm them.

Resistance to American Values

The United States is not just the world's strongest country, of course. It is also a society with a distinct set of political values and institutions and a singular vision of its historic world role. As the world's dominant economic and military power, the United States casts a large cultural shadow. In contrast to some other Great Powers (such as the former Soviet Union), U.S. society is also adept at producing cultural icons with enormous worldwide appeal—think of Coca-Cola, Michael Jordan, Hollywood movies, or television—as well as institutions of higher education that serve as powerful intellectual beacons.

As discussed in chapter 1, the appeal of American ideals and the long shadow cast by American culture reinforces America's position of primacy. Unfortunately, America's political values and cultural products are not universally appealing. The ideals that America stands for, and the cultural practices that it transmits to the rest of the world, can also be a powerful source of anti-American sentiment, especially when the global balance of power is so heavily weighted in America's favor.

At one extreme, anti-Americanism arises from the belief that American society and culture are inherently evil or immoral. Religious fundamentalists and other extremists condemn the hedonism and sexual explicitness of American popular culture and point to its high rates of divorce, out-of-wedlock parenting, and other social ills. Thus, when the late Sayyid Qutb, a leading intellectual of Egypt's Muslim Brotherhood and a continuing influence on today's Islamic radicals, visited the United States in the late 1940s, he was repelled by what he saw as America's individualism, commercial greed, and sexual licentiousness. As he put it, "Humanity today is living in a large brothel. . . . One has only to glance at its press, films, fashion shows, beauty contests. . . . Or observe its mad lust for naked flesh, provocative pictures, and sick, suggestive statements in literature, the arts, and the media!"[40] More recently, Osama bin Laden has sought to capitalize on similar feelings of revulsion by denouncing the United States for "gambling," for "practicing the trade of sex in all its forms," for "exploiting women like consumer products," and for "producing, trading and using intoxicants and drugs," not to mention President Clinton's "immoral acts" in the Oval Office.[41] Such critiques are not confined to foreign radicals, of course; homegrown fundamentalists also regard contemporary American society as morally bankrupt and in need of a radical religious revival.[42]

Less extreme versions of this same tendency reject the individualism, materialism, and glorification of violence in American popular culture, as well as some of the more obvious failings of the American social and political system. In particular, foreign critics point to the comparatively high levels of violent crime in the United States, an incarceration rate that is significantly higher than in other industrial democracies, and its continued reliance upon the death penalty. As one French commentator explains it, "In European eyes, America is still a barbaric country, a Wild West that does not know how to police its population and control its judges and sheriffs."[43]

Paradoxically, concerns about U.S. primacy also arise from the fear that American culture is *too* attractive, and that the spread of American values will extinguish other ways of life. Here the concern is not that U.S. culture is inherently repellent; rather, the concern is that it is so seductive that it will eventually replace existing cultural systems. When the French worry about the spread of English, fast food, or Walt Disney, or when developing countries complain about "cultural genocide," they are expressing a fear that the dynamic thrust of American norms, business practices, and cultural products will eventually compromise their own cultural identity. As the Pew Global Attitudes Survey noted in 2002, "Publics in every European country surveyed except Bulgaria are resentful of the American cultural intrusion in their country. . . . In the Middle East, overwhelming majorities in every country except Uzbekistan have a negative impression of American ideas and customs. . . . The sentiment also appears throughout Latin America and Asia (with the exception of Japan and the Philippines)."[44]

In these cases, opposition to the United States does not necessarily arise from a direct concern about its power. Rather, the common thread in these different types of anti-Americanism is an aversion to specific American political and social values and a desire to contain—or, in some cases, reverse—their spread.

Upon reflection, concerns about the contagious spread of U.S. values and practices should not surprise us. The U.S. political system is based on a set of universal claims about individual rights and human liberty, claims that by definition transcend the borders of existing states. Moreover, U.S. leaders have long declared the promotion of these ideals to be a fundamental U.S. interest. In 1989, for example, President George H. W. Bush declared, "Nothing can stand in the way of freedom's march," and he later proclaimed, "No society, no continent, should be disqualified from sharing the ideals of human liberty."[45] Some ten years later, Bush's son began his own *National Security Strategy* by declaring that "these values of freedom are right and true for all people everywhere." Thus, the United States openly identifies itself as a universal model for all societies and sees itself as a superior alternative to all nonliberal social orders.[46]

Like other universal ideologies, therefore, American liberalism threatens the legitimacy of alternative social orders merely by existing.[47] Even if the United States did not try to spread its ideals abroad, other states would still worry that the ideas might spread spontaneously. The stronger and more successful the United States is, the longer the shadow it will cast on others and the more illiberal states will fear the power of the U.S. example.[48]

Furthermore, the United States has not been content to be merely a "shining city on a hill." Instead, the United States actively seeks to spread its ideals abroad, sometimes with a vengeance. The combination of a universalist political philosophy and a strong evangelical streak is understandable, for if one genuinely believes that one's own political principles are universally valid, then it is easy to conclude that one has an obligation to carry them to others. John Quincy Adams may have famously warned Americans not to venture abroad "in search of monsters to destroy," but he was writing when the United States was still a weak and isolated power whose survival as an independent country was far from certain.[49] American leaders have long seen the United States as a model for the rest of the world, and their ambitions have grown as U.S. power has increased. Upon joining the ranks of the other Great Powers, the United States sought to combine the pursuit of power with the loftier goal of recasting the world in America's image.[50] Between 1900 and 2000, in fact, the United States used force to impose democratic institutions on other countries at least twenty-five separate times, albeit with varying degrees of success.[51]

U.S. power is now unmatched, and the belief that primacy should be used to promote democratic ideals enjoys broad support across the political spectrum. Thus, neoconservatives such as William Kristol and Lawrence Kaplan ask, "What's wrong with dominance in the service of sound principles and high ideals?" and the Bush administration declares that "the great strength of this nation must be used to promote a balance of power that favors freedom."[52]

Nor is this ambition confined to conservative Republicans. The Clinton administration also advocated using U.S. power to "enlarge" the sphere of democratic rule, and contemporary liberals remain as committed to this goal as their neoconservative counterparts. Thus, Michael McFaul of the Carnegie Endowment for International Peace believes U.S. foreign policy should be guided by a "Liberty Doctrine," which in turn requires the United States to maintain its current position of primacy. "To effectively promote liberty abroad over the long haul," he writes, "the United States must maintain its overwhelming military advantage over the rest of the world."[53]

Unfortunately, the combination of great power, universal principles, and a bipartisan consensus in favor of imposing these principles on others is bound to be alarming to other countries, including some of our fellow democracies. Even societies that admire certain U.S. values may not want to adopt all of them—and especially not at the point of a gun. As noted at the beginning of this chapter, for example, the world's industrial democracies share similar commitments to individual rights and the rule of law, and many of their citizens see the United States as a "land of opportunity" and admire many of its achievements. Yet these same populations oppose the spread of American-style democracy and business practices and regard the less-admirable features of American society with a combination of fear and disdain. In particular, although European publics (and especially European elites) clearly believe "globalization" is a good thing, sizable majorities reject the U.S. economic system as "too inequitable" to be a good model for their own countries. According to a 2002 study by the State Department's Office of Research, "Half or more in Britain, France, Germany and Italy say that the U.S. economic system 'neglects too many social problems because of a lack of job security and few employment benefits for many workers.'"[54] Similarly, a *Eurobarometer* survey in 2003 showed that French, German, and British citizens by overwhelming margins rejected "copying the American economic model." There are many "varieties of democratic capitalism" in the world today, and the inhabitants of other Organization for Economic Cooperation and Development (OECD) countries want to keep it that way.[55]

Equally important, much of the world is not democratic at all. For these regimes, the combination of preponderant power and ideological zeal that now drives U.S. foreign policy is undoubtedly alarming. When President George W. Bush declares that "it is the policy of the United States to seek and support the growth of democratic movements and institutions in every nation and culture," he is in effect saying that the United States is committed to making the whole world move toward the American vision of an ideal social order.[56] And when his administration justifies regime change in Iraq by claiming that it will spark a wave of democratic transformation throughout the Middle East, it is in effect declaring that all nondemocracies are illegitimate and deserve to be replaced.[57] Not surprisingly, the Bush administration's "Greater Middle East Initiative"—a program intended to promote democracy and good governance—provoked a decidedly negative reaction in the Arab world when it was announced in the spring of 2004. Jordan's foreign minister declared that "our objective is for this document never to see the light," and a columnist in Egypt's semi-official newspaper, *al-Ahram*, commented that "there is no difference between what was said by the British, French, Belgian, and Dutch colonizers . . . and what the modern colonial empires are saying."[58] Indeed, it would be astonishing if the leaders of nondemocratic states did not view America's efforts to spread democracy as an imminent threat to their own positions.

It is hardly wrong, of course, for Americans to favor liberty, democracy, free markets, the rule of law, or the vibrant diversity of American cultural life. Nor is it necessarily wrong for the United States to use its power to encourage others to adopt these ideas. But the truths that Americans hold to be "self-evident" are not "self-evident" elsewhere. This is one more reason why American power worries others: Not only can they not be sure what we are going to do with it, some of the things we say we intend to do are deeply troubling.

Is It "What We Are" or "What We Stand For"?

At this point, it may be tempting to conclude that foreign hostility is simply unavoidable, either because other states are worried about American power or because they are hostile to American ideals. In this view, anti-Americanism is an inescapable part of being the dominant global power. Thus, the Pentagon's 2005 *National Defense Strategy* acknowledges that America's "leading position in world affairs will continue to breed unease, a degree of resentment, and resistence," and neoconservative pundit Max Boot writes that "resentment comes with the territory."[59]

As one would expect, this interpretation is popular among those who believe the United States should pursue an ambitious global role, as well as those who believe the United States should pay little attention to the concerns of other countries. Thus, Robert Kagan and William Kristol write that "the main issue of contention between the United States and most of those who express opposition to its hegemony is not American 'arrogance.' It is the inescapable reality of American power in all its forms."[60] Similarly, historian Bernard Lewis maintains that "Muslim rage" is a response to the past failures of the Islamic world, rather than a reaction either to past Western actions or current U.S. policies.[61] Neoconservative Arabist Fouad Ajami offers much the same view, suggesting that anti-Americanism is the " 'road rage' of a thwarted Arab world—the congenital condition of a culture yet to take full responsibility for its self-inflicted wounds," and he recommends that "there is no need to pay excessive deference to the political pieties and givens of the region."[62] If anti-American extremism is primarily a reaction to perceived weakness and past humiliation, then the United States should do what it thinks is right and not worry very much about whether the rest of the world agrees.[63]

A milder version of the same argument sees European opposition to American unilateralism (and especially its opposition to preventive wars in places like Iraq) as a reflection of European resentment at their own impotence and envy for America's current global dominance. This explanation was a central theme of Robert Kagan's *Of Paradise and Power*, which famously claimed, "Americans are from Mars; Europeans from Venus." Or as columnist Charles Krauthammer put it, Europeans who object to the active use of U.S. power are part of an "axis of petulance . . . the real problem is their irrelevance."[64] These arguments carry an obvious implication: If there is nothing the United States can do to alleviate foreign hostility, why try?

As the previous pages have suggested, there is a grain of truth in these arguments. Some degree of foreign opposition to U.S. primacy is a reaction to America's dominant material position and the alien and potentially threatening effects of American values and culture. Such attitudes are reinforced by the destabilizing effects of globalization, for, as Benjamin Cohen puts it, "Globalization is seen by many as not benevolent but malign . . . [and] since America is identified with globalization as its patron and its principal beneficiary, that view means that America is the enemy too."[65] To an extent, therefore, anti-Americanism is "hard-wired" into the system as long as the United States remains number one.

Yet it would be a grave error to see this as the whole story, or even the most important part.

First, this interpretation cannot explain the downward trend of the past decade, and especially the deterioration of America's international position after 2000. The United States has been the "unipolar power" since the early 1990s (at the latest), but its international standing remained high throughout the entire decade. Although a number of foreign leaders expressed concerns about the asymmetry of power in U.S. hands, solid majorities around the world held "favorable" opinions of the United States, and both George H. W.

Bush and Bill Clinton enjoyed good working relations with a wide array of foreign leaders. Indeed, in 2000 Clinton became only the third American to win the Charlemagne Prize, awarded annually to the individual who had made the greatest contribution to European unity.[66] If U.S. power were the main source of the problem, America's image in the world should have declined much sooner. Instead, the chief source of contemporary opposition is global reaction to specific U.S. policies—and especially the actions of the Bush administration—and is not simply a response to U.S. power or American values.

Second, the belief that it is just "who we are" ignores the testimony of some of America's most fervent opponents. Take Osama bin Laden, for example. Although bin Laden is sometimes critical of American culture, his actions throughout his career have been inspired primarily by opposition to the specific policies of particular states. In the 1980s, he went to Afghanistan to aid the *mujaheddin* resistance to the Soviet Union. In the 1990s, he organized al Qaeda in response to the U.S. military presence in the Persian Gulf—and especially in Saudi Arabia—and in opposition to U.S. support for Israel.[67] It is not simply America's *existence* that fuels his hatred. It is also his belief that the United States "has been occupying the lands of Islam in the holiest of places . . . , plundering its riches, dictating to its rulers, humiliating its people, terrorizing its neighbors, and turning its bases in the [Arabian] Peninsula into a spearhead through which to fight the neighboring Muslim peoples." Indeed, bin Laden emphasized in October 2004 that he and his followers were not at war against "freedom," which is why they did not strike countries like Sweden. Rather, he attacked the United States to "punish" it for its "unjust" actions in the Middle East. His enmity, in short, is a reaction to U.S. foreign policy, and not to U.S. power per se or to America's underlying values.[68]

Bin Laden's opposition is extreme, of course, but he is not alone. According to the Pew Global Attitudes Survey, for example, "antipathy toward the United States is shaped more by what it *does* in the international arena than by what it *stands for* politically and economi-cally."[69] Similarly, an authoritative study by the Pentagon's Defense Science Board concluded that "Muslims do not 'hate our freedom,' but rather they hate our policies," noting further that in the eyes of the Muslim world, the "American occupation of Afghanistan and Iraq has not led to democracy there, but only more chaos and suffer-ing."[70] According to the State Department's Advisory Group on Pub-lic Diplomacy for the Arab and Muslim World, "Arabs and Muslims . . . support our values but believe that our policies do not live up to them."[71] When citizens of six Arab countries were asked if their atti-tude toward America was shaped by their feelings about American values or U.S. policies, "an overwhelming percentage of respondents indicated that policy played a more important role."[72] Or, as former Palestinian chief negotiator Saeb Erekat put it, "Most of the Arab public admires U.S. freedoms and democracy and bears no hostility to the Americans as a people. But that same public is both horrified and angered by an American foreign policy which does little, if any-thing, to promote similar freedoms and democracy in the Middle East.[73] Similarly, Egyptian President Hosni Mubarak has testified that "there exists a hatred [of America] never equaled in the region," in part because Arabs "see [Israeli Prime Minister] Sharon act as he wants, without the Americans saying anything."[74]

In particular, the most violent forms of anti-American terrorism seem to be inspired primarily by reactions to U.S. actions and policies rather than by a fundamental animosity to U.S. values or culture or even U.S. power itself. For example, a 1997 study by the Defense Sci-ence Board found "a strong correlation between U.S. involvement in international situations and increased terrorist attacks on the United States."[75] Prominent examples of these essentially reactive attacks include Libya's hijacking of Pan Am flight 73 in September 1987 and the December 1988 bombing of Pan Am flight 103, the bombing of the World Trade Center in 1993, and a rocket attack on U.S. military facilities in Japan in 1991. Similarly, the terrorist attack on the Madrid subway system in 2004 was not inspired by antipathy toward Spanish values or Spanish culture; it was a deliberate response to Spain's support for the U.S. invasion of Iraq and its continued presence among the occupying forces. In other words, international terrorists have not attacked the United States or its allies because they are opposed to U.S. values, or even primarily because they are worried about U.S. power. Instead, they have targeted the United States because they oppose its global military presence and the policies that presence is supporting.[76] And even here, the vast majority of terrorist groups are not attacking the United States directly; rather, they are primarily motivated by local grievances and target Americans only when U.S. power is actively engaged in their neighborhoods. It is not just "who we are," in short, it is what we do and where we do it.[77]

Third, the claim that foreign opposition stems solely from "who we are" is simply too convenient. Americans find it an appealing thesis, of course, because it absolves us of any responsibility for the fear, hatred, or resentment that others direct at the United States. In this view, it is not our fault that we are so powerful, and we have nothing for which to apologize if our democratic values pose a threat to corrupt and oppressive dictatorships around the world. The appeal of this interpretation was repeatedly demonstrated in the aftermath of the September 11 attacks, when government spokesmen (and especially the president) repeatedly portrayed them as an assault on "liberty," and anyone who suggested that the attacks might also be a reaction to prior U.S. activities was likely to be condemned for being unpatriotic.[78]

Unfortunately, once we embrace this explanation for foreign opposition, we cease asking how the United States can act in ways that might make its position in the world either better or worse. If they hate us solely for what we stand for, and what we stand for is basically good, then there is nothing we can or should do about it, and the only question is how we can win the inevitable struggle.

To recognize the U.S. role in generating foreign opposition is not to imply that U.S. foreign policy is necessarily wrong, and it certainly does not mean that anti-American terrorism is justified. Rather, the point is that opposition to the United States is not based solely on concerns about U.S. power and does not arise primarily from some abstract opposition to U.S. values (including its support for "freedom"). Instead, anti-Americanism is the price the United States is paying for its current global position and the specific ways it uses its power, and the real question is simply whether the benefits outweigh the costs.[79]

In short, anti-American attitudes and anti-American behavior are not just a defensive reaction to America's superior power or a reflection of some fundamental rejection of U.S. values. Instead, we must also consider what the United States has done to other countries, and what it is doing today.

What the United States Has Done and What It Is Doing

Historic Grievances: The Legacy of the Past

The belief that American primacy is good for the world and should be welcomed by others rests on the claim that the United States is an unusually benevolent Great Power. According to columnist Charles Krauthammer, "The American claim to benignity is not mere self-congratulation. We have a track record."[80] He has a point. U.S. global leadership has produced a number of important successes, including the reconstruction of Europe and Japan, the creation of multilateral institutions for global economic management, the containment and eventual defeat of the Soviet Union (without a Great Power war), and the growing acceptance of democracy and human rights worldwide. The United States does not deserve all the credit for these events, but it surely played a major role. American power has deterred conflict on the Korean Peninsula, dampened rivalries in Europe and Asia, helped bring peace to Bosnia and Kosovo, and eased the simmering dispute between India and Pakistan. And, unlike earlier Great Powers, it has done these things without amassing a vast overseas empire and without ruling vast colonies and millions of people by force. As German foreign-affairs expert Josef Joffe put it (albeit before the invasion of Iraq): "America is a hegemon different from all its predecessors. America annoys and antagonizes, but it does not conquer."[81]

Yet America's "track record" is not perfect, and the rest of the world knows it. Even before the Cold War, the United States sometimes used force in heavy-handed and self-serving ways, although it did so primarily within its own hemisphere.[82] During the Cold War, the United States supported armed rebels in Nicaragua, Afghanistan, Angola, and elsewhere, and actively worked to undermine communist rule whenever and wherever it could. Along the way, the United States helped overthrow at least nine freely elected governments, while turning a blind eye to the brutal behavior of an unsavory array of anticommunist dictators, including some of its authoritarian allies in the Middle East and Persian Gulf.[83] After the Cold War ended, the United States imposed a series of one-sided agreements on its defeated Cold War adversaries, fired cruise missiles into Sudan and Afghanistan in a failed attempt to prevent future terrorist attacks, maintained crippling economic sanctions and conducted repeated air strikes against Iraq, and continued to subsidize Israel's occupation of the West Bank and the Gaza Strip. It also overthrew governments in Afghanistan, Haiti, Serbia, and most recently Iraq, killing thousands of civilians in the process.

Even if each of these actions were entirely defensible, this history provides fertile ground for anti-Americanism. If another country believes the United States has acted aggressively in the past—and especially if U.S. actions seemed particularly hostile or callous—then it is likely to be even more suspicious of U.S. conduct and especially worried by U.S. primacy.

This tendency may seem somewhat puzzling at first. Why should one nation care what some other nation did to it in the past? Why incur present-day costs and risks because of some unfortunate behavior long ago? Why should Armenians continue to dwell on the past crimes of the Turks? Why do Serbs obsess about their own historic misfortunes? Why can't East Asians forget what Japan did a half-century ago? Why not let bygones be bygones, bury the hatchet, and move on?

There are at least two reasons why past grievances can still shape current attitudes and behavior. First, states may use another country's past behavior as a guide to its future conduct.[84] As with a mutual fund, past performance is no guarantee of how a state will act in the future. Nonetheless, other states are likely to draw inferences from past behavior in order to forecast how others are going to behave in the future. States that have behaved benevolently (or at least with a degree of restraint) will be seen in a more favorable light; those that have acted badly will be viewed with more suspicion. And governments that commit great crimes—such as Nazi Germany or Imperial Japan—may place their nations under a shadow of suspicion lasting for decades. Even when there are no immediate signs of revanchism, historical memories will encourage others to make sure that subsequent generations never gain the opportunity to repeat the crimes of their ancestors. Remembrance of past atrocities fueled Serb and Croat violence following the breakup of the former Yugoslavia and gave nationalist leaders like Franjo Tudjman and Slobodan Milosevic a potent weapon for stoking nationalist fervor.[85]

Second, even if the victims do not believe that past behavior is necessarily a guide to future conduct, past crimes can also generate a desire for vengeance. This desire might be explained on purely rational grounds (i.e., states want to punish crimes against humanity in order to reinforce norms and deter similar acts in the future), but it may also arise from the desire to make the guilty parties suffer as others have suffered. A purely rational explanation for retaliation ignores the role of anger and rage: when you have wronged me, I may want to hurt you, even if doing so does nothing to deter future harm and may even add fuel to the fire. The desire for vengeance seems to have played a role in the Balkans and the Israeli–Palestinian conflict, and it is a key ingredient in contemporary terrorist violence.[86]

Iran's troubled relationship with the United States illustrates both tendencies. As James A. Bill and others have noted, the long and intimate association between the United States and the Shah of Iran led many Iranians to believe the United States was constantly manipulating Iranian domestic politics for nefarious purposes. Even after the Shah fell, therefore, U.S. efforts to reach a modus vivendi with the revolutionary regime were hamstrung by Iranian suspicions that the United States was inherently hostile and untrustworthy. The result was a Catch-22: U.S. warnings or threats confirmed Iranian suspicions, but friendship or attempts at accommodation were regarded as duplicitous attempts to reassert U.S. control. At the same time, Iranian hostility was also fueled by genuine anger over past U.S. support for the Shah, and by a desire to undermine U.S. interests wherever possible.[87]

Under what conditions will historical grievances foster hatred or resentment of the United States? The answer is not immediately obvious, because there is no clear or direct relationship between the intensity of past conflicts and the present state of U.S. relations with other countries. In the Korean War, for example, violent conflict among the United States, North Korea, and the People's Republic of China solidified existing suspicions and led to a long period of hostility. U.S. interventions in Latin America have had similar effects, helping to explain why virulent anti-American movements emerged in Cuba, Nicaragua, and elsewhere.[88]

Yet other cases underscore the complex relationship between past conflict and current attitudes. The United States waged all-out war against Germany and Japan in World War II, killed tens of thousands of civilians in each society, and eventually dropped two atomic bombs on Japan. Yet relations improved dramatically once the fighting was over, and these two countries have been among America's closest allies for over half a century. The United States caused far less suffering in Iran—despite its lengthy involvement with the Shah—yet Iran has remained suspicious of the United States ever since the ouster of the Shah in 1980.

These examples show that past behavior is neither a necessary nor sufficient condition for the emergence of anti-Americanism. There are at least four other conditions that will affect whether or not past U.S. behavior will be a powerful source of present-day resentments.

First, U.S. actions will provoke greater fear, hatred, and resentment when the United States uses force and when its use of violence is seen as unprovoked. As the examples of Germany and Japan suggest, other states are less likely to resent what the United States has done when they recognize that their own actions were at least partly responsible for the damage U.S. power ultimately inflicted upon them. Although many Germans and Japanese died as a result of American military action, these societies also understood that the United States was retaliating for their own acts of aggression. Although Germans and Japanese have been critical of certain U.S. actions, they do not see U.S. participation in World War II as a historic crime.[89]

By contrast, U.S. interventions in Latin America have generated enduring anti-American attitudes because these actions were rarely (if ever) a response to Latin American aggression against the United States. Instead of responding to a direct attack on the United States itself (or on vital U.S. interests), the United States intervened in Cuba, Mexico, Chile, the Dominican Republic, Guatemala, Nicaragua, and elsewhere in order to protect U.S. business interests, to preserve U.S. political influence, or to prevent the emergence of leftist governments. Although Americans usually regarded these actions as justified, the victims of U.S. intervention saw them as unwarranted interference.

Arab and Muslim hostility toward Israel and the United States has similar origins. The Zionist movement was a response to centuries of anti-Semitism in the Christian West, and its ultimate success was partly a response to the tragedy of the Nazi Holocaust in World War II. The Arab inhabitants of Palestine were not responsible for European anti-Semitism or the Nazi genocide, yet it was their land that was lost when Israel was created. Moreover, the establishment of Israel involved considerable violence and atrocities on both sides, including officially sanctioned "ethnic cleansing" during the War of Independence and organized terrorist attacks by Israelis and Palestinians alike.[90] Israelis (and many Americans) may regard the creation of Israel as a miraculous solution to an enduring historical problem, but Palestinian Arabs understandably resent having to pay the price for other people's crimes.[91]

Second, and following from the first point, historic grievances are more likely to fester into long-term hostility when the United States either does not recognize that its actions were wrong or refuses to admit that its policies have harmed others. America's troubled relationship with Iran was not helped, for example, when President George H. W. Bush responded to the mistaken U.S. downing of an Iranian airliner in July 1988 by saying, "I will never apologize for the United States of America—I don't care what the facts are."[92] Failure to acknowledge past crimes is troubling to others in part because it implies that the victims do not merit an apology; it compounds the original injury by treating the victims with contempt. Equally important, failure to acknowledge past sins reinforces the fear that these crimes will be repeated. When a state does not admit that it did something wrong, those to whom the wrong was done will rightly conclude that the transgressor either does not know what proper behavior is or does not care whether or not it "follows the rules." Being treated with contempt is likely to generate additional rage and resentment, and victims may also conclude that a state that would blithely ignore well-established norms will not be bound by moral constraints in the future.

Third, this tendency will be compounded when the United States takes some action that harms another state, and when doing so violates principles that the United States had previously declared to be important. This sort of hypocrisy suggests that the United States regards the victims of its policies as inherently inferior, because it is acting as if its own cherished principles do not apply when its own behavior is involved. Thus, U.S. support for third-world dictators during the Cold War provoked widespread criticism partly because these rulers were frequently brutal and corrupt, and also because this behavior was at odds with the ideals that U.S. leaders proclaimed to be all-important. Similarly, many people in the Arab and Muslim world cannot understand why the United States supports self-determination in places such as Eastern Europe or the Balkans yet continues to support Israel's occupation of the West Bank and the Gaza Strip and maintains close ties with assorted Arab dictatorships. As the Pentagon's Defense Science Board noted in November 2003, "When American public diplomacy talks about bringing democracy to Islamic societies, this is seen as no more than self-serving hypocrisy."[93] It appears equally hypocritical when President George W. Bush condemns suicide bombings by Palestinian groups like Hamas and simultaneously hails Israeli Prime Minister Ariel Sharon as "a man of peace." As Emad Eldin Adeeb, host of an Egyptian TV call-in show, put it, "When somebody comes and tells me that Mr. Sharon is a man of peace, and then you want me as a TV presenter to come out and try to defend American policy, I have nothing. I'm speechless. I have no weapons to answer my public opinion back."[94] Small wonder, then, that Osama bin Laden was quick to seize upon Bush's statement as part of his own efforts to rally Muslim support.[95]

Fourth, U.S. actions will provoke greater resentment when they harm others without leading to some greater good.[96] When the United States does something that harms others but also brings clear and significant benefits, foreign resentment (including the anger of the victims) will be tempered by the recognition that this policy was motivated by laudable aims and ultimately led to a more desirable state of affairs. In the minds of others, at least, desirable ends can justify costly means. But when the United States harms another country solely to advance its own narrow self-interest, or when its actions harm others but do not produce any compensating benefits, then the victims (and possibly onlookers) are more likely to harbor a powerful sense of historical grievance.

Here it is useful to compare NATO's 1999 intervention in Kosovo with America's subsequent invasion of Iraq in 2003. Although NATO's military campaign killed a number of innocent civilians in Kosovo and Serbia, many residents in Bosnia and Kosovo saw the intervention as necessary to end a festering civil conflict and to help remove a brutal and dictatorial regime. Although some countries were critical of NATO's action—and especially its decision to intervene without authorization from the UN Security Council—awareness that NATO was not acting for selfish reasons, and that intervention had improved the lives of many local residents, helped mitigate foreign concerns somewhat.

The situation in Iraq is quite different. For Americans, the costs of toppling Saddam Hussein appeared to be justified by the benefits of eliminating a brutal dictator, the eradication of Iraq's alleged WMD programs, and the concern that Hussein might be collaborating with al Qaeda. Even if the invasion did entail some degree of suffering (mostly for Iraqis), these costs might have been justifiable if the occupation removed an imminent threat, led to a rapid improvement in the lives of the Iraqi people, and sparked positive political developments elsewhere in the region.

For the rest of the world, however, this calculus of means and ends was not very convincing before the war and has grown more dubious over time. Hardly anyone is sorry that Saddam is gone from power, but the failure to find WMD and the growing conviction that the Bush administration misled the world about the nature of the Iraqi threat has reinforced global opposition to the U.S. action. Nor have the war and the occupation led to a rapid improvement in the lives of ordinary Iraqis. Unless the United States can point to significant and unmistakable improvements in the lives of Iraqis in the years ahead, the invasion will appear increasingly illegitimate, and foreign condemnation will perforce increase.

Of course, a sense of historical grievance can arise even when the United States bears little or no responsibility for some unfortunate historical event. Distorting the past is easiest when governments control key sources of information (i.e., the press, educational institutions, etc.), but even democratic governments have many tools for shaping the way past events are perceived. Even when the United States is largely innocent, therefore, it may still face populations who genuinely believe that it has done them harm. Thus, some Arabs probably accepted Egypt's erroneous claim that U.S. warplanes had participated in Israel's preemptive strike against Egypt's air force during the 1967 Six-Day War, just as some Africans now believe HIV/AIDS is the result of a Western or American plot.[97] The problem is even worse when the United States is not blameless, however, because its actions will give opponents valuable ammunition in their efforts to stoke anti-American attitudes. And, as we shall see, America's own propensity for historical amnesia exacerbates this problem by making it more difficult for Americans to understand why any society might have legitimate grounds for wishing them ill.

What We Are Doing Today

As the case of Iraq reminds us, anti-Americanism is not just a response to actions the United States has taken in the distant past, or to the ways that its past behavior has been interpreted. It also reflects what the United States is currently doing, in terms of both its stated ambitions and the content of its policies. U.S. officials can proclaim benevolent intentions as often as they wish, but other countries are likely to pay more attention to what the United States does. In world politics, as in other realms of life, actions ultimately speak louder than words.

As discussed above, the evidence is now unmistakable that current

U.S. policies are undermining its global standing. U.S. primacy was apparent to all by the mid-1990s, but there was only modest erosion in the U.S. position until the arrival of the second Bush administration. There were signs of strain in traditional U.S. alliances, openly expressed ambivalence about U.S. "hyperpower," and a gradually rising number of terrorist attacks on U.S. forces overseas. On the whole, however, America's standing in most of the world remained strong.

Needless to say, this is no longer the case. The dramatic decline in favorable attitudes toward the United States coincides perfectly with the Bush administration's increasingly unilateralist foreign policy.[98] Not only did the United States reject a number of well-publicized international conventions, but it did so in an especially irritating fashion. The Bush administration did not merely reject the Kyoto Protocol; it declared that the United States would never sign the treaty and declined to offer an alternative approach to global warming until many months later. And the justification that was given—that the treaty was "not in the United States' economic best interests"—was unlikely to appeal to a world that knows the United States is both a wealthy country and the largest producer of greenhouse gases.[99] The administration did not just announce that it would not ratify the agreement establishing the International Criminal Court; it took the further (and unnecessary) step of "removing" the earlier U.S. "signature" from the treaty and then launched an aggressive diplomatic campaign to compel other states to reject the convention as well. The Bush administration took the lead in opposing a stiffer verification protocol for the Biological Weapons Convention (largely to protect the interests of U.S. drug companies and its own bioweapons research program), and abrogated the 1972 Anti-Ballistic Missile (ABM) Treaty, despite deep misgivings from long-standing U.S. allies. The United States also showed scant regard for global opinion when it decided to invade Afghanistan and Iraq. Although the United States unsuccessfully sought UN Security Council authorization for the Iraq invasion, it made clear from the outset that it did not regard such authorization as necessary. Indeed, National Security Advisor Condoleezza Rice later acknowledged that the decision for war was made even before the UN was consulted, and the failure to obtain UN authorization did not slow the march to war.[100]

Explicit U.S. unilateralism provokes foreign opposition for two different reasons. On the one hand, unilateral U.S. actions can harm other states' interests, and it should hardly surprise us when they react negatively. Conflicts of interest are inevitable in world politics, and sometimes the United States cannot accommodate other states' concerns without sacrificing its own interests. In some cases, in short, the United States will have to defend its own interests even if this requires abstention from multilateral cooperation and acceptance of greater foreign hostility.

But shouldn't Americans expect their elected officials to do their utmost to make sure that U.S. interests are protected, before worrying about what others think? Of course they should. But focusing solely on U.S. interests and paying scant attention to the interests of others is not without costs. In fact, the United States may pay a large—and unnecessary—price for treating the rest of the world as if it is merely an obstacle in its path. When top officials declare that the United States will do whatever it wants—even if the rest of the world is outraged—they are in effect saying to the rest of the world, "Your opinions are not worth considering." If the United States consistently acts this way, its citizens should not be surprised if others resent it, or if others are pleased whenever something bad happens to the United States. Nor should Americans be surprised if some of their opponents retaliate when and where they can.

Democracy and Double Standards

Other countries will be especially resentful when the United States acts hypocritically, applying different standards to its own conduct than it expects from others. For example, U.S. leaders often emphasize their commitment to "the rule of law" and tend to be quick to condemn others whenever established legal principles are violated. Yet, like most other countries, the United States has also been willing to bend (or break) international law when it was in its interest to do so. Thus, the United States refused to acknowledge a World Court verdict condemning its covert campaign against Nicaragua in the 1980s, and it has been widely criticized for its plans to try suspected al Qaeda members in secret military tribunals. The U.S. decision to hold suspected terrorists incommunicado—and indefinitely—as "enemy combatants" has been equally controversial, and it reinforces the sense that America's commitment to the rule of law is overly flexible.

Indeed, examples of U.S. hypocrisy are numerous. U.S. leaders routinely invoke the principle of free trade and condemn trading partners for erecting barriers to U.S. goods, yet they abandon these principles when powerful U.S. interest groups are threatened by foreign competition. The United States pressures other countries not to acquire or test weapons of mass destruction, and it went to war against Iraq in order to keep Saddam Hussein from having them. Yet the United States has conducted more than a thousand nuclear tests and has more than 7,000 operational thermonuclear weapons of its own—a position hardly consistent with its efforts to deny them to others.[101] While extolling its virtues as an apostle of freedom and democracy, the United States tolerated the apartheid government in South Africa for many years. It supported brutal dictators like Saddam Hussein when it was in its geopolitical interest to do so, and it now backs pro–U.S. dictatorships in Pakistan, Uzbekistan, and elsewhere.

Finally, the United States has long adopted a double standard regarding the use of force. Americans were understandably outraged when al Qaeda attacked the World Trade Center in September 2001, and they were quick to condemn Osama bin Laden for al Qaeda's attack on innocent civilians. Such a reaction is entirely appropriate, but it betrays a certain ignorance of America's past conduct. The United States deliberately attacked thousands of civilians during World War II (including dropping two atomic bombs on Japan), and it did so with the explicit aim of sowing terror among the civilian population.[102] Japan had started the war, of course, but the victims of these attacks were no more responsible for their government's policies than the victims in the World Trade Center were responsible for the conduct of U.S. policy in the Middle East and the Persian Gulf. Yet, like most countries, the United States rarely acknowledges any moral similarity between its own "regrettable but necessary" actions and the "brutal and unwarranted" acts of its foes.

My purpose here is not to shine a spotlight on America's past sins; it is simply to recognize that the United States often adopts one standard for its own behavior while demanding a different standard from others. As one would expect, the gap between what the United States prescribes for others and what it demands for itself has not gone unnoticed abroad. Indeed, it is a key theme of many of Osama bin Laden's denunciations, for he knows that accusing the United States of acting hypocritically is a potent weapon in the struggle for hearts and minds around the world.[103]

A hypocritical foreign policy creates several problems for the United States, especially given its dominant world role. First, instead of demonstrating that the United States is a principled nation—that is, a nation whose conduct is guided by certain ethical principles and whose word can be counted upon—hypocritical behavior casts doubt on America's moral stature and the credibility of U.S. promises. It makes U.S. primacy less legitimate in the eyes of other countries, for they will regard it as especially unfair when the world's most powerful country lacks virtue. Second, when the United States ignores the norms that it expects other states to observe, it is suggesting that the United States is unwilling to be bound by rules and more likely to use its considerable power without restraint. In addition to fostering foreign resentment, such behavior is likely to add to underlying fears about U.S. power itself.

Why Don't Americans Understand This?

Unfortunately, most Americans do not fully understand why the rest of the world is worried about U.S. primacy and alarmed by specific U.S. policies. Although U.S. officials are aware that many states worry about U.S. power and know that some states (or groups) are deeply hostile, Americans still underestimate the degree of fear, resentment, and hostility that the United States provokes and do not fully comprehend its origins. As National Security Advisor Condoleezza Rice replied when asked why Germany and France had opposed U.S. policy on Iraq, "I'll just put it very bluntly. We simply didn't understand it."[104] Why?

The Consequences of Asymmetric Power

One reason why the United States underestimates the level of foreign resentment is the sheer size of America's global impact. Paradoxically, American power both creates foreign resentment and makes it more difficult for the United States to recognize why it occurs.

First, as noted in chapter 1, because the United States is so large, wealthy, and powerful, it invariably affects other states more than they affect it. Actions that U.S. leaders regard as trivial may have major effects on states that are much smaller and weaker. A protectionist tariff may benefit some narrow interest group here in the United States while having little overall effect on the U.S. economy, but it may well have quite severe effects on the economy of a small country that depends on exports to the United States.

Even when the United States *is* affected by its own actions, its policies tend to have an even greater impact elsewhere. U.S. involvement in the Korean and Vietnam Wars cost billions of dollars and more than 100,000 U.S. lives, but the effects on Korea and Indochina were much larger and more enduring. Similarly, the U.S.-backed "*contra*" war was politically controversial at home but in fact cost the United States relatively little in either blood or treasure. It was a major event in Nicaraguan history, however, killing at least 30,000 Nicaraguans.[105] To put these figures in perspective, Nicaragua's losses were the equivalent of America's suffering approximately 1.8 million dead—a number far exceeding U.S. deaths in any of its past wars. Thus, Americans underestimate foreign hostility because we do not feel the full impact of our own actions, and thus we do not notice what we are doing to others and how they are responding.

Second, a preponderant power like the United States inevitably has a short attention span. With a world to run, Washington cannot devote as much attention to each part of the world as other states are likely to pay to their own situation and their own neighborhoods. Given America's size and influence, other states devote plenty of time and effort to observing what the United States is up to, and they work hard to influence what the United States decides to do with its power. Smaller states such as Israel, Colombia, Kenya, and Singapore do not define their interests in global terms, and their foreign-policy agendas are limited by their resources. As a result, smaller states (and even medium-size powers such as Italy and Germany) tend to focus their attention on a finite set of issues.

By contrast, the United States has commitments and concerns in virtually every corner of the globe, and it tries to influence outcomes in a wide range of policy domains. Other states pay lots of attention to what *we* do, but U.S. leaders are inevitably distracted by events all over the world and focus on particular issues or areas only when they are compelled to do so. With our attention divided and distracted, we Americans may not even notice the full impact of our actions in any one area or on any one issue.

This problem is compounded both by the decentralized nature of the U.S. foreign-policy bureaucracy and the diverse nature of U.S. power. The management of U.S. foreign policy is divided among a host of competing government agencies, and coordination among them is notoriously imperfect and erratic.[106] Moreover, some U.S. actions abroad are either poorly publicized or deliberately covert, which means that many Americans—including members of the U.S. government—will be unaware of them. If the left hand of the U.S. government does not know what the right hand is doing, and if U.S. citizens do not know what either is up to, then we cannot hope to understand why other states are responding as they are.

This problem is even more severe when U.S. foreign policy is conducted in secret. Government officials and U.S. citizens cannot hope to understand the origins of foreign opposition if they are unaware of the policies that have provoked foreign ire. Chalmers Johnson refers to this phenomenon as "blowback," which he defines as "the unintended consequences of policies that were kept secret from the American people." Even when Americans are partially aware of what their country is doing in one part of the world, they may miss the connection between what is happening in one place and the negative consequences that subsequently occur somewhere else. We may be aware that the United States supported Turkey's anti-Kurdish campaign, bombed Libya in 1986, sent cruise missiles into Sudan in 1998, and conducted counterterrorist operations in Pakistan, the Philippines, and Indonesia in 2003, but we may not see how these activities led to negative repercussions later. As Johnson puts it, "The unintended consequences of American policies and acts in Country X are a bomb at an American embassy in Country Y and a dead American in Country Z."[107]

Foreign perceptions of the United States are not driven solely by the official policies of the U.S. government, of course. America's role in the world also includes the activities of U.S. corporations, foundations, media organizations, and various nongovernmental organizations, including the increasing use of private security firms in such far-flung places as Iraq and Afghanistan. Yet few of us will be aware of many of these activities. When a U.S. corporation decides to relocate an offshore manufacturing plant from one developing country to another, for example, it is an individual corporate decision that may not even be noticed by most of the company's shareholders. Yet this decision could have large negative effects on some local community in another country. A plant closing in the United States might attract publicity here at home, but a plant closing in Malaysia, Guatemala, or Thailand will go unnoticed back in the United States. If this sort of corporate behavior generates anti-American attitudes, however, U.S. citizens will have no way of knowing where they came from or whether they have a legitimate basis. Even worse, when a private security firm like Dyncorp—which has a government contract to help protect Afghan President Hamid Karzai—uses abusive and heavy-handed tactics, the people it mistreats are likely to see it not as misconduct by a private corporation but rather as a direct reflection on the United States. Americans are likely to think that Afghans should be grateful that we are protecting Karzai, but Afghans themselves may dislike Americans because of the ways these U.S. firms are behaving.[108]

Finally, America's image in the world is also shaped by the behavior of its allies and clients. When a pro-U.S. dictatorship represses its own people—as was done by the Pahlavi regime in Iran and the Somoza government in Nicaragua—its actions will also hurt America's standing among the local population and in the eyes of foreign observers. When a close ally like Israel denies the national aspirations of the Palestinians and uses massive force against them, it reinforces Arab and Muslim hostility to the United States itself, even if the United States occasionally tries to distance itself from specific Israeli actions. Americans may be aware of these connections, but they are unlikely to recognize the degree to which their own reputations are shaped by the actions of others.

Historical Amnesia

As noted earlier, if other states believe that the United States has hurt them in the past, and especially if U.S. actions were unprovoked and cruel, they are likely to be suspicious of future U.S. behavior and prone to resent U.S. power. The memory of past humiliations and suffering fades slowly, and victims are likely to remember their sufferings long after the perpetrators have forgotten them. In extreme cases, a prior history of U.S. interference can create a deep reservoir of ill will and make it extremely difficult to build a positive relationship.

Unfortunately, the same events that others remember are the ones that the United States has probably gone to considerable lengths to forget. All countries sanitize their own history, of course, and are prone to downplay or deny their worst transgressions. Even when states recognize that they have committed egregious acts, they tend to portray them as necessary for their own security and as justified by the equally egregious actions of the other side. Open societies such as the United States may be less prone to the worst forms of historical falsification, but they are hardly immune.

For example, U.S. leaders have routinely justified their own actions by claiming they were provoked by others, while downplaying the possibility that the United States might have been partly responsible for the alleged provocation. During the Korean War, for example, the United States interpreted China's entry into the war as a case of deliberate communist aggression and failed to recognize that it was primarily a reaction to the U.S. advance to the Chinese border.[109] The result was two more years of war, and the conflict helped harden Sino-American hostility for nearly twenty years, yet U.S. citizens never recognized that U.S. policy had helped produce this result. In 1964, President Lyndon Johnson used a North Vietnamese attack on U.S. naval vessels in the Gulf of Tonkin to justify escalating the war, but key U.S. officials failed to tell the U.S. Congress (or the American people) that the alleged North Vietnamese attack was itself a response to a series of covert U.S.-led raids on North Vietnamese territory. Today, we see global terrorism as motivated by radical animosity to U.S. values, and we discount the possibility that certain U.S. policies might be of equal (or greater) importance in provoking violence against us.

In each of these cases (and there are plenty of others), U.S. leaders claimed that the use of force by the United States was a defensive reaction to someone else's unprovoked aggression. In each case, this interpretation was at best debatable and at worst simply incorrect. The issue is not whether U.S. policies were correct or not; the issue is that Americans were being told a false version of events. As a result, the targets of U.S. actions—that is, the foreign populations who were attacked by the United States—were certain to come away from these events with a very different understanding of what happened than Americans had. By portraying these incidents as examples of foreign aggression, and by justifying the American response as purely defensive, the United States had in effect blinded itself to how these events appeared to others.

But the problem is even broader than the ways in which U.S. leaders justify specific applications of military force. As in most countries, U.S. textbooks and public rhetoric tend to glorify our past achievements, give the United States too much credit for positive international developments, and omit or minimize the nation's worst foreign-policy transgressions.[110] As a result, U.S. leaders—and the general public—are often simply unaware of what the United States has actually done to others.

The consequences of this sort of historical amnesia can be severe, especially in an era when countries around the world are even more attentive to U.S. behavior and even more worried about what the United States might do. When the United States teaches a false version of the past, it is unable to understand why other societies may have valid reasons to be suspicious or hostile. Many Americans may have "forgotten" about their many interventions in Latin America, for example, but the inhabitants of these countries have not. The anti-American attitudes of Castro, the Sandinistas, and Hugo Chavez did not emerge solely from the misguided wellsprings of Marxist theory; they were also produced by the historical legacy of prior U.S. occupations and prolonged U.S. support for the Batista and Somoza dictatorships. Similarly, the sense of bitterness expressed by Mexican President Vicente Fox—which helps explain Mexico's refusal to support the invasion of Iraq—reflects both his disappointment at being ignored by the Bush administration and the legacy of 150 years of U.S. dominance.

Furthermore, by portraying its international role as uniformly noble, principled, and benevolent, the United States teaches its citizens that the rest of the world should be grateful for the many blessings that Americans have (allegedly) bestowed upon them. When others do not offer us the gratitude we think we deserve, however, we conclude that they are either innately hostile or inspired by some sort of anti-American ideology, alien culture, or religious fanaticism. And once we have reached that conclusion, it is but a short step to believing that such groups deserve harsh treatment in return. By exaggerating our own virtues (and forgetting our past mistakes), we become less able to comprehend why others may mistrust or resent us and more likely to react in ways that will make existing conflicts of interest worse.

Conclusion

This chapter has identified the main reasons why U.S. primacy arouses concern, fear, and resentment around the world. Few countries seem willing to confront the United States directly, but many are increasingly uncomfortable with U.S. primacy and some are openly opposed.

But does any of this really matter? Those who favor the unilateral exercise of U.S. power sometimes acknowledge that others may not like it, but they quickly conclude that there is nothing that others can do about it. As former *New Republic* editor Andrew Sullivan puts it, the only thing America needs is "political will and public support. . . . The only thing that can stop America now is American resistance, revolt, or restraint."[111] Or, as historian Niall Ferguson commented, "The threat to America's empire does not come from embryonic rival empires. . . . [But] it may come from the vacuum of power—the absence of a will to power—within."[112] As long as the United States is strong and resolute, so the argument runs, the fear of U.S. power will keep everyone else in line. As Deputy Secretary of Defense Paul Wolfowitz wrote several months before taking office, global leadership requires "demonstrating that your friends will be protected and taken care of, that your enemies will be punished, and that those who refuse to support you will live to regret having done so."[113] If other nations cannot be cowed, in short, then they can be ignored or crushed. This view of U.S. foreign relations assumes that hostile states can do little to harm us, so there is little reason to worry about anti-Americanism abroad. President Bush himself downplayed the danger of U.S. isolation by noting that in the war on terror, "at some point we may be the only ones left. That's okay with me. We are America."[114] From this perspective, the United States is strong enough to take on its remaining opponents and fashion a world that is conducive to U.S. interests and compatible with U.S. ideals, even if forced to act alone.

This view also assumes that most states have interests that are compatible with our own, and it ignores the possibility that these states are in fact trying to use U.S. power in ways that may benefit them but could harm the United States. In effect, it assumes that pro-American countries are fully supportive of U.S. foreign-policy goals either because they genuinely share them or because they know that resistance is futile.

The next two chapters will show that this smug overconfidence is misplaced. Both friends and foes have many ways of dealing with American power, and the United States is neither so powerful nor so wise that it can afford to disregard what others may do.

CHAPTER 3

STRATEGIES OF OPPOSITION

Serbian President Slobodan Milosevic led a country whose population was 3 percent the size of the U.S. population. Serbia's GNP was roughly 0.2 percent that of the United States, and it spent roughly $1.6 billion on defense in 1998 (compared with $271 billion spent by the United States). Yet Milosevic did not seem troubled by his Lilliputian stature. When U.S. diplomat Richard Holbrooke met with Milosevic in October 1998 to negotiate the status of Kosovo, Holbrooke tried to impress the Serb leader by bringing along Air Force Lieutenant General Michael Short, who would later command the air war against the Serbs. At their first meeting, Milosevic greeted Short by remarking, "So you are the man who is going to bomb me." And when Short told the Serbian president that he had "U2s in one hand and B-52s in the other, and the choice [of which I use] is up to you," Milosevic "just sort of nodded." Milosevic was given a detailed briefing describing what an air war would do to Serbia, but he ultimately rejected NATO's proposals and chose to face war instead.[1]

This story reminds us that some states sometimes choose to resist U.S. primacy, even against what appear to be overwhelming odds.

Countries that align with the United States are sometimes vexing for U.S. policymakers, but the more serious challenges arise from other states that are reluctant to embrace *Pax Americana*, and especially from those that feel threatened by U.S. primacy and would like to find ways to keep American power in check. If the United States cannot make its position of primacy acceptable to others, the number of countries in this category will grow and the world will be a more contentious and unpleasant place. It would also be a world in which it would be more difficult for the United States to achieve its core foreign-policy goals.

States that oppose U.S. power do so for three main reasons. First, and most obviously, states that regard the United States as fundamentally hostile—and whose basic interests are at odds with ours—will reject alignment with the United States and are likely to adopt a policy of open defiance. The obvious examples here are the so-called rogue states singled out by the Clinton administration, or the three "axis of evil" nations identified by President Bush in his 2002 State of the Union speech.

Second, some states may oppose U.S. policy on a limited set of issues, while trying to maintain good relations with Washington in other areas. As long as the differences do not become too great, such frictions are part of the normal give-and-take of international life. Even in these relatively benign contexts, however, other countries will be interested in finding ways to counter U.S. power, if only to get a better bargain for themselves.

Third, states may also choose to resist the United States because they are worried about the broader implications of American primacy. This motivation may reflect the fear that the United States will use its power to get its way on specific issues today, but it also reflects the broader concern that U.S. power will be used in ways that might harm others' interests in the future. It is, in short, the general fear of unchecked power in a world where there is no overarching authority that can prevent strong states from acting as they please. As Russian

President Vladimir Putin said in February 2003, "We believe here in Russia, just as French President Jacques Chirac believes, that the future international security architecture must be based on a multipolar world. That is the main thing that unites us. I am absolutely confident that the world will be predictable and stable only if it is multipolar."[2] Former European Commission President Romano Prodi explained cooperation between the EU and China in similar terms, saying, "We are building new relationships, and it's clear it's a commitment for us and for China. Both of us want a multipolar world in which we have many active protagonists. This is a Chinese priority and it is a European interest." Or, as South African leader Nelson Mandela put it, South Africa cannot accept one state "having the arrogance to tell us where we should go or which countries should be our friends. . . . We cannot accept that a state assumes the role of the world's policeman."[3]

But how do you stop an eight-hundred-pound gorilla? What can other states do to restrain a country as powerful as the United States? Trying to resist the United States is fraught with peril—as Milosevic, the Taliban, and Saddam Hussein have all learned to their sorrow. The combination of economic, technological, and military resources at America's disposal does not enable it to do everything, but U.S. power can make it costly for other states to defy its wishes. Even states that have little reason to fear a U.S. invasion have to worry that the United States might punish their defiance in less vivid but still painful ways.

Yet states do defy the United States—and sometimes violently— and the record of the past decade shows that even far weaker states do have options. Just as children routinely disobey their parents, just as slaves sometimes defied their owners, and just as inmates find small ways to evade the rules imposed by their jailers, so too will weaker states in today's international system employ various methods either to evade U.S. control or to limit the ability of the United States to have its way. These strategies may not undermine America's dominant position—at least, not in the short term—but they complicate its diplomacy and form much of the context in which U.S. foreign policy must now be conducted. Let us first consider when states are likely to challenge America's dominant position, and then consider the different strategies they can employ.

When Will Other States Challenge U.S. Primacy?

Given the preponderance of power in America's favor, why would any state risk courting the direct opposition of the world's most powerful country? The obvious answer, of course, is when there are profound conflicts of interest between the United States and some other country—conflicts so fundamental that appeasement or accommodation is impossible. But even when serious conflicts are present, other states have to consider whether defying Washington's wishes is still prudent. Whether resistance makes sense will depend on three major conditions.

1. How Big Is the Disagreement?

States (or nonstate actors) are more likely to reject accommodation and oppose U.S. dominance when there are fundamental conflicts between their foreign-policy goals and those of the United States. During the Cold War, for example, the long rivalry between the United States and the Soviet Union was partly based on the balance of power—that is, on the fact that they were the two most powerful states in the system—but also on unbridgeable ideological differences. The American and Soviet visions of an ideal social order were fundamentally at odds, which made it hard to imagine either one voluntarily aligning with the other.

In the post–Cold War world, states that have chosen to defy the United States openly have generally been those whose foreign-policy objectives clashed sharply with U.S. preferences. The most obvious examples were the members of the Bush administration's "axis of evil"—Iraq, Iran, and North Korea—but several others (e.g., Serbia, Syria, Libya) have defied U.S. pressure as well. Although there were important differences among these regimes, each was committed to foreign-policy objectives opposed by the United States, and several of them were also seeking to obtain weapons of mass destruction, a goal that U.S. leaders have emphatically opposed.

Finally, some states will seek to oppose the United States on particular issues, or will merely be looking for ways to keep U.S. power in check. Thus, Japan and South Korea want the United States to act with restraint in dealing with North Korea's nuclear ambitions, and France, Russia, China, and several others have openly opposed the Bush administration's emphasis on preventive war, and especially its decision to launch one against Iraq. States such as these do not oppose the United States on many (or even most) global issues, but they are clearly willing to defy Washington on occasion and to look for ways to give their opposition greater weight.

2. Will the United States Find Out?

States will be more inclined to oppose U.S. dominance when they think they can get away with it. Their ability to do so depends in part on whether the United States is likely to detect what they are up to. Governments cannot punish criminals if they are either unaware that a crime has occurred or do not know who did it, and prison wardens cannot punish inmates whose infractions have not yet been discovered. Similarly, the United States cannot sanction other states when it is not aware of their transgressions or is unable to identify exactly who is responsible.

The ability to detect foreign resistance depends on the relative balance between U.S. surveillance and intelligence capabilities and an opponent's capacity for concealment and deception. In some cases, of course, defiance is impossible to conceal, as when Serbian President Slobodan Milosevic rejected NATO's ultimatum at the Rambouillet (France) summit and began forcibly expelling the Albanian population of Kosovo. In other cases, however, defiance of the United States may be deliberately concealed or left inherently ambiguous. States that are trying to develop weapons of mass destruction are likely to conceal their activities, or they will claim that their nuclear programs are intended solely for legitimate peaceful purposes. An even more subtle variation occurs when a foreign government takes a public position in line with U.S. preferences but does not devote much effort or energy to implementing the agreement. Whether such regimes are "cooperating" or not depends on how much cooperation one can reasonably expect, which makes a definitive assessment of their performance more difficult.

In most cases, of course, U.S. officials will be well aware when other states are resisting. Opposition is obvious when foreign leaders publicly complain about U.S. positions, when they take actions that the United States has sought to prevent, or when they encourage other states to join them in defying U.S. wishes. U.S. leaders may underestimate both the scope and the intensity of foreign opposition (if only because some states will be reluctant to declare it openly), but it is unlikely to come as a complete surprise.

3. Will the United States Respond?

Other states are more likely to defy the United States if they believe that America will be unable or unwilling to respond—either because the United States does not have usable options or because the costs of retaliation outweigh the benefits. During the Cold War, for example, the risks of escalation made it more dangerous for the United States to threaten Soviet client states directly. This constraint helps explain why the United States never invaded North Vietnam, why Soviet allies such as Syria and Iraq could resist U.S. pressure, and why India could ignore U.S. opposition to its dismemberment of Pakistan in 1971. But as the recent wars in Serbia, Afghanistan, and Iraq suggest, the ability of the United States to threaten some regimes is greater now, both because potential opponents cannot get help or protection from a rival superpower and because U.S. armed forces are increasingly capable of projecting overwhelming force over great distances. Although the U.S. experience in Afghanistan or Iraq could not be duplicated against more capable foes, there is little question that the direct cost of U.S. military action against opposing states is significantly lower than it once was.

When military force is not an option, the United States can also use economic sanctions or other forms of economic pressure in order to compel obedience. Sanctions are a popular response when leaders feel that they have to "do something," but they are no panacea. Economic sanctions usually require broad international cooperation to be effective, and they will have little effect when the potential target has minimal ties to the United States. Political scientist Daniel Drezner calls this phenomenon the "sanctions paradox": Economic sanctions work best against countries where there is a close and potentially long-term economic relationship—because each side has a lot to lose—but these states tend to be close U.S. allies and thus are the states that U.S. leaders are least disposed to punish. Sanctions are more likely to be used against hostile regimes, but such regimes are unlikely to be close economic partners and thus will have less at stake. In other words, economic weapons work best where they are least likely to be employed, and they work least well in the cases where they are most frequently applied.[4] U.S. leaders will also be reluctant to employ sanctions when doing so will hurt U.S. firms, and especially if it will give foreign competitors new market opportunities.

Even when the United States does have viable options for countering or punishing foreign opposition, it is not going to respond to every single act of foreign opposition. When choosing whether or not to punish an act of opposition, U.S. leaders have to decide whether the benefits of retaliation will exceed the costs. Will retaliation today deter a new challenge tomorrow, or will it inspire greater resentment and lead to further acts of defiance? Is the issue involved largely symbolic, or are there more vital interests at stake?

Will retaliation make it easier for us to achieve other important objectives, or make it more difficult to respond to new challenges elsewhere? Because U.S. policymakers have to weigh both the costs and the benefits of reacting to each act of defiance, other states will sometimes be able to ignore or defy U.S. wishes without facing a direct U.S. response.

When deciding to resist U.S. power, therefore, other states must calculate the probability that the United States will choose to use its power to punish them. Even if they know their actions will be detected, and even if they are aware that the United States has usable options, they may still conclude that the United States is *unlikely* to react, especially if the costs of retaliation are likely to exceed the expected benefits.

This consideration suggests that other states can affect the probability of a hostile U.S. response by limiting the scope of the challenge, or by carefully "designing around" a particular deterrent warning.[5] Weaker states that are worried about U.S. retaliation will try to challenge the United States in ways that undermine its position, but never so much that the United States is compelled to respond with overwhelming force. Even if the United States does react, it may not go all-out if the infraction is fairly minor.

As Thomas Schelling noted some years ago, this is the basic problem of "salami tactics." When retaliation is costly, weaker actors may be able to evade the rules just enough to get some of what they want, but without going so far that they provoke a harsh response. If a weaker challenger is persistent and clever, it may win a series of concessions by making each incursion just a little too small to justify a response. Each marginal infraction is not worth punishing, but the cumulative effect—if unchecked—can be enormous.[6]

For the United States, which faces potential challenges virtually everywhere, the problem becomes one of credibility. Can the United States deter a wide range of potential challenges by responding forcefully to a few minor ones? Just as dominant corporations sometimes fight costly "price wars" in order to deter rivals from trying to enter their markets, the United States will be tempted to fight "credibility wars" designed to show challengers what will happen if they defy U.S. wishes.[7] This strategy makes sense if the costs are low, and if they do not encourage more and more states to see the United States as the main threat that needs to be thwarted or contained. But this strategy can backfire if the costs of reacting are unexpectedly high, if taking action in one area makes it impossible to react somewhere else, or if the use of force by the United States magnifies foreign resentment and inspires additional acts of resistance.

This point reminds us that the size and scope of resistance matters. U.S. primacy does not prevent weaker states (and nonstate actors) from challenging its power, provided that they can do so without threatening core U.S. interests. From this perspective, al Qaeda's attack on the World Trade Center and the Pentagon on September 11, 2001, may have been a strategic blunder. Osama bin Laden and his network had attacked U.S. military targets in the Arab world on several occasions, including the bombing of the USS *Cole* in October 2000. In response, the United States had arrested several al Qaeda associates, fired cruise missiles at terrorist training camps in Afghanistan and Sudan, and formulated more ambitious plans to capture bin Laden himself. But until September 11 occurred, neither the Clinton nor the Bush administration chose to go all-out against al Qaeda.[8] Had al Qaeda continued to operate far from the U.S. homeland, the United States might never have decided to invade Afghanistan (thereby eliminating its main sanctuary) or made a "war on terrorism" the defining focus of its foreign policy. By attacking U.S. soil directly and with such dramatic effect, however, al Qaeda made a forceful U.S. response virtually inevitable.[9]

States are also more likely to defy the United States when it is already busy elsewhere and thus less able to respond to a new challenge. In any hierarchy, subordinates are more likely to engage in acts of defiance, resistance, or noncompliance when their supervisors are distracted. Workers are more likely to shirk when the foreman is monitoring another part of the jobsite and prisoners in one cell block will have greater latitude when the guards are busy elsewhere. By the same logic, countries that seek to defy the United States will look for moments when the United States is already tied down. Even a state as powerful as the United States cannot devote equal attention and effort to all problems, and the more heavily engaged the United States is in one area, the greater the latitude enjoyed by states in other regions. Unless a particular act of resistance constitutes a clear and immediate threat, it will be harder to move the problem up the bureaucratic agenda when other issues are already dominating policy debates.

In short, states that seek to challenge U.S. primacy will look for windows of opportunity. The temptation to exploit these windows will increase even further when they enable other states to alter the balance of power in some tangible and enduring way. Defying the United States is inherently risky, but it makes more sense to run these risks if the act of defiance itself may place the state in question in a fundamentally stronger strategic position.

Consider three examples. The first is Iraq's decision to invade Kuwait in 1990. Although this decision is often portrayed as evidence of Saddam Hussein's reckless expansionism, it is more properly understood as a "rational" response to the combination of threats and opportunities that Iraq faced at that time. Relations between Iraq and Kuwait were already poor, and Iraq's economic position was increasingly dire. By seizing the defenseless sheikhdom, Iraq could eliminate a key creditor, gain control of oil revenues worth roughly 40 percent of Iraq's own GDP, and enhance its ability to intimidate neighboring states such as Saudi Arabia. And it could achieve all of these things in a few hours, with little or no risk that its army would be defeated— provided that outsiders did not come to Kuwait's assistance. There seemed to be little danger of that happening, however, given that the United States was preoccupied with the collapse of the Soviet empire and U.S. diplomats had unwittingly signaled that the United States was not committed to protecting Kuwait. Although the invasion did not work out as Saddam expected, his decision to invade was neither reckless nor surprising.[10]

An even clearer example of this sort of behavior was North Korea's decision to restart its nuclear development program in 2003. Relations between Washington and Pyongyang had deteriorated under the Bush administration, and the 1994 "Agreed Framework" halting North Korea's nuclear program had largely collapsed by the end of 2002. The Bush administration was aware of North Korea's nuclear ambitions, but its preoccupation with Iraq gave North Korea an ideal opportunity to accelerate its nuclear development activities. With the United States busy in the Gulf, there was less danger of a preventive strike on the Korean Peninsula. Equally important, this window might permit North Korea to acquire enough nuclear material to make it too dangerous to challenge later. In other words, North Korea seized a window of opportunity in order to achieve a small but significant shift in the Asian balance of power.

Much the same logic seems to be guiding Iran's own pursuit of a nuclear capability. During 2003, coordinated pressure from the United States and the European Union made some progress in slowing—and possibly halting—Iran's nuclear development program. The invasion of Iraq reinforced this effort at first, because it seemed to suggest that Iran would have to take U.S. military threats seriously. Once the Iraqi insurgency ensnared the United States in a prolonged occupation, however, the threat of additional military action evaporated and Iran returned to a more defiant position. Tehran announced in August 2004 that it was resuming construction of enrichment centrifuges and declared that it would not allow "others to deprive us of our natural and legal rights." As Gary Samore of the International Institute for Strategic Studies explained: "The US is bogged down in Iraq, the conservatives control the Iranian parliament and Iran does not feel that sanctions are likely. So it has reneged on a key part of [its earlier] agreement."[11] Like the North Koreans, in short, Iran exploited the window of opportunity created by the Iraq debacle in order to press ahead with its nuclear programs.[12]

The moral of these (and other) stories is simple. U.S. power confers many advantages on the United States and creates many options for U.S. leaders—options that no other state can even contemplate. Yet primacy does not mean that all (or even most) states must invariably accommodate Washington's wishes. Although the United States enjoys an unprecedented asymmetry of power, other states still have options. If conflicts of interest are large enough, if resistance can be concealed, or if there are good reasons to believe that the United States either cannot or will not respond, then other states do not have to accommodate to U.S. power and can pursue various strategies of opposition or resistance instead. What are the main strategies available to them, when will they be chosen, and how well are they likely to work?

Balancing

According to realist theories of world politics, states respond to unbalanced power by balancing *against* the dominant country. In the words of Kenneth Waltz: "As nature abhors a vacuum, so international politics abhors unbalanced power. Faced with unbalanced power, some states try to increase their own strength or they ally with others, to bring the international distribution of power into balance."[13] States may balance *externally*, by combining their capabilities with others, or they may balance *internally*, by mobilizing their own resources in ways that will enable them to resist stronger states more effectively. Or they may do both. In any case, the goal is the same: to ensure that a more powerful state (or coalition) cannot use its superior capabilities in ways that the weaker side will find unpleasant.

Traditional balance-of-power theory focuses on the distribution of material capabilities, such as population, economic wealth, military power, and natural resources. It predicts that states will normally balance against the most powerful state—i.e., the one with the greatest material resources. Applying it to the current era, balance-of-power theory leads us to expect America's existing alliances to become more fragile and harder to lead, and predicts that other countries will either mobilize internal resources to counter the U.S. advantage or join forces in order to limit U.S. freedom of action.

The Relative Absence of External Balancing

At first glance, the standard realist view seems to face an immediate challenge. Although there are modest signs of anti-American balancing, there is much less than the theory leads us to expect. To be sure, the end of the Cold War and the arrival of the second Bush administration have been accompanied by growing tensions between the United States and its European allies, with experts on both sides of the Atlantic warning that NATO can no longer be taken for granted.[14] During the 1990s, French Foreign Minister Hubert Vedrine repeatedly complained about America's position as a "hyperpower" and proclaimed that "the entire foreign policy of France . . . is aimed at making the world of tomorrow composed of several poles, not just one." German Chancellor Gerhard Schroeder offered a similar warning in 1999, declaring that the danger of "unilateralism" by the United States is "undeniable."[15] Schroeder then won reelection in 2002 by openly distancing himself from the United States over the issue of war with Iraq, and even the successful incorporation of several new NATO members in 2003 could not disguise the growing gulf between the two sides of the Atlantic.[16]

Concerns about American power have also led to tentative efforts at multilateral cooperation *against* the United States. The European Union is seeking to reduce its dependence on the United States by improving its own defense capabilities, amid continued calls for institutional reforms that will permit Europe to speak with a unified voice in foreign affairs. China and Russia have reacted to U.S. preponderance by seeking to resolve existing points of friction and increasing other forms of security cooperation—a process that culminated in the signing of a formal treaty of friendship and cooperation in July 2001. Although the treaty was not directed at a specific country, it was explicitly intended to foster a "new international order," and Russian commentators described it as an "act of friendship against America." Russian President Vladimir Putin has also labored to improve Russia's relations with India and with Europe, based in part on the explicit desire to "help create a balance in the world." There can be little doubt as to which state he thinks needs to be balanced *against*. Even lesser states would like more limits on U.S. primacy: as Venezuelan President Hugo Chavez put it in 2000, "The twenty-first century should be multipolar, and we all ought to push for the development of such a world. So long live a united Asia, a united Africa, a united Europe."[17]

The tendency to join forces against U.S. power reached a new peak in early 2003, when a loose coalition of France, Germany, Russia, and several small states combined to deny UN Security Council authorization for America's preventive war against Iraq. Not surprisingly, the ouster of Saddam Hussein also encouraged increased security cooperation between Syria and Iran, especially after prominent U.S. officials made threatening statements toward both countries.[18] And when U.S. President George W. Bush was reelected in November 2004, French President Jacques Chirac responded by saying, "European cohesion is naturally the right way to deal with . . . the worries or concerns" of the election, adding, "Europe today has more need than ever to reinforce its unity and dynamism."[19]

If one is looking for signs of balancing against U.S. power, in short, they are not difficult to find. Yet it is striking how limited these efforts have been. Responses to U.S. primacy pale in comparison to the encircling coalitions that Wilhelmine Germany or the Soviet Union provoked, where most of the other major powers made formal or informal alliances to defeat or contain these powerful expansionist states. U.S. allies have long resented their dependence on the United States and the unsubtle hand of U.S. leadership, but the old cry, "Yankee, Go Home," is still largely unheard in Europe and Asia. Instead, the United States is still formally allied with NATO (whose membership has grown to twenty-six, with other aspirants in the wings), and it has renewed and deepened its military relationship with Japan. Its security ties with South Korea, Taiwan, and several other ASEAN countries remain intact, even though opinions of the United States have declined sharply in recent years, and an announcement that the Pentagon was planning major troop redeployments in Europe and Asia provoked a decidedly mixed reaction in both regions.[20] U.S. relations with Russia are sometimes contentious but still far better than they were during the Cold War, and relations with China improved as soon as the United States started worrying more about terrorism and less about China's possible emergence as a future peer competitor. Similarly, U.S. ties with India are warmer and deeper than ever before, despite America's continued embrace of General Pervez Musharraf's Pakistan. To date, at least, no one is making a serious effort to forge a meaningful anti-American alliance.

Meanwhile, who have been America's principal adversaries? Instead of America's facing a combined coalition of major powers united by a common desire to contest U.S. primacy, its main enemies have been a stateless terrorist network and the isolated and oppressive regimes in Cuba, Serbia, Iraq, Afghanistan, Libya, Iran, and North Korea. Even taken together, these states possess little power and even less international support.[21] With enemies like these, one might ask, who needs friends?

From the perspective of classical balance-of-power theory, this situation seems anomalous. Power in the international system is about as unbalanced as it has ever been, yet balancing tendencies have been comparatively mild. Although a number of states are engaged in various forms of *internal* balancing (discussed below), there have been only modest efforts at *external* balancing through the creation of an anti-U.S. coalition. Such efforts do exist, of course, but one has to squint pretty hard to see them. How can we account for this apparent violation of classical international-relations theory?

The anomaly of states failing to balance U.S. power vanishes when we focus not on power but on *threats*.[22] Although the United States is enormously powerful relative to other states, it has not been perceived as a major threat by most other powers. To begin with, the United States profits from its geographic isolation in the Western Hemisphere, which makes it more difficult for the United States to engage in ambitious wars of territorial expansion.[23] Moreover, because the other major powers lie in close proximity to one another, they tend to worry more about each other than they do about the United States. Indeed, as discussed in chapter 4, this explains why the United States is still an attractive ally for states in Europe and Asia. U.S power ensures that its voice will be heard and its actions will be felt, but it lies a comfortable distance away and does not threaten to conquer or rule its allies directly.

Much the same logic applies in much of Asia, which is why America's Asian allies prefer a U.S. presence even though U.S. power dwarfs their own.[24] Geographic proximity also explains why it would be exceptionally difficult to construct a cohesive anti-American coalition of Russia, China, and India—unless the United States behaves in an especially bellicose and shortsighted manner. These three Asian giants worry as much about each other as they do about the United States.

Anti-American balancing has also been muted because U.S. *intentions* have been perceived as comparatively benign, at least until very recently. Although the United States has used force on numerous occasions—and sometimes with less-than-compelling justification— most of the world's major powers have not seen the United States as an especially aggressive country. Instead of seeking to conquer and dominate large sections of the globe—as the European Great Powers did during their imperial heyday—the United States has generally acted as an "offshore balancer."[25] It has intervened in Eurasian affairs with some reluctance, and only when local powers were unable to maintain a stable equilibrium on their own.

This behavior, however, stands in sharp contrast to U.S. conduct in North America and the Western Hemisphere, where it proceeded to conquer a continent, subjugate the indigenous inhabitants, evict the other Great Powers, and openly proclaim its own hegemony over the region. Not surprisingly, the United States *is* seen as a hostile power in much of Latin America—where it has intervened on numerous occasions to maintain its hegemony—even though it has enjoyed remarkably good relations with its allies in Europe and Asia. Good fences make good neighbors, and two vast oceanic moats help insulate the United States and much of the world from each other. The United States may be self-righteous, hypocritical, and occasionally trigger-happy, but most states have had little reason to believe that it might try to conquer them. As a result, they have been less inclined to balance America's daunting capabilities than we would otherwise expect.

Here again, one may draw a useful contrast between Presidents George H. W. Bush and William Clinton, on the one hand, and President George W. Bush on the other. Under the first two, the United States generally acted within the framework of existing security institutions and sought to advance its influence largely by incorporating new states into these arrangements. U.S. power was used *defensively*— in response to specific acts of aggression—and for the most part only after careful international consultation. By contrast, the second Bush administration was openly skeptical of many existing institutions and willing to initiate the use of force in order to alter the status quo in its favor. As one would expect, this more assertive policy also encouraged other states to begin balancing somewhat more vigorously.

Other states remain reluctant to balance the United States because such a policy is not without risks. Forming a balancing coalition requires trust: each member of a balancing coalition must be confident that its allies will contribute to the common objective (in this case, the containment of American power), and each must be reasonably sure that the others will not defect at the first sign of trouble and leave one isolated against a powerful adversary. This concern gives the United States yet another advantage: Because its power is ample and diverse, and because it is not very dependent on *any* allies at present, it can play a strategy of "divide and conquer" whenever a countervailing coalition threatens to emerge.

Last but not least, other states are reluctant to form an overt anti-American coalition because such an alliance would still be substantially weaker than the United States itself, at least initially. Although a coalition of medium powers (i.e., Europe, Russia, India, Japan, and China) possesses a combined GDP exceeding that of the United States, as well as a formidable nuclear arsenal, its military capabilities would still trail the United States by a wide margin, and it would be plagued by the rifts and uncertainties that habitually undermine alliance cohesion. Unless U.S. foreign policy becomes even more bellicose, therefore, other states are unlikely to construct a formal anti-American alliance.[26]

"Soft Balancing"

Instead of forming formal alliances to contain the United States, other states generally have opted for "soft balancing."[27] "Hard balancing" focuses on the overall balance of power and seeks to assemble a countervailing coalition that will be strong enough to keep the dominant power in check. By contrast, soft balancing does not seek or expect to alter the overall distribution of capabilities. Instead, a strategy of soft balancing accepts the current balance of power but seeks to obtain better outcomes within it. In the current era of U.S. dominance, therefore, soft balancing is the *conscious coordination of diplomatic action in order to obtain outcomes contrary to U.S. preferences—outcomes that could not be gained if the balancers did not give each other some degree of mutual support.* By definition, "soft balancing" seeks to limit the abil-

ity of the United States to impose its preferences on others. To practice soft balancing, therefore, other states must coordinate their
actions with this aim explicitly in mind.

A strategy of soft balancing can have several objectives. First, and
most obviously, states may balance in order to increase their ability to
resist U.S. pressure, including the use of military force. In recent
years, for example, several states that were directly threatened by U.S.
power have shared intelligence information designed to enhance
each other's ability to stand up to U.S. pressure. Serbia received
information on U.S. air-warfare tactics from Iraq prior to the war in
Kosovo, which helped the Serbs prepare for NATO's air offensive.[28]
Other reports suggest that the People's Republic of China provided
fiber-optic technology for Iraq's command-and-control system,
thereby enhancing Iraq's air defense capabilities. Although commercial benefits may have been the primary motivation for these programs, the potential of complicating U.S. activities in the Middle
East and Persian Gulf may have struck the Chinese government as a
desirable bonus. Similarly, North Korea is reported to have sold fluo-
rine gas, a requisite material for making uranium hexafluoride, to
Iran, a step that is both profitable and further complicates U.S.
antiproliferation efforts.[29] Nonstate actors (e.g., terrorist groups) have
also provided each other with various forms of mutual support, while
retaining their own independent identities and political agendas.

Second, joining forces with others is a way of improving one's
bargaining position in global negotiations—whether the issue is
trade, regulation of genetically modified foods, environmental safeguards, labor regulations, or even issues of "high politics" like the
use of military force. Thus, soft balancing may arise in response to
some discrete issue, or it may be used when states are bargaining
over the broad institutional arrangements that regulate international
behavior. Within the World Trade Organization, for example, a
coalition of twenty-one developing countries—led by Brazil, China,
India, and South Africa and representing more than half the world's

population—has come together to pressure developed countries to make significant reductions in their farm subsidies and other trade barriers. South African representative Alex Erwin called the move a "historic moment, when we have been able to unify our positions across economies." This concerted effort paid off in July 2004, when the developed countries were forced to make a series of concessions on agricultural subsidies that paved the way for a new trade round. As Brazilian Foreign Minister Celso Amorim put it, "This is the beginning of the end of all subsidies."[30] A unified stance enhanced the weaker states' bargaining positions, so the wealthier powers could not get the concessions they wanted without making concessions in exchange.[31]

Third, soft balancing can also be intended as a diplomatic "shot across the bow," to remind the United States that it cannot take for granted the compliance of other states. The Sino-Russian "Friendship Pact" of 2001 seems to have been intended for this purpose; by demonstrating that they had other options (even if neither state really wanted to pursue them very far), Russia and China sought to remind Washington that excessive unilateralism could lead to "harder" balancing in the future. In December 2004, in fact, the two countries announced that they would conduct joint military exercises involving land, air, and naval forces, a move that one analyst termed "a symbolic gesture aimed at the United States, intended to show that Russia has other allies." Similarly, Russia and Iran have quietly expanded their own strategic partnership since 2000, at least partly in response to the increased U.S. presence in the region. As one analyst comments, "Russia and Iran have joined efforts to limit the influence of the United States and its allies (Turkey and Israel) in central Asia and the Caucasus. . . . Iran's partnership with Russia . . . is . . . a strategic response to U.S. efforts to develop influence in the area through its ties with Turkey, Georgia, Azerbaijan, and Uzbekistan."[32]

A potentially more significant illustration of this sort of soft balancing is the expanding strategic partnership between the EU and

China. Not only is each now the other's largest trading partner, but Chinese leaders now hold regular meetings with European officials and each now speaks openly of their strategic "partnership." Plans are underway for military exchanges, several European countries have already conducted search-and-rescue exercises with Chinese naval forces, and other forms of strategic dialogue are increasingly frequent. Perhaps most important of all, the EU is about to lift the arms embargo it imposed after Tiananmen Square—despite strong U.S. pressue to keep it in force—a step that will facilitate China's efforts to increase its military power. These developments are still relatively modest and are probably not inspired by a desire to balance U.S. power directly, but the trend highlights Europe's increasing independence from the United States and its willingness to take steps that could complicate U.S. strategic planning in East Asia. Given their shared preference for a more multipolar world in which U.S. power is at least somewhat constrained, it is hardly surprising that Europe and China are beginning to move closer together.[33]

Fourth, soft balancing is also a way to hedge one's bets in the face of growing uncertainty about relations with the United States. A classic example of this type of balancing, as Robert Art suggests, is Europe's gradual effort to create a genuine European defense capability. Although the original motivation for this policy was not anti-American, Europe's ability to chart its own course in world politics—and to take positions at odds with U.S. preferences—will be enhanced if it becomes less dependent on U.S. protection and able to defend its own interests on its own.[34] A more unified European defense force would also increase Europe's bargaining power within existing transatlantic institutions, which is why U.S. officials have always been ambivalent about European efforts to build autonomous capabilities.

The feasibility of both hard and soft balancing depends in part on each state's expectations of what other potential balancing partners will do. No state wants to face the United States alone—even in a purely diplomatic context—and soft balancing is therefore more likely to occur when several states are looking to check U.S. power and are confident that the others will be steadfast. Up to a point, therefore, successful soft balancing is self-reinforcing: the more states that are worried about U.S. power and U.S. policy—and the more obvious and deeply rooted their concerns are—then the more willing each of them will be to coordinate a common effort to contain American action.[35] In this sense, therefore, soft balancing could also lay the groundwork for more fundamental challenges to U.S. power. States that coordinate positions on minor issues may become more comfortable with each other and thus better able to collaborate on larger issues, and repeated successes can build the trust needed to sustain a more ambitious counter-hegemonic coalition. Thus, successful soft balancing today may lay the foundations for more significant shifts tomorrow.

As already suggested, the Bush administration's failure to obtain UN Security Council authorization for its 2003 preventive war against Iraq illustrates perfectly the various dynamics of soft balancing. Although there was broad agreement that Saddam Hussein was a brutal tyrant, and broad opposition to Iraq's weapons programs, the United States was able to persuade only three other states to support its call to arms within the UN Security Council. This failure was partly due to widespread concerns about U.S. power and the Bush administration's heavy-handed diplomacy, but also because France, Russia, and Germany were able to convince the rest of the Security Council that they were going to hang together on this issue.[36]

The antiwar coalition did not "balance" in the classic sense (i.e., it did not try to resist U.S. armed forces directly or send military support to Iraq), but its collective opposition made it safer for lesser powers such as Cameroon and Mexico to resist U.S. pressure during the critical Security Council debate. The result was classic soft balancing: by adopting a unified position, these nations were able to deny the United States the legitimacy it had sought and thereby impose greater political and economic costs on Bush's decision to go to war. Their actions also made it less costly for a state like Turkey to refuse U.S. requests to use Turkish military bases during the war.

Yet the diplomacy of the Iraq war also illustrates the limits of soft balancing. Defeat in the Security Council did not prevent the United States from going to war, and the Bush administration was able to obtain political support (as well as symbolic military partici- pation) from Great Britain, Spain, Italy, Japan, Poland, Hungary, Bul- garia, Romania, and a number of other countries.[37] These successes remind us that NATO expansion has made it easier for the United States to use a divide-and-conquer strategy within the alliance, because expansion has brought in a set of new members who are more interested in close ties with the United States than NATO's more established members are. Secretary of Defense Donald Rums- feld's dismissive remarks about "old Europe" and his praise for "new Europe" were needlessly provocative, but his comment contained more than a grain of truth.

Even so, one should not dismiss soft balancing as purely symbolic. During his European tour in early 2005, for example, President Bush tried to persuade Britain, France, and Germany (the so-called EU-3) to take a harder line toward Iran's nuclear programs. The Europeans had long favored a diplomatic approach to Tehran, partly to restrain Iran and partly to make it harder for the United States to take unilat- eral action (such as a preventive military strike). Bush failed to drive a wedge between the three European powers, however, and in the end he chose to endorse their diplomatic efforts without participating in them fully. Thus, "soft balancing" by Britain, France, and Germany forced the United States to adjust its own policies, and made the pre- ventive use of military force less likely, at least in the short term.[38]

There is an important lesson here. If the United States acts in ways that fuel global concerns about U.S. power—and, in particular, the fear that it will be used in ways that harm the interests of many oth- ers—then the number of potential "soft balancers" will grow. This number may increase because the United States takes on several different adversaries at the same time—thereby giving them reasons to help each other—or because third parties conclude that the United States is dangerous and needs to be kept in check through concerted action. And if that number increases, these potential balancers will have more partners from which to choose and greater confidence that other states share their concerns and will be willing to cooperate against Washington. If this trend were to continue, anti-American balancing (both hard and soft) could become more widespread. We may be some distance from such a "tipping point" today, but we cannot discount the possibility entirely.

Fortunately for Americans, the United States has many ways to discourage the formation of hostile coalitions. The United States does not want to give up its position of primacy and cannot alter its geographic location, but it can pay close attention to how others perceive its intentions. Above all, U.S. leaders should seek to convince most states that they have little to fear from U.S. power unless they take actions that directly threaten vital U.S. interests. In other words, the United States can best discourage both soft and hard balancing by making its behavior—and not just its rhetoric—contingent on the behavior of others. States that cooperate with the United States must be confident that they will be heeded and rewarded; states that remain aloof but do not threaten the United States must be left alone; and only those states that actively threaten U.S. interests should fear the sharp end of U.S. power.[39]

Internal Balancing

As noted at the beginning of this section, weaker states can balance a stronger power either by forming alliances with others or by mobilizing their own internal resources in ways that limit the stronger state's ability to pressure or thwart them. Although *external* balancing remains relatively muted for the reasons just discussed, a number of states and nonstate actors are trying to oppose U.S. power through various forms of *internal* balancing.

When facing a much more powerful opponent, however, the weaker side should not try to beat the stronger power at its own game. If forced to compete with Tiger Woods, for example, most of us should pick virtually any activity other than golf. And if forced to compete with Tiger at golf, we would be better off on a practice green than a driving range. We would almost certainly lose, but at least we'd have a slim chance.

The same logic applies for weak states (and nonstate actors) who find themselves facing the overwhelming power of the United States. Instead of trying to beat the United States at the things it does best, weaker actors will employ some form of *asymmetric strategy*, seeking to shift the competition into areas where they enjoy a relatively better position. According to the Pentagon's 2005 *National Defense Strategy*: "The U.S. military predominates in the world of *traditional* forms of warfare. Potential adversaries accordingly shift away from challenging the United States through *traditional* military actions and adopt asymmetric capabilities and methods."[40] In particular, weaker actors should look for specific U.S. vulnerabilities that they can exploit, and should seek to avoid arenas of competition where the United States is particularly strong. They should try to operate in novel ways that the United States has not anticipated—using new weapons, employing different tactics, and attacking unusual or unexpected targets. The objective of this strategy is not to defeat the United States directly; rather, "adversaries employing irregular methods aim to erode U.S. influence, patience, and political will. Irregular opponents often take a long-term approach, attempting to impose prohibitive human, material, financial, and political costs on the United States to compel strategic retreat from a key region or course of action."[41]

In the present era of U.S. primacy, states that choose to resist the United States through internal balancing have three broad options. First, they can develop conventional military strategies designed to negate or counter specific U.S. strengths. Second, they can use terrorism—a classic "weapon of the weak"—in order to impose additional costs on vulnerable U.S. targets at home or abroad. Needless to say, this is also a strategy that nonstate actors are likely to adopt, because it requires the fewest resources. Third, they can acquire weapons of mass destruction, in order to gain some measure of immunity from U.S. conventional military capabilities. Let us briefly consider each in turn.

Conventional warfare: exploiting the "contested zone." Throughout history, weaker adversaries have tried to devise military strategies and tactics that can maximize their own effectiveness while minimizing the effectiveness of their opponents. During the War of Attrition in 1970–71, for example, Egypt did not try to defeat the Israeli air force in direct air-to-air combat. Instead, Egypt and its Soviet patron built a dense network of ground-based air defenses near the Suez Canal, which made it impossible for Israeli aircraft to operate freely in this area. Similarly, guerrilla armies usually avoid direct battlefield engagements with regular army troops until their own strength has grown to a point where they can meet their opponents directly.[42]

For the foreseeable future, weaker states will try to avoid meeting the United States in the arenas where America enjoys near-total mastery. The United States is unchallenged in several realms of military action, including the military use of outer space, air operations above 15,000 feet in altitude, armored engagements at ranges beyond one or two kilometers, and "blue water" naval battles. According to military expert Barry Posen, these advantages give the United States "command of the commons": it can use the "common areas" of the globe with near-impunity and deny them to its adversaries more or less completely. These advantages allow the United States to bring military power to bear against a wide array of potential adversaries, and in virtually any corner of the globe.[43]

At the same time, however, U.S. advantages are much less pronounced in other areas of military competition, such as urban warfare, close-range infantry combat, air operations below 15,000 feet (where antiaircraft weaponry becomes more lethal), and naval operations in shallow waters or along the ocean littoral.[44] U.S. superiority declines further when operating in unfamiliar territory, and against adversaries with local knowledge of terrain and weather, and when adversaries can fight on the defensive from concealed positions. The effectiveness of U.S. military power may also be compromised by a reluctance to cause civilian casualties, by legal constraints on the use of force, or by its own sensitivity to U.S. casualties.[45] Astute adversaries will therefore seek to avoid meeting the U.S. military in realms where its advantage is greatest; instead, they will try to tailor their own capabilities and tactics so as to force the United States to operate in this "contested zone," where America's technological, logistical, and material preponderance will be less decisive.

Not surprisingly, this type of asymmetrical response is increasingly evident on the battlefield. During the Kosovo and Gulf Wars, for example, the Serbs and Iraqis did not even attempt to challenge U.S. air superiority through direct air-to-air combat. Instead, they relied upon surface-to-air missiles (SAMs) and antiaircraft artillery, often employing them in ways specifically intended to complicate U.S. efforts to suppress them. The Serbs proved especially adept at camouflage as well, and their tactics appear to have reduced significantly the lethality of NATO air attacks.[46] The Iraqi military learned from its crushing defeat in 1991 and made little or no attempt to meet the U.S. invasion in 2003 directly. Instead, Iraq relied primarily on a combination of harassing attacks, irregular forces (including suicide bombers), and sabotage to resist the U.S. invasion force. These tactics could not prevent the fall of the Ba'ath regime, but they imposed unexpected costs on the occupying forces. Saddam and his associates had also laid the groundwork for a protracted insurgency by dispersing arms and money to loyal subordinates, and this response soon derailed the Bush administration's original plans for reconstructing Iraq and "transforming" the entire Middle East. Finally, U.S. efforts to destroy or capture Taliban and al Qaeda forces in Afghanistan were thwarted by unexpectedly effective resistance during the battles of Tora Bora and Operation Anaconda. The al Qaeda forces used their superior knowledge of the terrain to negate many U.S. advantages (such as airpower and high-tech reconnaissance capabilities), and eventually forced the U.S. forces into a costly close-quarters firefight. Both battles were at best a draw for the United States—despite its enormous overall superiority—and enabled the al Qaeda and Taliban forces (and possibly Osama bin Laden himself) to escape.[47]

Internal balancing and an asymmetrical response are also apparent in the military preparations of potential U.S. adversaries. For example, China is not trying to forge a balancing coalition at the present time, but it is increasing its military capabilities and trying to develop a capacity to deal with U.S. military forces in the Far East.[48] Chinese military experts have studied U.S. military operations extensively, and have sought to fashion conventional military options that could enable a much-weaker China to hold its own—or at least impose high costs—in a direct confrontation with superior U.S. forces. According to the authors of one Chinese study (entitled *Unrestricted Warfare*): "We are much poorer than the United States. So we think China needs to begin to adjust the way it makes war. It's like Mao said to the Japanese: 'You fight your war and I'll fight mine.'"[49] In addition to contemplating a variety of nonmilitary actions (such as terrorism and environmental degradation), China has deliberately sought to acquire military capabilities (such as anti-ship cruise missiles) that would make it more difficult for the U.S. Navy to operate close to China (e.g., in defense of Taiwan). Chinese military officials also emphasize the need for electronic and cyberwarfare techniques in order to exploit U.S. reliance on information technology; the use of mines, cruise missiles, and submarines to blockade key ports or straits; and the development of sophisticated air defenses that can negate America's current airpower advantage. Once again, the aim is neither to defeat the U.S. outright nor to challenge the U.S. position as the dominant global power; rather, the goal is "to develop politically useful capabilities to punish American forces if they were to intervene in a conflict of great interest to China."[50]

Terrorism. Today, America's most fervent opponents are not states at all, but rather nonstate groups like al Qaeda. Lacking the resources of an organized polity, such groups are naturally drawn toward the strategy of terrorism. Terrorism is a strategy that weaker actors use because it allows them to avoid the superior armed forces of its stronger opponents, and thus to target the more vulnerable elements of society itself. Deliberate targeting of civilian populations is a classic "weapon of the weak"—rebel groups do not need to use terrorist tactics if they are strong enough to obtain what they want directly. Open societies such as the United States may be especially vulnerable to terrorist action, precisely because it is more difficult for them to impose the laws and procedures that would make terrorism more difficult.[51] Hostile forces can also use terrorist tactics (such as suicide bombings) in order to attack U.S. military forces, seeking to penetrate U.S. defenses by masquerading as innocent civilians rather than by openly engaging U.S. forces on the battlefield.

Like other asymmetric strategies, terrorism does not seek to defeat the stronger opponent directly. Terrorism is a *political* strategy that achieves success by attacking the stronger opponent's resolve and by encouraging sympathizers to rally to the terrorists' banner. By increasing the costs faced by a stronger power, and especially by imposing costs on the larger society as a whole, a terrorist strategy seeks to alter the stronger power's behavior by persuading it that its current policies are too expensive to sustain. For example, in seeking to remove the U.S. military presence from the Arab and Islamic world, al Qaeda attacked U.S. forces in the region as well as the U.S. homeland. These actions sought to persuade the United States to reduce its presence in the region and to catalyze more widespread resistance around the Muslim world.[52]

It follows that terrorist strategies are more likely to succeed when the target is not defending vital interests (and thus is not likely to be as highly motivated as the terrorists are). It is not surprising, therefore, that terrorism (and especially suicide terrorism) is overwhelmingly directed against what the terrorists perceive as foreign military occupations. The IRA in Northern Ireland, the nationalist rebels in Chechnya or Kashmir, and the various Palestinian groups that have conducted suicide bombings in Israel are all motivated by a desire to force a foreign occupier to withdraw from what they regard as their own territory. And the strategy rests on the belief that native inhabitants care more about regaining their homelands than foreign occupiers care about keeping it.[53]

The effectiveness of terrorism as an asymmetric balancing strategy will depend in large part on who is able to win the "hearts and minds" of the larger populations from which terrorist movements arise. If the groups that are now using terrorism against the United States can convince others that they are heroes acting in a noble cause, and if they can successfully portray U.S. responses as heavy-handed efforts to preserve injustice, then their efforts are more likely to succeed. If the United States responds in a harsh and indiscriminate manner, therefore, it will merely vindicate the terrorists' own use of violence and reinforce their image as heroic opponents of foreign oppression. By contrast, if the United States can portray those who use terrorism as criminals driven largely by a selfish desire for power, then a terrorist campaign is more likely to fail.

Weapons of mass destruction (WMD). Instead of trying to counter U.S. conventional forces directly, states that are worried about U.S. military power may decide to acquire military capabilities that would make it difficult-to-impossible for the United States to use its superior conventional forces against them. In particular, they may try to deter the use of U.S. conventional forces by acquiring an arsenal of nuclear, chemical, and/or biological weapons.[54]

Why would a weak or impoverished state want to acquire WMD? For the same reasons that the United States and the Soviet Union did: to deter potential or actual enemies from threatening its vital interests. That is the main reason why Israel, India, and Pakistan eventually acquired nuclear weapons of their own, and similar motives inspire the pursuit of WMD today.[55] In particular, several states have sought (or are seeking) WMD in order to make it more difficult for the United States to use its conventional forces to coerce or overthrow them.[56] As Iranian President Muhammad Khatami remarked in April 2003, "They tell us Syria is the next target [after Iraq], but according to our reports, Iran could well follow." Or as Iranian reformer Mostafa Tajazadeh observed just prior to the war in Iraq, "It is basically a matter of equilibrium. If I don't have a nuclear bomb, I don't have security."[57]

As these statements reveal, weaker states are aware that a WMD arsenal can offset some—though of course not all—of the advantages that stronger states would otherwise possess. Weapons of mass destruction—and especially nuclear weapons—are extremely effective instruments of basic deterrence, because it is too dangerous to threaten a WMD-owning state with conquest or "regime change." As a result, states that do acquire significant WMD arsenals will gain considerable protection against the more extreme forms of U.S. pressure. Specifically, states with WMD (and some capacity, however unreliable, to deliver these weapons against U.S. targets) could probably deter the United States from trying to overthrow them by force. A U.S. president might be willing to risk nuclear attack in order to defend the U.S. homeland, or perhaps to protect some vital overseas interest, but no U.S. president is likely to risk a nuclear bomb on American soil simply to overthrow a foreign government that had not attacked us first. Obtaining a WMD arsenal is a classic "asymmetric response"—it cannot negate all the instruments of U.S. power, but at least it can prevent the United States from using its power with impunity. And that, of course, is why states such as Iran and North Korea want them, and why Saddam Hussein wanted them too.

It follows that current U.S. efforts to compel various states to abandon their WMD programs face enormous obstacles. Earlier efforts to halt the spread of nuclear weapons were only partly successful, and they required the United States to offer considerable inducements to would-be proliferators (including security guarantees, access to nuclear technology, and a U.S. pledge—in the Nuclear Non-Proliferation Treaty—eventually to reduce its own nuclear arsenal).[58] As one would expect, more recent efforts to halt proliferation by threatening suspected proliferators with "regime change" have been counterproductive, because such threats merely increase the target state's desire to find a way to deflect U.S. pressure.

Terrorism plus WMD. As mentioned briefly in chapter 1, the gravest form of asymmetric response would be a terrorist organization armed with WMD, and especially one that managed to acquire a nuclear weapon. Unlike states armed with WMD, a terrorist group has no obvious "return address." We know that some of these groups (e.g., al Qaeda) are willing to slaughter large numbers of people, willing to martyr themselves, and are openly interested in acquiring various sorts of WMD. Deterrence is unlikely to work against such groups, and there is every reason to think that these groups would try to use any weapons that they were able to acquire or manufacture.

A terrorist group's use of WMD against the United States would be the ultimate form of "asymmetric strategy." If a terrorist group were able to obtain and use a nuclear weapon against the United States, it would almost certainly do more damage than any other adversary ever had. The repercussions for America's economy, civil liberties, and foreign policy would be incalculable. Biological or chemical weapons in the hands of a terrorist could also inflict grievous harm, although probably not as severely as a nuclear weapon could. For this reason alone, denying anti-American terrorists access to the most destructive weapons technology may be America's single greatest foreign-policy priority.[59] And the fact that we can no longer dismiss this possibility underscores a key fact about the contemporary world: America's unmatched strength cannot guarantee its security against a number of nominally weak but dedicated and extremely hostile foes.

Summary

At first glance, the rest of the world does not appear to be balancing against U.S. primacy. Upon closer inspection, however, there are clear signs that U.S. power is making other states uncomfortable and encouraging them to search for various ways to limit U.S. dominance. At one level, states are forming informal diplomatic coalitions, in order to make it harder for the United States to use its power with impunity. At another level, several states (and some nonstate actors) are mobilizing their own resources and devising particular strategies designed to improve their ability to withstand U.S. pressure. These responses are the typical reaction to unbalanced power, and there is nothing about them that should surprise or perplex us.

Whether such efforts grow in number and in significance, however, will depend largely on what the United States chooses to do. The United States will remain the world's most powerful country for some time to come; the question is whether other states will view this situation favorably or not. In particular, will most states see U.S. intentions as comparatively benign, or will they believe that U.S. intentions are aggressive? If the latter, then efforts to balance the United States will increase and the United States will find itself increasingly isolated.

Balking

A close cousin of balancing is *balking*, which is a deliberate decision not to cooperate with a nation's requests or demands.[60] States that *balance* are trying to improve their position vis-à-vis the United States either by joining forces with others or by mobilizing their own internal resources; states that *balk* usually do so on their own and may not be trying to improve their relative position at all. Rather, they are merely trying to avoid taking some action that the United States wants them to take, because they do not think it is in their interest to comply. Saddam Hussein was balking when he refused to readmit

UN weapons inspectors to Iraq in the late 1990s, and both India and Pakistan balked when the Clinton administration tried to get both countries to refrain from testing nuclear weapons in 1998. Balking is the international equivalent of "just saying no," and it can be a surprisingly effective way to tame American power.

Balking can take several distinct forms. The simplest form is to refuse to do what the United States asks, in the hope that America lacks either the will or the capacity to compel obedience. An obvious example is Turkey's refusal to give U.S. military forces access to Turkish bases prior to the invasion of Iraq in 2003, a decision that forced the United States to attack Iraq solely from the south and made the entire operation more difficult.

A second variation is to agree formally to take some action, but to do the absolute minimum necessary as slowly as possible. It is the international equivalent of "dragging one's feet," or "working-to-rule." Thus, Israel says it will dismantle its settlements in occupied territories, but it does so very slowly (while simultaneously expanding others), and the Palestinian leadership promises to crack down on suicide bombers but in fact takes little concrete action against them. This form of balking can be especially effective because it does not involve open or public defiance; rather, the balking parties are acting as if they intend to comply. The onus for any subsequent diplomatic confrontation thus rests on the United States, and U.S. leaders may be tempted to look the other way rather than risk a costly confrontation or let others see that they can be defied openly.

A third form of balking is "free-riding." In this variant, a state genuinely supports U.S. policy but doesn't want to contribute its share of the costs. This is akin to "foot-dragging," except that free-riding states are not trying to thwart U.S. objectives—they are simply trying to make the United States (or others) pay for them. The classic illustration of this form of balking is burden-sharing within international alliances, but it also applies to other forms of collective goods, such as the current effort to control international terrorism, or the various initiatives to improve the global environment.[61] Most states would like to reduce the danger of terrorism and protect the global environment, but they would also like someone else—e.g., Uncle Sam—to foot the bill.

Why do states balk? In some cases, they balk because there is a genuine conflict between their interests and those of the United States. For example, the United States has pressed Russia to stop helping Iran build a large nuclear reactor at Bushehr, but the cash-strapped Russian government wants the money and has politely refused repeated U.S. requests. Similarly, South Korea balked when the United States contemplated a preventive strike against North Korea's nuclear facilities in 1994, because the South Koreans worried that military action might spark a damaging war on the Korean Peninsula. Governments may also balk because domestic opinion opposes cooperating with the United States (as it did in Turkey before the war with Iraq), or because leaders believe they can rally nationalist sentiment by openly defying the world's only superpower. And states may also balk simply to force the United States to pay a higher price to gain their compliance, or to make sure that the United States does not take them for granted. Finally, by forcing the United States to bear a disproportionate share of the costs of any foreign-policy action, and by making it spend lots of political capital in order to achieve its objectives, balking can be another way to sap U.S. power over the longer term. Here balking borders on balancing, if it becomes a way for weaker states gradually to narrow the U.S. advantage.

And, like "soft balancing," balking can be self-reinforcing. The more that states balk, the more overextended the United States will become and the easier it will be for other states to balk as well without worrying about U.S. retribution. Balking is an especially effective strategy in an era of American primacy, because even a superpower like the United States cannot force or intimidate all other states into doing its bidding.

Binding

States that do not necessarily want to balance the United States still hope to restrain Washington's ability to use its preponderant power. But instead of forming a direct counterpoise to U.S. power and trying to deter the United States from acting as it wishes, many states now hope to constrain U.S. behavior by *binding* the United States within an overarching set of international institutions. "Binding" seeks to exploit America's own commitment to a world order based on effective norms and the rule of law, in order to encourage American restraint and insulate other states from the full effects of U.S. preponderance. Unlike balancers, who in effect pull away from the United States in order to oppose its dominant position, binders embrace the United States in the hopes of ensnaring it in a shared framework of norms and rules.[62]

The familiar metaphor for binding, of course, is Gulliver lying on the beach, lashed down by a horde of tiny Lilliputians. The Lilliputians are too small to resist Gulliver directly, so they bind him with hundreds of minuscule ropes. The story also suggests the limitations of this strategy: binding worked for the Lilliputians because Gulliver was asleep. It is hard to imagine that they would have succeeded had Gulliver been awake and alert to what they were doing.

The logic of binding rests on the belief that international institutions play a powerful role in sustaining international cooperation. According to the prevailing orthodoxy, states that would like to cooperate can do so more effectively if they establish general rules, norms, and procedures to regulate their interactions.[63] These rules make it easier to negotiate agreements, help states determine whether their partners are living up to the specified terms, and can provide mechanisms for distributing the benefits of cooperation more equally. As Michael Hirsh, former chief diplomatic correspondent for *Newsweek*, puts it: "We are the chief architects of a vast, multidimensional global system that consists of trading rules, of international law, of norms for economic and political behavior. . . . It is overwhelmingly in our national interest to stay engaged in the global system shaped by these ideas and values, to strengthen it and nurture it."[64]

Equally important, international institutions can also confer legitimacy on actions taken by the most powerful states, particularly with respect to the use of force. If weaker states believe that the strongest powers will only use their strength when there is broad international backing (signified, for example, by UN Security Council authorization), they will be less worried about asymmetries of power. Thus, by agreeing to be bound within a set of rules, powerful states can reassure weaker partners that the weakness will not be exploited (or at least not too much), thereby discouraging the formation of countervailing coalitions and making it easier for the dominant power to obtain voluntary compliance. If correct, then the liberal order constructed after World War II can endure in a period of U.S. primacy, because it still confers great advantages on the United States and its partners alike.[65]

There is little doubt that other states have tried to use existing institutions in order to place limits on the unilateral exercise of U.S. power. Throughout the 1990s, for example, a number of other states sought to confine the resolution of key international problems to existing institutional forums—most notably the United Nations—even when this made it much more difficult to reach an effective solution. As neoconservative pundit Charles Krauthammer complains, this is "the whole point of the multilateral enterprise: to reduce American freedom of action by making it subservient to, dependent on, constricted by the will—and interests—of other nations. To tie down Gulliver with a thousand strings. To domesticate the most undomesticated, most outsized national interest on the planet—ours."[66]

As the full extent of U.S. primacy has become apparent, and as the Bush administration has used U.S. power more unilaterally, efforts to "bind" the United States have become both more explicit and less successful. The most obvious example, of course, was the French, German, and Russian effort to use the institution of the United Nations Security Council to prevent the United States from invading Iraq in early 2003. The heart of the dispute was a disagreement about policy: The Bush administration favored preventive war against Iraq while most other states preferred containment. Equally important, however, was a basic disagreement about the role of norms and institutions in legitimating the use of force by Great Powers. As a number of foreign leaders made clear, they sought to reinforce the general principle that the use of force should be regulated by international law and by existing institutions. Not surprisingly, weaker states prefer a world where the dominant world power cannot invade other countries without the formal approval of the Security Council (or some other equally authoritative international body), even if the cause is just. As Jean-Marie Colombani wrote in *Le Monde*, "While there may be good reasons for wanting to deal with the Iraqi problem swiftly, the manner in which the United States is trying to achieve this—as a chance to disengage itself from the obligations incurred by a newborn international order—is simply not acceptable."[67] Thus, the protracted contest in the Security Council was both an example of soft balancing and an explicit attempt to bind U.S. behavior within an existing international institution. America's opponents sought to prevent the use of force in this particular instance, while simultaneously strengthening the authority of the UN system.

Yet this incident also showed that binding is not a very effective strategy, at least not in matters of national security. In the end, the United States invaded Iraq without approval from the Security Council, just as it had gone to war in 1999 against Serbia. In both cases, Washington was able to assemble "coalitions of the willing" to provide a thin veil of legitimacy for its actions. In both cases, and especially in the case of Iraq, U.S. leaders made it clear that they did not regard UN approval as a prerequisite for the legitimate use of force. Indeed, the official U.S. *National Security Strategy* (2002) now declares that the United States "will not hesitate to act alone, if necessary, to exercise our right of self-defense by acting preemptively" against terrorists or other threats. It further asserts that the United States "will take the actions necessary to ensure that our efforts to meet our global security commitments and protect Americans are not impaired by the potential for investigations, inquiry, or prosecution by the International Criminal Court, whose jurisdiction does not extend to Americans and which we will not accept."[68] No matter what one thinks of this particular policy, it illustrates America's deep reluctance to be bound by institutions, especially when doing so would require it to forego actions it believes to be in its own short-term interest. International institutions may be good for many things, but controlling the United States in its current condition of primacy is not one of them.

The U.S. attitude toward international law shows similar tendencies. The United States has always taken a somewhat ambivalent stance toward international law, and this ambivalence has grown over the past decade.[69] On the one hand, the U.S. government has played a key role in the development of new international legal statutes, and it consistently affirms its commitment to the "rule of law" at home and abroad. But on the other hand, the United States often places significant limits on its own adherence to these same statutes, either by refusing to sign or ratify them or by insisting on special reservations that sharply limit the impact of the statutes on U.S. behavior. Indeed, the United States has made such extensive use of reservations that other states have sought to ban them outright from treaties such as the Ottawa Convention banning landmines or the convention establishing the International Criminal Court. Predictably, the United States has simply refused to ratify these treaties. This policy reduces the impact and effectiveness of the resulting convention, but it also means that the United States may have less and less influence over the emerging international legal environment.[70]

These trends reveal the inherent limits in the strategy of "binding." The United States was willing to "bind itself" within various multilateral institutions during the Cold War because it needed allied support and wanted to keep the Soviet Union isolated. Now that the Cold War is over and the United States is perched on the pinnacle of power, however, it is loath to let its allies restrict its freedom of action and less interested in multilateral approaches. Thus, when America's NATO allies took the unprecedented step of invoking Article V of the NATO treaty (the mutual-defense clause) in the wake of the September 11 terrorist attacks, the United States welcomed the gesture but rather brusquely rejected the proffered help. One Bush administration official explained the decision to decline assistance from its NATO allies by saying: "The fewer people you have to rely on, the fewer permissions you have to get."[71] It is equally unsurprising that the United States was reluctant to share authority in Iraq following the ouster of Saddam Hussein, even when the postwar occupation proved far more difficult and expensive than its architects had predicted. The United States eventually turned to the United Nations for help, but only to provide a fig leaf of legitimacy for the establishment of a new interim government.

This position is not surprising. Weaker states may want to use institutions to bind the strongest power, but the dominant power will try to use the same institutions to magnify its power and to advance its own interests. Institutions cannot force strong states to behave in certain ways, and when the dominant powers no longer want to be bound, the strategy of binding is not likely to work.

In the end, faith in the binding capacity of existing institutions rests on the hope that U.S. leaders will prefer to keep existing institutional arrangements intact and that they will be willing to restrain their own behavior in order to do so. If U.S. leaders recognize that primacy will not last forever, they may decide it is better to "lock in favorable arrangements that continue beyond the zenith of its power."[72] But why? Once the balance of power changes and the United States is no longer in a position of primacy, then it will be less able to shape the institutional order, and other states will begin remaking that order to suit their own preferences. Thus, the hope that future competitors might one day be bound by existing institutions is not a compelling reason for the United States to accept institutional arrangements whose main purpose is to bind U.S. power today.

Using formal institutions to "bind" the United States is especially ineffective in areas where the U.S. advantage is especially pronounced—such as the use of military power—and where important security interests are at stake.[73] Outside the security arena, however, the broad strategy of binding is somewhat more effective. Indeed, a recent survey of U.S. participation in international organizations concludes that there "is more evidence of unilateralism in the area of security than there is in that of economic cooperation."[74] Why is this the case?

First, and most obviously, the United States is bound by institutions that perform a "constitutive" role—that is, by institutions that *define* some set of activities or social relations. If a particular status or activity has no meaning outside of the institution that establishes it (as the status of "husband" or "wife" is defined by the institution of marriage), then all who participate in this activity will be constrained by the established institutional principles, even if they had no direct hand in creating them. For example, America's status as an independent, sovereign state depends in part on the general recognition by others that statehood is a meaningful concept that is conferred on some groups (e.g., current UN members) but withheld from others (e.g., the Taiwanese, Kurds, Palestinians, Chechens, etc.). The United States cannot decide the "terms" of sovereignty for itself, or decide on its own which political groups will enjoy this status, although it can withhold its own recognition and encourage others to do the same.

Second, like all states, the United States can be "bound" by others in areas that are regulated by specific norms and procedures, and where it is necessary for participants to follow the rules in order for the activity to take place. Driving a car would be nearly impossible if most drivers didn't follow traffic laws most of the time, and the same is true for international air travel, postal regulation, the functioning of the Internet, and the conduct of international trade. Once established, the conventions that regulate these activities limit the autonomy of even the most powerful members. Although states can "opt out" of these arrangements, doing so threatens the benefits of sustained cooperation and may even be harmful. Any of us can choose to drive on the wrong side of a busy highway if there is no policeman around to arrest us, but it will rarely be the best or safest way to reach our destination.

Of course, the United States has considerable influence over the design and implementation of most international institutions, and its bargaining position is strengthened by its ability to negotiate bilateral deals (such as bilateral free-trade agreements) when more ambitious multilateral efforts are stymied. U.S. Trade Representative Robert Zoellick warned of this after the breakdown of the WTO talks in Cancun in September 2003: "As WTO members ponder the future, the US will not wait: we will move towards free trade with can-do countries."[75] Yet because other states must consent to the terms, and because U.S. primacy is not as pronounced in the economic arena as it is in military affairs, America's ability to set the rules in these realms is more limited. The design of the WTO conforms to U.S. preferences in many ways, for example, but the United States was forced to compromise on a number of issues in order to help bring the WTO into existence. The WTO dispute-settlement procedure is not controlled by the United States, and it frequently issues rulings unfavorable to the United States. These are compromises that America must live with, unless it wants to jeopardize the entire regulatory structure of the world trading system. As one commentator observes, "The WTO has greatly increased value for a global trader like the United States. The reduced commercial weight of the United States in the WTO today precludes the option of going it alone."[76] And, as noted above, the United States and the EU could not make substantial progress in the latest round of trade negotiations until they were willing to make genuine concessions to nominally weaker trading partners. In some realms, at least, "binding" can be an effective strategy.

Indeed, building new institutions may even be an effective tactic when the United States refuses to play along. If the United States chooses not to engage in "international rulemaking," or if other states become convinced that the United States will reject some new convention no matter how it is written, they may decide to go ahead anyway, without further input from Washington. If their efforts succeed, the United States could end up being at least partly bound by "the power of the first draft." Even if the United States were to join in at a later date, its ability to reshape the existing conventions could be limited by the existing arrangements. The Kyoto Protocol is certainly not the "last word" in the global effort to control greenhouse gas emissions, for example, but it is the "first word." To the extent that it succeeds (despite its many flaws), its underlying principles are likely to shape subsequent negotiations and limit America's ability to dictate a radically different approach. Much the same could be said for the Ottawa Convention on landmines and the statute establishing the International Criminal Court (ICC). U.S. opposition to these initiatives has not prevented other states from working to bring them to life, paying less and less attention to U.S. concerns as they proceed. According to one observer of the Rome negotiations on the ICC statute, "The other delegations felt that it would be better to stop giving in to the United States; they believed that the United States would never be satisfied . . . and ultimately would never sign the Treaty . . . [so they] decided to go ahead with [the] proposed compromise package."[77] Over time, the basic principles that underlie these conventions may take on a life of their own, gradually molding prevailing legal practice and normative understandings.[78] Indeed, this is probably the main reason why the Bush administration has gone to such lengths to weaken and discredit the ICC, for if the ICC becomes a legitimate and effective part of the international legal order, the United States will have even less ability to shape its future evolution, and the costs of remaining aloof will increase.

These examples remind us that the United States is not omnipotent, and that the rest of humanity can and does impose certain constraints on the exercise of American power. Nonetheless, in an era of primacy, the ability of other states to "bind" the United States is limited. Because the United States does not need allies as much as it did during the Cold War, and because U.S. leaders see freedom of action as essential to defending vital U.S. interests, they are less willing to bind themselves within formal international institutions and reluctant to cede autonomy on critical issues of national security. In the more mundane, day-to-day areas of international affairs, however, the United States is bound to abide by a broad set of constitutive and regulatory norms that are easier to follow than to defy or dismantle, even when defiance might be tempting in the short term.

Blackmail

The *Oxford English Dictionary* defines blackmail as "any payment or other benefits extorted by threats or pressure." A blackmailer threatens to take some action that the victim would like to prevent, but offers to refrain if the victim complies with the blackmailer's demand. Although it might seem implausible to think that a weak state could successfully blackmail a country as strong as the United States, it can be an attractive strategy under certain conditions. For one thing, it makes more sense to blackmail a rich country than a poor one—if you can get away with it—for the same reasons that it is more tempting to blackmail a rich person than a poor one. The question is: How can a weak state gain sufficient leverage over the United States so that the latter will give in to its demands?

In order to force the United States to "pay up," a potential blackmailer has to meet several demanding conditions.[79] First, the blackmailing state must be able to take some action that the United States regards as dangerous or threatening—in other words, the blackmailer must have the capacity to harm U.S. interests. Second, the threat must be credible—i.e., U.S. leaders must believe that there is some reasonable chance that the blackmailer might execute the threat if they did not comply. If executing the threat would be equally harmful to the blackmailer, then the threat is less credible and less likely to work.[80] By contrast, if carrying out the threat would be in the blackmailer's interest no matter what the United States did, then the threat will be quite credible and more likely to trigger U.S. concessions. Third, the threatened action must be one that the United States cannot easily prevent via other means. A victim threatened with the exposure of embarrassing evidence (such as compromising photographs) could try to steal the photographs. If this strategy worked, the blackmailer's leverage would evaporate. Similarly, the United States will not have to make concessions if it can use its own capabilities to prevent a blackmailing state from carrying out its threat—unless meeting the blackmailer's demands would be easier and cheaper.[81] Finally, the blackmailer must be able to convince U.S. leaders that the threat will disappear once its demands are met. If a potential victim believes that paying off the blackmailer will merely invite repeated demands, then giving in may be less attractive than rejecting the demand and suffering the consequences.

Thus, weak states can successfully employ a strategy of blackmail when: (A) they have the ability to do something that the United States does not want; (B) the United States cannot easily prevent it; (C) their demands are not too large; and (D) the United States has reason to believe that complying with the demands will in fact prevent the threat from being carried out.

Since the Cold War ended, the undisputed world champion in the "effective use of blackmail" category is North Korea. North Korea is a tragic failure by most standards: its per capita income is less than $1,000 per year; it is increasingly isolated diplomatically; its people are exposed to recurring famines; and it remains a brutally repressive dictatorship. By contrast, South Korea is a modern industrial power and has gradually moved toward full-fledged democracy. Although North Korea still maintains a large army, its military forces are primitively armed and poorly trained, and would be no match for the South Korean armed forces, especially if the U.S. military were also involved.[82]

Yet since the early 1990s, North Korea has successfully managed to extort a number of key concessions from the United States, even though U.S. power dwarfs North Korea's.[83] Beginning in 1994, a consortium of the United States, Japan, and South Korea agreed to provide North Korea with two light-water nuclear reactors free of charge, along with a package of economic assistance, fuel, and food aid. The Clinton administration also began steps to normalize relations with North Korea and came close to authorizing an exchange of high-level visits.

Why did the United States agree to these gifts, when far more deserving regimes received far less attention from Washington? The answer, of course, is that North Korea had an active nuclear-weapons program. The package of aid was not a reward for good behavior, it was a payoff inspired by the threat of continued *bad* behavior.

North Korea's nuclear blackmail worked because it met virtually all of the conditions identified above.[84] First, North Korean acquisition of nuclear weapons was seen as a potentially serious threat to U.S. interests, and especially the broad U.S. goal of limiting nuclear proliferation. If North Korea got the bomb, it might be difficult to prevent South Korea and Japan from following suit, thereby triggering a potentially dangerous arms race in the Far East. Moreover, given North Korea's long history of provocative behavior, U.S. leaders also worried that its acquisition of nuclear weapons would lead to more aggressive activities on the Korean Peninsula or elsewhere.[85] Thus, North Korea possessed the first component of successful blackmail: It could do something that U.S. leaders very much wanted to prevent.

Second, North Korea's threat to develop nuclear weapons was quite credible. Given the collapse of the Soviet Union, China's gradual opening to the West, and North Korea's own economic deterioration, it was easy to imagine why North Korea would want a nuclear "insurance policy" against the threat of regime change. Although there is no evidence that any of North Korea's neighbors actively sought to bring down the regime—if only because doing so would make them responsible for North Korea's impoverished population—the government in Pyongyang could not be sure of this, especially since it seems to be afflicted with a healthy dose of xenophobia and paranoia. North Korea had good reasons to want nuclear weapons, in short, so its threat to "go nuclear" had to be taken seriously.

Third, the United States could not easily prevent nuclear acquisition by North Korea through other means (such as military force). Although the United States could have launched preventive air strikes against North Korea's various nuclear facilities, U.S. planners were not certain they could eliminate the entire program in this way. Equally important, a preventive attack ran the risk of triggering large-scale fighting between North and South Korea. Although the United States and South Korea were virtually certain to win such a clash, the damage to South Korea (whose capital, Seoul, lies within artillery range of the border) might be considerable. Furthermore, a major war would almost certainly lead to the collapse of the North Korean regime, forcing South Korea to begin a massive reunification and reintegration effort under the worst possible circumstances. For these and other reasons, both South Korea and Japan were dead set against preventive military action by the United States. Although the Clinton administration did undertake extensive planning for a possible preventive strike, these various concerns made a diplomatic solution appealing, even if it meant paying off the North Korean government.

Fourth, U.S. leaders also had reasonable grounds for believing that the solution—the so-called Agreed Framework of 1994—would stick at least long enough to make the effort worthwhile. North Korea was in desperate financial straits, which gave Pyongyang an obvious incentive to cut a deal. U.S. negotiators were also careful to build in extensive verification procedures, so that any violation of the Agreed Framework could be detected. The agreement also involved commitments that would take several years to fulfill, thereby giving each side—and especially North Korea—additional incentives to abide by the agreement, for fear of jeopardizing the full package of benefits.

Yet the Agreed Framework broke down in 2002–2003, with each side claiming (with some justification) that the other had failed to fulfill its commitments.[86] The Bush administration received intelligence reports suggesting that North Korea had resumed covert weapons-development efforts, and it eventually confronted North Korea with these revelations in October 2002. For its part, North Korea accused the United States of failing to deliver the promised light-water reactors on schedule, and a North Korean official warned in February 2001: "If [the United States] does not honestly implement [the Agreed Framework], there is no need for us to be bound by it any longer."[87] North Korea was also angry when President Bush included it in the "axis of evil" in his 2002 State of the Union speech, and annoyed by additional administration comments suggesting that the United States favored "regime change" in North Korea.[88] The new U.S. emphasis on "preemption," as codified in the 2002 *National Security Strategy*, was undoubtedly a source of concern for Pyongyang as well. North Korea promptly reverted to its earlier tactics: removing International Atomic Energy Agency (IAEA) safeguards, restarting the Yongbyon reactor, and eventually declaring that it had already had a nuclear capability and intended to increase it.

The sequel is instructive, because it demonstrates that blackmail is less likely to work if the blackmailer refuses to stay bought. The danger posed by North Korea's nuclear-weapons program had, if anything, increased since the 1990s—especially given the possibility that the cash-strapped North Korean regime might sell nuclear material to others—and North Korea's threat to go nuclear was as credible in

2003 as it had been ten years earlier. Similarly, a preventive strike against the North Korean facilities was no more attractive in 2003 than it was in 1993–94, especially given that U.S. military forces were already preoccupied with the invasion and occupation of Iraq.

Yet the U.S. government has been reluctant to play the same game twice. This reluctance was partly due to the presence of a new administration (key officials in the Bush administration had been extremely critical of the Agreed Framework prior to taking office), but it also reflected valid concerns about North Korea's willingness to keep a bargain once it had been made. Accordingly, the United States responded to North Korea's resumption of its nuclear program by suspending existing aid programs and rejecting any further concessions. Although the administration eventually agreed to hold talks with North Korean officials, it insisted that these talks be multilateral and gave no indication that it was willing to offer North Korea anything until the nuclear issue was resolved.[89]

North Korea is not the only example of successful blackmail, merely the most dramatic. Blackmail is also a strategy that allies can employ in order to persuade more powerful patrons to accede to their wishes. The basic logic is the same: A weaker ally threatens to do something that its patron opposes, in the hopes of persuading the patron to give it something in exchange for acceding to the patron's preferences. During the Cold War, for example, Soviet and American client states were able to extract greater benefits from their respective patrons by threatening to realign or resign, or even by threatening to collapse completely. Egyptian leader Gamal Abdel Nasser persuaded the Soviet Union to increase its military support in 1970 by threatening to resign in favor of a pro-American president, and South Vietnamese leaders like Ngo Dinh Diem and Nguyen Van Thieu repeatedly obtained additional U.S. aid by tacitly threatening to go under (and leave Vietnam to the communists) if they did not get more help.[90] Because both superpowers were convinced that their interests and prestige were bound up in the fate of these clients, the threats were taken seriously and were often successful in eliciting greater support. Similarly, South Korea, Taiwan, and Japan have used veiled threats to "go nuclear" themselves in order to obtain conventional military support and security guarantees from the United States.

Since September 2001, several other states have exploited the U.S. preoccupation with terrorism in order to extract additional concessions from Washington. Because the United States needed cooperation from Uzbekistan, Pakistan, and Russia in order to wage war in Afghanistan, it has turned a blind eye to human-rights conditions in these countries, and has given economic and political support to each of these governments. The Pakistani case is especially revealing: although Pakistan is actively developing nuclear weapons and President Pervez Musharraf is a military dictator who has done relatively little to rein in Muslim extremists within Pakistan, the collapse of his regime could easily usher in a far more radical government. Thus, the Bush administration has had little choice but to back him to the hilt, despite well-founded concerns about his domestic and foreign policies.

Blackmail can be an effective strategy in some circumstances, but (fortunately) not very often. Successful blackmail is rare because it only works under unusual conditions and because all states are reluctant to acknowledge that they can in fact be coerced into making major concessions. Blackmail is also a high-risk strategy; you can't get the United States to make significant concessions unless you threaten important U.S. interests, but if you do, the United States may decide it would rather fight than pay.

Among other things, this means that the fear that rogue states might use nuclear weapons (or other WMD) to "blackmail" the United States is far-fetched.[91] In order for this form of blackmail to work, the blackmailer must make it clear that it is willing to use its weapons if it does not get its way. But this strategy is feasible only if the blackmailer has WMD and neither the target state nor its allies do, and history suggests that even an overwhelming nuclear advantage is hard to translate into direct political leverage.[92] If a nuclear-armed rogue state tried to blackmail the United States or one of its allies, the threat would be an empty one, because the blackmailer could not carry out the threat without triggering its own destruction.[93] Threatening to *acquire* WMD can be a credible instrument of blackmail, but threatening to *use* WMD against the United States or its allies is not.

The United States has an additional incentive to prevent other states (and especially relatively weak states) from using WMD for blackmail or coercion, or as a shield for conventional aggression. Nuclear weapons have been a profoundly *defensive* force throughout the nuclear age, and this tendency has been an important cause of peace among the major powers.[94] To permit a weak rogue state to alter the status quo through the use of nuclear blackmail would reverse this equation and would send a powerful signal that these weapons were in fact an effective instrument of expansion or aggression. The consequences for world politics would be tremendous: Incentives to proliferate would grow apace, revisionist powers would be quick to repeat their efforts to intimidate others, and war as a result of miscalculation would become much more likely. Neither the United States nor the other Great Powers has any interest in allowing such a world to emerge, which means that they have ample reason to help defend any states facing a threat from a nuclear-armed rogue.[95]

Ironically, blackmail may be easier for allies rather than adversaries. Allies can threaten to take some unwanted action in the hopes of gaining a concession, but without worrying that they will provoke a war, whereas enemies may push the United States over the edge if they push too hard. North Korea's successful manipulation of nuclear brinkmanship is all the more remarkable in light of this consideration. The United States would probably be delighted to foster regime change in Pyongyang, if it could only think of a way to do it quickly and inexpensively. But because an easy solution remains elusive, the world's mightiest superpower continues to be tormented by a small country that can build nuclear weapons but cannot reliably feed its own people.

Delegitimation

All political orders depend to some degree on the belief that they are *legitimate*. When members of a society regard existing arrangements as "natural" (i.e., as the expected or normal state of affairs), they will be less likely to question them or even to imagine that they might be altered. Similarly, when they regard the existing order as desirable (in either material or moral terms), they are unlikely to challenge it. Thus, the belief that kings ruled by "divine right" reinforced monarchical authority: if one's subjects saw the royal position as an expression of God's will and believed that aristocratic status reflected "noble" character, then the idea of reordering society along different (i.e., democratic) lines would seem both heretical and impractical. Not surprisingly, therefore, efforts to level traditional social and political hierarchies also entailed active efforts to portray them as unnatural, evil, or corrupt. In order to dismantle the *ancien regime*, one first had to make it seem unworthy.[96]

Similar issues arise when one state enjoys a dominant position in the international system. If other states see the existing structure of power as broadly "legitimate" (for whatever reason), they will be less likely to challenge the dominant state and may even regard its position of primacy as "natural" or inevitable. By contrast, if the rest of the world sees the existing distribution of power as inherently unfair, they will look for opportunities to alter it. Similarly, if other states regard the dominant state's behavior as generally beneficial and consistent with established moral standards, they will be less likely to fear or resent the asymmetry of power in its favor and less likely to want to undermine it.

As the dominant world power, the United States has much to

gain from the perception that its privileged position is legitimate. The United States would like to maintain its position of primacy for as long as it can, and with as little effort as possible. It should try, therefore, to persuade others that its present position is morally acceptable, and perhaps even desirable. In other words, U.S. leaders want the rest of the world to see us as Tony Blair does—as "a force for good"—so that other states will accept the U.S. position instead of trying to undermine it.

By contrast, the enemies of U.S. primacy will portray it in much more malignant terms. Instead of seeing America as a benevolent hegemon, those who oppose the United States will seek to depict it as selfish, venal, capricious, lacking in wisdom, devoid of virtue, and generally unsuited for world leadership. In other words, they will try to portray U.S. primacy and U.S. foreign policy as inherently *illegitimate*, in order to persuade others that U.S. primacy ought to be resisted. A strategy of *delegitimation* does not seek to challenge U.S. power directly—i.e., by forming a countervailing coalition—instead, the main goal is to undermine the belief that U.S. primacy is either "automatic" or morally acceptable. In essence, delegitimation seeks to make more people resent U.S. dominance, so that they become more willing to take action against it and so that the United States has to work harder to win their support.

But where does legitimacy come from? What characteristics or behaviors make one country's position "legitimate" in the eyes of other states, and what traits or actions will tend to call into question one's legitimacy? There are at least four possible sources of international legitimacy, and the struggle to either legitimate or delegitimate U.S. primacy is fought along every one of these fronts.

Conformity with Established Procedures

In politics, actions may be legitimate because they result from a previously agreed-upon process. In a democracy, for example, the authority of political leaders is established by winning a fair election, just as new statutes are legitimate if they emerge from normal legislative procedures. By the same token, the legitimacy of an elected official (or a new law) will be compromised if agreed–upon procedures appear to have been violated or ignored.[97]

It follows that U.S. primacy will be seen as more legitimate when the United States acts in accordance with established international procedures. To take the most obvious example, the 1991 Gulf War with Iraq was widely regarded as a legitimate use of U.S. power, because the use of force was specifically authorized by the United Nations Security Council. By contrast, the decision to attack Iraq in 2003 undercut the legitimacy of U.S. primacy, because the United States failed to gain Security Council authorization yet went to war anyway.

The more well–established the process is, the greater the expectation that states should follow it. In challenging the new U.S. doctrine of preemption, for example, UN Secretary-General Kofi Annan explicity noted that this policy clashed with procedures and principles that the international community had endorsed for more than five decades. In his words, the logic of states that "reserve the right to act unilaterally, or in ad hoc coalitions . . . is a fundamental challenge to the principles on which, however imperfectly, world peace and stability have rested for the last 58 years."[98] Annan's challenge to U.S. policy rested on the fact that the world community has an *established procedure* for legitimating the use of military force, a procedure that the U.S. doctrine of preemption violates.

The desire to delegitimate American dominance also lies at the heart of global complaints about U.S. "unilateralism." Until recently, the United States had endorsed multilateralism as its preferred approach to addressing many international problems, and especially problems that affect many other states.[99] In effect, this approach makes U.S. actions more legitimate by letting others participate in the decisionmaking process and giving them a stake in the outcome. Not surprisingly, therefore, the abandonment of multilateralism in several key issue-areas sparked a chorus of foreign criticism. To be sure, some of the complaints about U.S. "unilateralism" merely reflect opposition to policies that threaten other states' interests. Thus, other countries complained when the United States imposed tariffs on foreign steel, rejected the Kyoto Protocol, and sought to undermine the International Criminal Court, because these decisions made it more difficult for them to achieve their own objectives.

But at a deeper level, the charge of "unilateralism" is also designed to place the United States in an unflattering light and to nurture further resentment of U.S. power.[100] Other states may not be able to stop the United States from pursuing particular policies, but accusing Washington of acting "unilaterally" is a way of imposing additional political costs. This goal helps explain why some states have been willing to develop conventions and protocols on a variety of issues, even when they are aware the United States will reject them, and when they know its rejection will render the agreements largely ineffective. By negotiating, signing, and ratifying the Kyoto Protocol, the landmines convention, the Rome Statute on the International Criminal Court, and so on, the rest of the world is in effect saying to America: "Sure, you can do what you want, and we can't stop you. But we can make you look bad, and over time, more and more people will yearn for the day when the United States is not so powerful."[101]

Positive Consequences

A second source of legitimacy derives from the effects of a particular policy: Actions will be seen as legitimate if they are broadly beneficial for others. From this perspective, U.S. primacy is more likely to be seen as legitimate if it is in fact good for the rest of the world, and especially if U.S. foreign policy decisions are *perceived* as being a force for good.

As discussed in chapter 2, Americans tend to see the United States as a positive force in world affairs, and U.S. leaders routinely invoke this sort of argument in order to defend America's current position.

Presidents and cabinet officials are fond of reciting the positive benefits that U.S. global leadership has produced, such as the reconstruction and rehabilitation of Germany and Japan, the expansion of the world economy after World War II, the spread of democracy and human rights in the 1980s and 1990s, and the liberation of certain countries or peoples. This line of defense helps legitimate America's structural position as the dominant world power, by suggesting that world politics would be even nastier if the U.S. position were weaker.[102]

Similar arguments are also used to defend specific U.S. policies, by arguing that their net effect is positive. Thus, both the Bush and the Clinton administration justified going to war in the absence of UN Security Council authorization by arguing that the net effect of the wars in Kosovo and Iraq had been beneficial. As President Bush told the UN General Assembly in September 2004: "Because a coalition of nations acted to defend the peace, and the credibility of the United Nations, Iraq is free, and today we are joined by representatives of a liberated country. . . . Across Iraq, life is being improved by liberty. Across the Middle East, people are safer because an unstable aggressor has been removed from power. Across the world, nations are more secure because an ally of terror has fallen."[103] Such efforts to defend the legitimacy of U.S. primacy may acknowledge that these actions have had unfortunate consequences (such as the deaths of innocent civilians) but nonetheless maintain that the overall balance of costs and benefits has been positive.[104]

Just as predictably, of course, U.S. opponents challenge the legitimacy of U.S. primacy by suggesting that the net effects of its actions have been largely negative. In the case of Iraq, for example, critics highlight the failure to find Iraqi weapons of mass destruction, the postwar sufferings of the Iraqi people, and the continued violence within Iraq in order to argue that the social and political costs of the war exceed the benefits claimed by President Bush and his supporters. At a more fundamental level, Islamic radicals such as Osama bin

Laden portray America's global role in wholly negative terms, accusing it of stealing Muslim oil wealth, imposing unjust economic sanctions on Islamic countries, installing military bases within the Muslim world, corrupting Muslim societies, and aiding Israel's "pillage" of Muslim territories.[105] Indeed, al Qaeda spokesman Suleiman Abu Gheith has claimed the right to kill at least four million Americans (half of them children) by arguing that "America is the head of heresy in the modern world . . . [It] is the leader of corruption and the breakdown [of values], whether moral, ideological, political and economic corruption," and by arguing that U.S. policies in the Middle East and elsewhere have caused the deaths of at least four million Muslims. For al Qaeda, U.S. primacy is inherently evil and illegitimate, and violent reprisals are therefore justified.[106]

A less extreme variation on this general theme blames the United States for causing a variety of global problems, or for failing to do enough to address them. U.S. rejection of the Kyoto Protocol is seen as especially damning from this perspective, given that the United States remains the single largest source of greenhouse gases. For critics, therefore, the United States is causing the problem but selfishly refusing to help solve it. Critics also point to America's niggardly foreign-aid budget, and to economic policies (such as agricultural subsidies and textile tariffs) that have limited the development prospects of some of the world's poorest nations. Thus, the United States can be damned both for what it does and for what it fails to do.

Finally, a number of world leaders have suggested that the concentration of power in U.S. hands is inherently undesirable—even if some U.S. policies are broadly beneficial to others—and argue that a return to a more "multipolar" distribution of power would be preferable.[107] A rapid return to multipolarity may be a vain hope, but such comments reinforce the idea that U.S. primacy is not a good thing and ought to be resisted.

In the broadest sense, the legitimacy of U.S. primacy will depend in part on whether its behavior is that of a *responsible fiduciary*.[108] U.S.

primacy will be more acceptable to others if the United States is in fact acting for the greater good, and especially when at least some of the actions for the greater good are not also in the narrow U.S. self-interest. A trust officer is not supposed to manage an estate so as to maximize the bank's profits; being a "responsible fiduciary" means managing the estate in order to serve the best interests of the benefi-ciaries. By the same logic, U.S. primacy will appear more legitimate when others can see that the United States is using its privileged position to do something more than just enhance its own power or well-being.

America's recent wars provide an ideal set of contrasts. The Gulf War of 1991 was broadly legitimate, both because the United States followed established procedures and because it did not appear to be acting *solely* in its own self-interest. NATO's interventions in Bosnia (1996) and Kosovo (1999) offered even clearer examples of fiduciary behavior, insofar as the United States did not stand to gain much for itself in either case. By contrast, the more recent war in Iraq was much less obviously "fiduciary" in nature, because the Bush adminis-tration's initial decisions to monopolize political control, to limit reconstruction contracts to U.S. firms, and to pursue long-term access to Iraqi military bases suggested self-serving rather than altru-istic motives.[109]

The U.S. response to the deadly tsunami that struck South Asia in December 2004 illustrates this issue in another way. Not only was the Bush administration slow to respond to the enormity of the disaster, but its initial pledge of $15 million in emergency assistance was promptly and justly condemned as niggardly by foreigners and Amer-icans alike. To its credit, the administration soon increased its pledge to $350 million and dispatched U.S. military forces to provide imme-diate help, but the fact that the U.S. government had to be shamed into a higher level of aid diluted the goodwill that the United States might otherwise have garnered. At the very least, the tragedy was a missed opportunity to demonstrate that the United States stood ready to act for the greater good, and thus a missed opportunity to bolster the legitimacy of U.S. primacy.

Conformity with Moral Norms

Actions that produce net positive consequences may still be illegitimate if they violate widely accepted moral principles. The removal of a despot might be wholly desirable, for example, but not if one has to slaughter hundreds of innocent children in order to do it. In other words, the ends do not necessarily justify the means. Even when its actions yield positive results, therefore, U.S. primacy will appear more legitimate if it also appears to conform to prevailing moral norms.

For those who seek to delegitimate U.S. primacy, accusing the United States of acting immorally is an obvious tactic. Recent examples include the efforts of a coalition of international lawyers and human-rights groups to prosecute the United States for war crimes committed during the 1999 Kosovo war and the 2003 war against Iraq, based on accusations that the United States targeted civilians and used weaponry (e.g., cluster munitions, depleted-uranium warheads, etc.) that violated existing laws of war. The United States was also criticized for failing to respond to humanitarian emergencies such as the Rwandan genocide—failures all the more striking in light of U.S. attempts to portray itself as "leader of the free world" and a beacon of hope for oppressed peoples. Both European and Arab critics argue that U.S. support for Israel's occupation of the West Bank and the Gaza Strip is inconsistent with the basic principle of self-determination, as well as more specific human-rights norms.

More recently, the U.S. refusal to designate battlefield detainees seized during the invasion of Afghanistan as "prisoners of war" (a decision that left the detainees outside the protections of the Geneva Convention), and its decision to subject them to military tribunals rather than civil prosecution, sparked complaints from many countries, further reinforcing the impression that U.S. policy was at odds with prevailing legal and moral principles.[110]

Perhaps the most damaging blow to the legitimacy of U.S. primacy, however, was wholly self-inflicted. I refer, of course, to the atrocities inflicted on Iraqi prisoners by U.S. personnel at Baghdad's Abu Ghraib prison, as well as the subsequent admission that as many as twenty-eight Iraqi and Afghan prisoners may have been murdered by U.S. soldiers. The public spectacle of U.S. soldiers and interrogators employing torture, intimidation, and explicit acts of sexual humiliation—recorded on film and available for viewing around the world—dealt a heavy blow to U.S. efforts to portray itself as a responsible global power with high moral ideals. Moreover, the fact that these actions may have been approved by higher authorities, and the Bush administration's tardy and ineffective responses to these revelations, reinforced global perceptions that this was far from an aberration.[111] Images of an Iraqi prisoner strung up for interrogation quickly became a graphic global icon, which the New York Times correctly called, "an ad for martyrdom, made in America."[112] A German TV station aired a documentary showing U.S. soldiers allegedly abusing Iraqi children, which led the head of the Norwegian Parliament's Foreign Policy Committee to call for "those politically responsible in the United States to step down."[113] President Bush tried to limit the damage by telling two Arabic TV interviewers that the torturers did not represent "the America I knew," but no senior officials resigned and Bush himself did not offer a formal apology.

Not surprisingly, commentators around the world felt U.S. behavior was abhorrent and the administration's response inadequate. The Financial Times Deutschland called Bush's interview "too late, much too late," and said it would be "impossible to regain moral authority." A conservative Italian media syndicate called the credibility crisis "devastating." The South China Morning Post said the scandal was "a stain on reputations too deep to wipe away"; the Philippine Daily Inquirer said that the U.S. presence in Iraq and involvement in the Middle East "had been stripped of all pretensions to legitimacy"; and the Globe and Mail in Canada saw "Bush's Moral High Ground Slipping Away." Reaction in the Arab and Islamic world was predictably harsh: Saudi newspapers declared that Bush's remarks "will convince almost no one in the Arab world that Washington has changed its ways"; a Lebanese journal commented, "Seeing George Bush talk, walk, move his arms, greet, repeat his nonsense, lie, promise, etc., has become torture itself"; and the official Syrian newspaper *Tishreen* declared, "Any cosmetic strategy will most likely be useless . . . [because] they are images of the crime of occupation and direct aggression in violation of international law and global legitimacy."[114] Americans may think these judgments are too harsh and hypocritical in themselves, but our opinions are not the issue. For Americans, the problem is that the Abu Ghraib scandal gave opponents of U.S. primacy a powerful weapon with which to challenge U.S. claims to morally legitimate conduct.

Efforts to challenge America's moral conduct are not confined to foreign policy, of course. Opponents seeking to delegitimate U.S. primacy also focus on America's various social ills—racial tensions, urban poverty, high rates of crime and imprisonment, etc.—while simultaneously condemning "immoral" U.S. practices such as the death penalty.[115] By 2001, European opposition to U.S. reliance upon the death penalty had become so persistent that a group of senior U.S. diplomats issued an open letter calling for an end to executions of the mentally retarded—a practice, they warned, that subjected the United States to "daily and growing criticism from the international community."[116]

More recently, the People's Republic of China has answered U.S. human rights criticisms by issuing its own report on the "Human Rights Record of the United States." The report documents America's high crime and incarceration rates, widespread gun ownership, persistent racism, homelessness, election fraud, mistreatment of foreign nationals, and several other social ills, and it emphasizes the "double standards of the United States on human rights and its exercise of hegemonism." According to Peter Edidin of the *New York*

Times, it "draws a picture of America that approaches caricature. But that doesn't mean it won't buttress the negative image of the United States held by its critics around the world." The Chinese report is a classic example of delegitimation, intended to tarnish America's reputation as a morally admirable society.[117]

It is less surprising that U.S. enemies also denounce the United States as a decadent and vice-ridden society worthy only of contempt. Thus, Osama bin Laden describes the United States as "the worst civilization witnessed by the history of mankind" and condemns its practice of usury, consumption of alcohol and drugs, sexual immorality, and gambling, among other vices.[118] His purpose is obvious: by portraying the United States as an immoral society, he encourages resistance to U.S. dominance and tarnishes the image of anyone who chooses to collaborate with Washington.

Efforts to undermine the moral stature of the United States can take subtler forms as well. The United States was denied a seat on the United Nations Human Rights Commission in 2001, for example, and the UN General Assembly has repeatedly voted for an end to the U.S. embargo of Cuba.[119] These actions are largely symbolic, of course, and unlikely to have much effect on America's overall power position or on efforts to advance human rights worldwide. But such actions do challenge the idea that the United States is in the vanguard of the human-rights movement, and they give weaker states a symbolic opportunity to "pay Uncle Sam back."

Global perceptions of America's moral legitimacy are also shaped by the ways that U.S. policy is described and by the particular rhetoric that foreign commentators use. When a prominent writer such as John le Carré tells readers of London's *Times* that "the United States has gone mad," it can only strengthen the image of the United States as an irrational bully unbound by moral norms. When the normally pro-American and right-of-center *Economist* asks, "Has George Bush ever met a treaty that he liked?" it reinforces the prevailing image of unfeeling U.S. unilateralism.[120] And when a Chinese newspaper editor explains his own country's wariness by saying that Americans "are too arrogant and high-handed to be tolerated," he casts doubt on whether it is desirable for the United States to control such a large share of world power.[121]

These forms of delegitimation have a straightforward purpose. If others can depict the United States as either acting immorally or as *being* immoral, the less legitimate its position of primacy will appear. And the less legitimate it appears, then the harder the United States has to work to gain support from others.

Consistency with the "Natural" Order

Social hierarchies are more legitimate when inequalities of status are believed to result from conditions that are seen as "natural" and/or immutable. We do not regard it as "illegitimate" or unfair that fifty-year-old tennis players never win Wimbledon, because we know that age inevitably erodes athletic performance. Perceptions of legitimacy can hinge, therefore, on whether existing conditions are consistent with our sense of the "natural" order of things.

To make its own position of primacy more acceptable to others, the United States would like them to see its dominance as the "natural" and inevitable product of particular American traits and virtues. For Americans, the nation's rise to world power is often portrayed as a direct result of the political genius of the Founding Fathers, the virtues of the U.S. Constitution, the emphasis placed on freedom and individuality, and the dedication and initiative of the American people themselves. In this narrative, it is entirely appropriate that the United States enjoys a position of primacy that no other country has ever reached. Other countries may envy America's position, and they may even believe that it is not good for the United States to be so powerful, but they should not question that the United States *deserves* to be where it is.

There is probably more than a grain of truth in this account, but those who question the legitimacy of U.S. primacy might tell a different tale. There is no denying that the United States is number one by a large margin, but this can also be portrayed as stemming from good fortune rather than from U.S. virtues. The Founding Fathers were lucky that North America was a continent rich in natural resources, lucky that the Native American populations were extremely susceptible to European diseases, and lucky to found a country far from the other Great Powers. They were also lucky that the European Great Powers were at war for much of the republic's early history—which facilitated U.S. expansion across the continent—and fortunate that later wars weakened the other Great Powers and helped destroy their overseas empires. This account of America's rise does not deny the role of U.S. virtues, but it sees U.S. primacy as a stroke of good luck rather than as a sign of "manifest destiny."

By emphasizing the contingent nature of U.S. primacy, this counter-narrative encourages others to see it as temporary—as a product of particular historical accidents rather than an immutable condition. It also encourages them to question U.S. global leadership, for if the United States is number one mostly because it was lucky (instead of being unusually virtuous, farsighted, or wise), then there is no reason to regard American advice as better than anyone else's. U.S. leaders may be able to use the power at their disposal to impose their preferences on others, but this interpretation implies that no one should accept U.S. advice uncritically, just because it happens to come from the world's most powerful country.

When Will Delegitimation Work?

As discussed in chapter 2, some degree of foreign fear and resentment is inevitable, simply because the United States is so much stronger than any other state. Efforts to delegitimate U.S. primacy are likely to vary, however, depending on how the United States uses its power and how it portrays itself to others. When will the United States be most vulnerable to a strategy of delegitimation, and what conditions will make such efforts especially effective?

First, and perhaps most obviously, U.S. power will appear less legitimate when it is arrayed against groups that are much weaker. No one likes Goliath, and underdogs often gain our sympathy even when they are acting in a provocative manner. Because the United States is objectively so strong and so secure compared with most other states, others expect it to behave with a greater sense of forgiveness and forbearance. Even when it is objectively "in the right," therefore, an excessive willingness to impose its will on especially weak states is likely to undermine global acceptance of U.S. power.

Second, challenges to U.S. legitimacy will be more telling when they come from authoritative, impartial, or morally distinguished sources. Criticisms from a hostile foreign government can be discounted as mere propaganda, but condemnation from a neutral organization like Amnesty International is likely to carry greater weight. Thus, an October 2004 study in the British medical journal *The Lancet*, which estimated that the U.S. war in Iraq may have caused 100,000 Iraqi civilian deaths, is potentially more damaging to U.S. legitimacy because its authors are professional epidemiologists with no apparent political axe to grind.[122] Similarly, if U.S. conduct is challenged by figures with commanding moral stature (e.g., Nelson Mandela, the Pope, the Dalai Lama, etc.), it is likely to do more damage to global perceptions of the U.S. role than accusations made by the leader of a country like Syria or North Korea. Even figures that we regard as evil (e.g., Osama bin Laden) may possess considerable moral stature with some populations, and their criticisms of the United States will strike a resonant chord wherever that is the case.

Third, the legitimacy of U.S. policy will be compromised whenever the proffered justification for its actions is palpably false. To take the most obvious recent case, America's legitimacy as a world leader was clearly damaged by the failure to find Iraqi weapons of mass destruction, and the subsequent recognition that its case for war in Iraq was based on distorted intelligence, worst-case analysis, and deliberate deception. When Deputy Secretary of Defense Paul Wolfowitz admitted that the administration's emphasis on Saddam Hussein's alleged WMD arsenal and links to terrorism was a "bureaucratic convenience," this confession was quickly trumpeted by critics and did further damage to U.S. credibility. *Le Monde* declared that the focus on WMD had been a "pretext," and a *Pravda* headline announced that Wolfowitz was "confessing the lies."[123] Not only did the United States bungle the postwar reconstruction and leave Iraq in a state of simmering discontent, but the original justification for war turned out to be fictitious. It is hard to build a strong case for America's global leadership role on such a foundation of falsehoods.

Fourth, the legitimacy of U.S. dominance will be challenged when U.S. behavior fails to live up to America's own professed ideals, or when the United States insists that others abide by standards that it refuses to accept for itself. As discussed in chapter 2, states (or individuals) that routinely employ double standards cast doubt on the reliability of their future conduct and undermine their own reputations for moral behavior. During the Cold War, racism in the United States was seen as a liability in the struggle against Communism, precisely because racial injustice made U.S. efforts to portray itself as the "land of the free" look hollow and thus undermined the U.S. image in Africa, Asia, and elsewhere.[124] Today, foreign critics are quick to highlight inconsistencies in what America asks of others and what it reserves for itself. According to Qazi Hussain Ahmad, head of Pakistan's Jamaat-e-Islami movement, "The most enduring factor of the U.S.–Islamic world relations is the sheer inconsistency between the high moral ideals that the United States advocates and the practice of successive U.S. governments in their relations with the Islamic world."[125] Similarly, there is an obvious contradiction between U.S. insistence that other states abandon their own nuclear programs and its own plans to build strategic missile defenses and to develop a new generation of nuclear weapons. As Iranian newspaper columnist Amir Mohebian argues, "The Americans say in order to preserve the peace for [their] children [they] should have nuclear weapons and [we] should not."[126] Foreign governments have also noted the contrast between America's insistence that other states establish "the rule of law" and the Bush administration's readiness to discard existing legal principles when dealing with suspected international terrorists. Needless to say, the abuses at Abu Ghraib prison have been a vivid example of U.S. hypocrisy, a fact not lost on foreign observers. As a Lebanese commentator put it (expressing a view widely echoed by others), "Everything that was said about dictatorship and Saddam's bloody rule will have to disappear before the sadistic American practices against prisoners, at a time when Washington has not stopped for even one day from shelling the Arabs with slogans of democracy and human rights."[127]

Last but by no means least, legitimacy in world politics also operates at the level of diplomatic "style." Just as unpopular monarchs are often condemned for their ostentation, venality, and arrogance, U.S. officials can undermine America's legitimacy by being insensitive to foreign concerns or by treating their foreign counterparts with contempt. While Teddy Roosevelt counseled that one should "speak softly, but carry a big stick," some U.S. officials seem to believe that "speak loudly and shake a big stick" is the more effective approach, with predictable results. Genuine disagreements are inevitable in world politics, and sometimes diplomatic confrontations must be brutally frank. It does little good and much harm, however, when U.S. representatives treat their foreign counterparts dismissively, as both Secretary of Defense Donald Rumsfeld and former Secretary of State Madeleine Albright were prone to do.[128] The United States may be able to get away with it for the time being, but such behavior is not going to make other societies happier about U.S. primacy.

Why Legitimacy Matters

But does any of this really matter? As long as the United States remains the world's dominant power, is it really a problem when U.S. actions appear illegitimate in the eyes of others? Doesn't this sort of resentment go hand in hand with being the world's sole superpower? Foreign nations may resent U.S. primacy and regard the U.S. position as undesirable and even illegitimate, but what can they do about it? In the end, isn't the preservation of U.S. power the only truly important objective? Challenges to U.S. legitimacy and complaints about U.S. behavior simply don't matter very much, as long as the United States is strong enough to impose its will when it has to, and as long as other states remain unwilling to challenge us directly.

This view is an article of faith among advocates of a muscular U.S. foreign policy that pays scant heed to the opinions of others.[129] It is also dangerously shortsighted. As many commentators have noted, even the world's strongest superpower cannot go it alone in every arena. In virtually every important policy realm, in fact—international trade, counterterrorism, human rights, nonproliferation, dealing with failed states or global environmental problems, and so on—effective solutions will require global cooperation.

Why, then, does *legitimacy* matter? It matters because America's ability to elicit active cooperation from other states is impaired when others see the U.S. position of primacy—and the policies the United States is using that position to pursue—as undesirable, shortsighted, or morally dubious. In particular, foreign governments will find it more difficult to support U.S. policy when their own populations regard the United States (and its actions) as inherently illegitimate or questionable. If international diplomacy were confined to the maneuvers of foreign offices and ruling elites—as it was in the classical era of European "cabinet diplomacy"—then public perceptions of international legitimacy might not matter very much. Today, however, most governments—and especially the governments of the most powerful states—must maintain popular support in order to keep themselves in power. And because people around the world have far greater access to information—through media, the Internet, the activities of NGOs, and so forth—their views on America's international conduct cannot be dictated from Washington.[130]

As a result, ruling elites who might themselves favor U.S. positions will find their freedom of action constrained by public skepticism or by outright opposition. In the fall of 2002, for example, German Prime Minister Gerhard Schroeder won reelection by distancing himself from key elements of U.S. foreign policy—and especially the simmering confrontation with Iraq—a position that resonated strongly with the German electorate. Schroeder was not being disloyal; he was simply responding to the opinions of his electorate. What else do we expect democratic leaders to do? Public opposition to the war in Iraq made it unwise for the Turkish government to permit U.S. troops free access to Turkish territory and military facilities, despite repeated U.S. efforts to obtain this permission and a U.S. offer of substantial economic assistance. And public opinion later drove Spanish and Philippine leaders to withdraw their own troops from the occupation forces. In Asia, public resentment of the U.S. military presence in South Korea and concerns about U.S. diplomacy in the region have complicated U.S. efforts to obtain a "united front" against North Korea's resurgent nuclear program. One could go on, but the basic point should be clear: The less legitimate U.S. primacy appears to others, the more resistance the United States will face and the more difficult it will be to attain any of its foreign-policy goals.

Finally, America's tarnished image may also affect the competitive position of U.S. firms in overseas markets. Surveys by the Global Market Institute suggest that anger over U.S. foreign policy has deterred significant numbers of foreign consumers from buying U.S. brands, with several prominent companies noting declining sales in key foreign markets. According to Keith Reinhard, chairman of the advertising firm DDB Worldwide, "Foreigners are transferring their anger at the U.S. government to anger at the U.S. and anger at U.S. business." Although definitive evidence of widespread consumer backlash is still lacking, it is clearly a growing concern for corporate America and yet another reason to worry about the legitimacy of American primacy.[131]

Delegitimation is a subtle and slow-moving strategy. It does not confront U.S. power directly, and it does not prevent other nations from cooperating with the United States when their interests are aligned with ours. Nor does it prevent the United States from bargaining, cajoling, and compelling others to do what it wants. But it does make everything more difficult. If U.S. primacy were seen as broadly legitimate, then other states would be more likely to join forces with the United States willingly and enthusiastically, based on the belief that doing so is "the right thing to do" and that it will be popular at home. When the United States is viewed negatively, however, and when its position of primacy seems unfair, unnatural, and undeserved, then foreign governments will face greater opposition if they are perceived to be too close to us. Because the United States is so powerful, it will still be able to get its way on many issues. But it will not be nearly as easy.

Conclusion

The strategies outlined above are not mutually exclusive, and states are likely to combine several of them in order to tame U.S. power. Soft balancing can make efforts to bind the United States more effective, and informal types of military cooperation (such as the exchange of information about U.S. military practices) can make it easier for weaker states to mobilize their own resources and develop effective asymmetric responses. Efforts to make U.S. primacy appear illegitimate will be more effective if they involve many diverse voices, and even efforts to blackmail the United States are likely to be facilitated if a blackmailer can gain foreign support.

Nor is the use of these strategies confined to avowed enemies of the United States. As noted throughout this book, even close U.S. allies are concerned about the concentration of power in U.S. hands, and some of them may try to use subtle versions of these different strategies either to limit U.S. autonomy or to gain particular advantages for themselves. U.S. allies can engage in subtle forms of balking or blackmail, for example, by withholding diplomatic support for some U.S. initiative unless or until the United States provides them with whatever it is that *they* want. Similarly, weak U.S. allies can extract concessions by threatening to collapse, as Afghan President Hamid Karzai did in order to get additional NATO and U.S. aid in February 2003.[132]

In the broadest sense, therefore, what is at stake is the basic character of the international political environment. For the foreseeable future, the United States is going to be the world's dominant military and economic power. If most states see its position as broadly beneficial and its actions as generally legitimate, then the United States will be operating in a comparatively *permissive* international environment. Such a world will not be free from conflict, but it will be one where U.S. preferences are broadly shared by others and where the United States will find it relatively easy to defend its vital interests and to advance its most important values.

Alternatively, if most states see U.S. primacy as a challenge and regard U.S. policies as "part of the problem" rather than "part of the solution," they will gravitate toward the strategies outlined in this chapter. If they do, then the United States will face an increasingly *resistant* international system rather than a largely permissive one. The United States will still get its way on many issues, and would still be the dominant world power, but it will find itself opposed on more and more occasions, and U.S. citizens are likely to see the world (and be seen by it) in a much more negative light.

For most of us, the first possibility offers a far more appealing vision. The primary task of U.S. foreign policy, therefore, is to ensure that Americans can live in a world that generally embraces U.S. values and welcomes the benevolent use of U.S. power, rather than a world that is constantly searching for opportunities to undermine, irritate, and restrain it. In chapter 4, I consider what states will do if they choose to accept U.S. primacy and turn it to their advantage.

CHAPTER 4

STRATEGIES OF ACCOMMODATION

I n chapter 1, I showed that the imbalance of power in America's favor is historically unprecedented, and argued that U.S. leaders have used this opportunity to pursue ambitious and self–interested policies designed to enhance and extend U.S. primacy. In chapter 2, I explained why other countries regard this situation and these policies with misgivings—even when their own preferences are not directly at odds with Washington's—and I suggested that the United States is likely to be the target of growing foreign resentment as long as it remains the dominant world power. Chapter 3 described the various strategies that states have employed to constrain or oppose U.S. primacy, even when they are no match for the United States in a direct test of strength, and warned that efforts to oppose the United States will increase if it acts in ways that threaten the interests of others.

Yet opposition is not the only way to deal with U.S. power, and both major and minor powers sometimes seem eager to accommo–date the American colossus. Consider the evidence of the last fifteen years. Since the breakup of the Soviet Union in 1991, a host of for–mer Soviet allies and satellites have actively pursued NATO membership, thereby aligning themselves formally with an alliance structure dominated by the United States. NATO's membership grew to twenty-six nations by 2004, with several additional candidates knocking at the door. Equally striking has been the rapprochement between the United States and India—after decades of frosty relations—a process that continued despite U.S. courtship of Pakistan following the September 11 terrorist attacks.

Security ties between the United States and a number of its existing allies expanded and deepened during this same period. The United States and Japan renegotiated their security treaty in 1996, while countries such as Singapore took steps to make themselves more attractive partners and to strengthen existing security ties with the United States.[1] Military-to-military contacts expanded throughout Central Asia and the Persian Gulf region (involving both traditional U.S. allies and a number of new partners), and this trend accelerated after the Bush administration declared war on al Qaeda and sought to enlist foreign governments in the campaign to root out this far-flung terrorist network. U.S. relations with several Latin American states also improved during the 1990s, reinforced by the spread of democracy in the region and a growing commitment to liberal market principles.

Relations with a number of former adversaries improved considerably as well. Although relations with Russia have been uneven, they still mark a dramatic improvement from the intense hostility of the Cold War. China and the United States remain divided over Taiwan, but they have continued to pursue mutually profitable economic ties and have avoided direct confrontation even when potential sources of tension were present.

Furthermore, concerns about U.S. power did not prevent the United States from garnering considerable international support (or at least acquiescence) on several critical foreign-policy issues. In 1990–91, the United States assembled a large and remarkably diverse coalition to oust Iraq from Kuwait. In 1999, the United States and its NATO allies successfully intervened to end Serbian oppression in Kosovo, a move that helped catalyze the removal of Serbian President Slobodan Milosevic. The Bush administration's decision to abrogate the 1972 ABM Treaty in 2001 provoked only modest protests from Moscow and U.S. allies in Europe, despite their prior warnings about the dangers of such a step. The United States was also able to obtain broad international support for the creation of the World Trade Organization, and on terms that were mostly favorable to its own interests.

Finally, foreign responses to the terrorist attacks in September 2001 were almost uniformly positive. NATO invoked Article V (the self-defense clause) for the first time in its history, the French newspaper *Le Monde* opined that "we are all Americans now," and countries such as Pakistan and Uzbekistan offered facilities and intelligence cooperation to aid U.S. efforts to oust al Qaeda and its Taliban hosts from Afghanistan. When President George W. Bush declared that states around the world faced a choice—"either with us or with the terrorists"—most countries quickly chose to line up behind the United States and against al Qaeda.

No matter where one looks, relatively few states seem willing to oppose the United States directly or give material aid to its enemies, and many states actually seem eager to curry favor with the dominant world power. This tendency is easy to understand; because the United States is so much stronger than any other power (or indeed, most combinations of powers), it can do more to punish or penalize any country that defies its wishes. Even where it cannot impose its will, it can certainly make opposition expensive. By the same token, the United States can also do more to reward states that accept its leadership and support its overall foreign policy. And in sharp contrast to the Cold War era, states that would like to resist U.S. dominance cannot obtain help from another superpower. So perhaps we should expect most states to accommodate themselves to U.S. primacy, based on the familiar logic: "If you can't beat 'em, join 'em."

Yet this simple explanation does not capture either the different forms that accommodation may take or the different motivations that might lead states to align with the United States. Nor does it tell us very much about how they will try to safeguard their own interests even as they cast their lot with Washington, often by trying to manipulate U.S. policy so that it serves their interests. What are the different strategies that states will employ when accommodating U.S. primacy, and what effects will their choices have on U.S. foreign policy?

Bandwagoning

"Bandwagoning" occurs when a state chooses to align with the strongest or most threatening state it faces. A state will bandwagon if it believes that the United States is powerful and potentially aggressive, and if it is convinced that aligning with the United States is the only way to avoid being pressed or punished. Bandwagoning is essentially a form of appeasement: instead of resisting the dominant power, the bandwagoning state realigns its foreign policy in order to support it. By bandwagoning, threatened states hope to convince a threatening power that they are in fact loyal supporters, so that it will leave them alone.[2]

Bandwagoning behavior has been historically rare, and generally confined to very weak and isolated states. The reason is simple: The decision to bandwagon requires the weaker side to put its fate in the hands of a more powerful state whom they suspect (usually with good reason) of harboring hostile intentions. By bandwagoning *with* the main source of danger, a threatened state in effect makes a potential adversary stronger, while hoping that its appetite is either sated or diverted.

The belief that states are strongly inclined to bandwagon lies at the heart of many hard-line prescriptions for U.S. foreign policy. The more that the United States demonstrates its military superiority and willingness to use force, so the argument runs, the more that other states will respect us and the more likely they are to support U.S. policy positions. At worst, talking loudly and carrying a big stick will make others reluctant to resist us; at best, it will encourage them to support us so as not to incur our wrath. Hawks such as Bush administration adviser Richard Perle and Deputy Secretary of Defense Paul Wolfowitz clearly subscribe to this view, arguing that displays of power and resolve by the United States will discourage further resistance and lead more and more states to conclude that it is time to get on our side. As Wolfowitz remarked in 1997: "A willingness to act unilaterally can be the most effective way of securing effective collective action."[3] Calling for war on Iraq in 2002, Perle argued that the successful ouster of Saddam Hussein would have a salutary effect on other U.S. adversaries. "We could deliver a short two-word message," Perle predicted. "You're next. You're next unless you stop the practice of supporting terrorism. . . . I think there's a reasonable prospect that . . . these regimes will decide to get out of the terrorist business." The *Wall Street Journal* later opined that the invasion of Iraq had done just that, proclaiming in April 2003 that the "demonstration effect" of Saddam's fall "is now being felt in Pyongyang, Damascus, Tehran," and elsewhere. The *Journal's* proclamation was clearly premature, but it illustrates the American right's tendency to believe that states are inevitably attracted to displays of strength and will.[4]

Yet contrary to these predictions, there are in fact relatively few examples of genuine bandwagoning, even in the current situation of American primacy. The United States has demonstrated its superior power on a number of occasions in the past decade, yet the targets of these threats—Iraq, North Korea, Serbia—and to a lesser extent Syria, Iran, and China—have not been visibly cowed. Moreover, earlier displays of U.S. prowess did not convince these states to abandon their policy preferences and bandwagon with Washington. The stunning U.S. victory over Iraq in 1991 did not convince Saddam Hussein to kowtow to the United States and did not make leaders such as Slobodan Milosevic and Hafez el-Assad more compliant with U.S.

demands. Similarly, Saddam's ouster in 2003 did not trigger the wave of pro-American shifts that advocates of "big-stick" diplomacy forecast. Although a number of neighboring countries muted their anti-American rhetoric temporarily, there are no clear-cut cases where states abandoned well-established policy positions because they feared U.S. pressure. Syria did not abandon its claims to the Golan Heights (or its continued espousal of the Palestinian cause), and as discussed below, the Bush administration's hints that Syria might be next in line after Iraq merely led Damascus to stop giving the United States valuable intelligence about al Qaeda.[5] North Korea did not become substantially more forthcoming in the multiparty negotiations over its nuclear programs; if anything, the invasion of Iraq probably increased North Korea's desire for a deterrent of its own and gave Pyongyang a bigger window of opportunity in which to pursue this goal.[6] Similar efforts to pressure Iran may have backfired as well, by undermining the reformist movement and strengthening Iran's hard-line clerics prior to the February 2004 parliamentary elections, and giving Teheran additional reasons to reject U.S. demands.[7] Operation Iraqi Freedom did demonstrate that the United States had unmatched military power—as if anyone had real doubts in 2004—but it did not provoke a wave of realignments toward the United States. And we should not forget that the United States has leaned on Castro's Cuba for more than four decades, yet the Cuban leader will probably go to his grave refusing to buckle under.

Did Libya "Bandwagon"?

But what about Libyan leader Muammar Ghaddafi's decision to dismantle his country's weapons of mass destruction (WMD) programs and end his three-decade-long policy of confrontation with the West? Doesn't this decision—which was announced following the invasion of Iraq—constitute a clear case of "winning through intimidation"? Certainly the Bush administration and its supporters have portrayed it in this light, in order to defend the decision to attack Iraq and the more forceful policies that they have followed since September 11. As President Bush told attendees at a Florida fund-raiser during the 2004 presidential campaign, "Because we acted [against Iraq], Libya got the message, and it now voluntarily decided to disarm."[8]

There may be a grain of truth in this claim, but even the Libyan case is not a very convincing example of bandwagoning. To begin with, the United States was not threatening to use military force against Libya. Libya was not included in the Bush administration's "axis of evil," and there had been no signs of military pressure under either the Clinton or the Bush administration. One reason for U.S. restraint was the fact that Libya had been actively trying to end its international isolation since the 1990s, largely in response to the economic sanctions imposed following the bombing of Pan Am flight 103 in 1988.[9] Furthermore, although Libya had imported a variety of equipment and matériel for its nuclear program, the program had achieved little and was not proceeding rapidly.[10] The relaxed pace of Libya's nuclear effort suggests that obtaining a nuclear capability was no longer a top priority for Ghaddafi. Instead, he seems to have concluded that the potential benefits were not worth either the economic or the diplomatic costs, which implies that he was giving up something that he no longer regarded as very valuable. Libya was also tempted by the prospect of economic benefits, particularly given the economic woes it had endured since the 1980s. As Ghaddafi's son, Saif ul-Islam Ghaddafi, explained, "The first reason [for the decision to give up WMD] is political, economic, cultural, and military gains that were promised by the Western party. . . . The temptation was really great." Thus, Libya "realigned" in order to end sanctions and obtain economic benefits, not because it feared a U.S. attack.[11] American power may have played some role in Ghaddafi's decision—in this sense, he was choosing not to resist the dominant global power—but it is not a compelling case of "bandwagoning."

Bandwagoning remains rare for two reasons. First, U.S. power is not a threat to most states most of the time. Although the United

States is extremely powerful and sometimes capricious, it is geographically separate from other major powers and not interested in conquering them. Although a number of countries do have reason to worry about U.S. intentions, the vast majority need not fear that U.S. military power will be directed at them. As we saw in chapters 2 and 3, this does not mean that all countries welcome U.S. primacy or are uninterested in constraining U.S. power. But it does mean that very few—if any—states will feel compelled to bandwagon with the United States in order to avoid incurring its wrath. Bandwagoning is alignment induced at the point of a gun, and the United States does not threaten that many countries that often.

Second, bandwagoning is most likely to occur when a very weak state believes that aligning with the dominant power will eliminate or deflect the threat and thereby advance its main interests. Yet military threats generally do not arise unless conflicts of interest are especially pronounced and compromise is largely impossible. Put differently, if the conflict of interest is relatively small and it is easy for a weaker power to adjust its policies, the stronger power will not have to make overt threats. Overt threats arise when the clash of interests is extreme, and regimes whose interests are sharply at odds with those of the United States are unlikely to abandon their basic goals, even if they may occasionally back down over specific issues.

To be sure, many states are mindful of U.S. power and wary of incurring Washington's wrath. But being prudent in the face of U.S. power is a far cry from bandwagoning, and such states do not endorse U.S. positions or lend direct support to U.S. foreign-policy efforts.

Regional Balancing

A far more common motivation for close ties with Washington is the desire for American protection, normally against some sort of regional threat. Thus, what might at first glance appear to be widespread "bandwagoning" (i.e., more and more states aligning with the strongest state in the world) is actually a form of balancing, where the threat to be countered is a neighboring power.

This tendency is not new, of course. Throughout the Cold War, local powers sought help from one of the superpowers (and sometimes both) in order to deal with nearby challenges. North and South Korea, North and South Vietnam, Israel, Egypt, Angola, Cuba, Pakistan, Ethiopia, Somalia, and a host of others all sought U.S. or Soviet support to meet a proximate threat from a neighboring power or to quell an internal challenge. The tendency for states to worry most about nearby threats was a great advantage for the United States, because the Soviet Union lay in close proximity to the other major world powers, while the United States was separated from Eurasia by two oceans. The United States was thus an especially attractive ally for the medium powers of Europe and Asia: it was strong enough to help deter the Soviet Union, but it was far enough away that it did not pose an equally serious threat. As a result, the United States was able to bring together the industrial powers of Western Europe and Japan (and eventually, to a lesser degree, China) in an anti-Soviet coalition, while the USSR was forced to rely on weak and unpopular regimes such as those in Angola, Ethiopia, South Yemen, and North Korea.

This same motivation is evident today. In Europe, U.S allies continue to favor an American military presence as an insurance policy against any future "renationalization" of foreign policy, a development that could turn Europe back toward rivalry and conflict. Although this possibility might seem remote, the fear has been real enough to convince many Europeans that keeping the American "night watchman" in place is still worth it.[12] Similarly, a desire to enhance their security against regional threats (including the long-term threat of a resurgent Russia) explains why Eastern European nations such as Poland, Hungary, and the Baltic states have been so eager to join NATO. According to Piotr Ogrodzinski, director of the America Department of the Polish Foreign Ministry, "This is a country that thinks seriously about its security. There's no doubt that for such a country, it's good to be a close ally of the United States." Or, as a leading Polish newspaper opined in 2001, "Poland has a tragic historical experience behind it, and it needs an ally on which it can depend."[13]

In Asia, the end of the Cold War did not eliminate the desire for U.S. protection. In addition to general concerns about the stability of governments in North Korea, Indonesia, and elsewhere, a number of Asian countries share America's concerns about the long-term implications of Chinese economic growth. If China continues to grow and develop, it is likely to translate that increased economic strength into greater military power and regional influence. In addition to Taiwan (which has long sought U.S. protection against pressure from the People's Republic of China), Asian countries such as Japan, Singapore, Vietnam, Malaysia, Indonesia, the Philippines, and India have welcomed closer strategic partnerships with the United States. Thus, when the United States lost access to its military bases in the Philippines in the late 1980s, Singapore signed a Memorandum of Understanding giving the United States access to facilities there and constructed berthing space (at its own expense) large enough to accommodate U.S. aircraft carriers. Prime Minister Lee Kwan Yew justified this policy by saying that "nature does not like a vacuum. And if there is a vacuum, somebody will fill it."[14] Malaysia endorsed Singapore's decision and eventually offered the United States access to some of its own military installations as well. As one senior Malaysian official commented, "America's presence is certainly needed, at least to balance other powers with contrasting ideology in this region. . . . The power balance is needed . . . to ensure that other powers that have far-reaching ambitions in Southeast Asia will not find it easy to act against countries in the region."[15] Fear of China was not the only motivation for these developments, of course, but it was clearly a key element in their calculations.

The desire for U.S. protection is also evident throughout the Middle East. This motivation is most obvious in the case of Israel—which has depended on a quasi-alliance with the United States since the mid-1960s—but it is also central to U.S. relations with Jordan, Saudi Arabia, and Egypt, as well as a number of smaller Persian Gulf states. Although security cooperation with the United States creates a number of domestic political difficulties for these regimes, they still see it as essential protection against a variety of internal and external challenges. As described in chapter 1, America's military role in the Persian Gulf and Middle East has grown dramatically since the 1991 Gulf War, in part because the smaller Gulf states (Kuwait, Qatar, Oman, Bahrain) are using U.S. power to counter their larger neighbors and to help quell potential domestic dissidents. According to Edward Walker of the Middle East Institute, "By seizing on the reform agenda the US has empowered these countries and given them the courage to stand up to the bigger countries."[16]

Last but not least, the heightened fear of international terrorism in the wake of the September 11 attacks has provided yet another incentive for close collaboration with the world's most powerful country. Whatever their other differences may be, most governments are understandably hostile to nonstate movements whose avowed aim is to overthrow existing regimes and foment international conflict, and whose preferred tactic is mass violence against innocent civilians. Cooperation against al Qaeda or its associates may fall well short of full alignment, but the shared fear of terrorism does provide another reason why states will collaborate with Washington despite reservations about U.S. policies and lingering concerns about U.S. primacy.

The United States does face a potential pitfall here, however. During the Cold War, brutal and corrupt dictators could get U.S. aid by convincing Americans that they were threatened by "international communism"; today, thuggish regimes can get U.S. help by claiming that they are battling "international terrorism." Thus, Russia has tried to portray the war in Chechnya as part of the broader struggle against international terrorism, and Israel justifies continued repression in the occupied territories by claiming that they, too, are simply going after "terrorists." In an even more brutal and bizarre twist, government officials in Macedonia reportedly tried to curry favor with the United States by murdering a group of refugees and claiming that they had in fact exposed a nascent terrorist "cell" within their own country.[17] The danger, of course, is that Americans will end up supporting the wrong governments for the wrong reasons, based on the indiscriminate application of a general "anti-terrorism" policy.

The strategy of regional balancing reflects a recognition of U.S. primacy—if the United States were not the dominant world power, its protection would be worth less—but it is not the same as "bandwagoning." In these cases (and others), states seek a close alignment with the United States in order to use U.S. power to protect themselves from other threats.

Bonding

In addition to gaining U.S. protection, some foreign leaders see a close personal partnership with U.S. officials as a way to gain greater influence over how the United States uses its power, and thus gain greater leverage over key international outcomes.[18] This motivation is implicit in the balancing alignments just discussed—by aligning with the United States, others hope to obtain U.S. protection—but some states may hope to accomplish even more than that. By cultivating a close strategic relationship with the United States—in effect, ingratiating themselves with key U.S. leaders—foreign officials hope to gain direct influence over U.S. policy deliberations and foreign-policy initiatives. "Bonding" with U.S. leaders can give foreign governments a "place at the table" and encourage U.S. leaders to consult them before launching major initiatives. Although America's junior partners cannot prevent the United States from taking actions to which it is strongly committed, states that manage to establish especially close links with U.S. leaders will have a greater opportunity to influence how America views problems and some hope of shaping the way these problems are addressed.

The most obvious example of this sort of connection is the "special relationship" between the United States and Great Britain, and the poster child for this strategy is British Prime Minister Tony Blair. Although Anglo-American relations were suspicious and conflictive until the end of the nineteenth century, earlier acrimony has been transformed into a durable—if decidedly unequal—partnership. The "special relationship" is partly a reflection of common traditions, language, and political culture, but it also reflects a conscious British choice to link its declining power to the rising power of the United States.[19] By cultivating close personal connections—and by serving as America's "link" to Europe—British leaders have sought to gain a degree of influence on American decisionmaking that their raw capabilities could not achieve. Thus, Winston Churchill went to great lengths to position England as America's closest ally in World War II, Prime Minister Harold Macmillan sought close ties with Dwight Eisenhower and especially John F. Kennedy, and Margaret Thatcher used her personal influence to good effect in the Reagan and first Bush administrations.[20]

This tendency has reached new heights under Blair, whose willingness to throw himself behind U.S. policies (and, in some cases, to play a leading role in selling them overseas) has led to repeated criticism that he is little more than George W. Bush's "poodle." The charge is not really fair, as Blair is nothing if not an equal-opportunity lapdog. His strategy for dealing with the United States is political, not personal, as Blair pursued virtually the same approach when Bill Clinton was president. Blair praised Clinton lavishly as the latter left office—calling him "the true leader of the Western world"—but declared in the very same speech that he expected Britain's "special relationship" to "flourish" under George W. Bush.[21] Blair has been Bush's staunchest ally ever since: denouncing anti-Americanism, defending the U.S.–led war on terrorism, and backing Bush to the hilt in his decision to invade Iraq. Blair has justified his intimate connection to Washington by claiming that this role gives England an ability to shape U.S. policy that is far greater than its raw capabilities might allow.[22] As British Foreign Secretary Jack Straw put it in November 2003, "The question is: how do we relate to America in the most constructive way possible and what influence can we bring to bear to ensure that this power is used for the better?"[23] Blair's answer is quite clear: "We should remain the closest ally of the U.S., and as allies influence them to continue broadening their agenda."[24]

Not every state can have a "special relationship" with Washington, of course. Trying to shape U.S. policy by visibly aligning oneself with U.S. preferences is likely to work only when underlying interests are in fact closely compatible, and when there is an underlying foundation of mutual respect and even affection between the two societies. As Blair himself acknowledges, "The price of influence is that we do not leave the U.S. to face the tricky issues alone," and it also means not airing serious differences in public.[25] But if genuine conflicts of interest arise, or if public support for a close embrace is lacking, then trying to ingratiate oneself with U.S. leaders can easily backfire. Leaders who get too close to Washington will pay a political price back home and may even be removed from office by a disgruntled electorate. The fate of former Spanish Prime Minister José Aznar is instructive: Although Aznar may have gained a modest degree of influence by associating himself with President Bush and the war in Iraq, this decision clearly undermined his position with Spanish voters and paved the way for his party's electoral defeat in April 2004.

To be successful, bonding also requires the United States to play along. When a foreign leader justifies close ties to the United States by claiming that doing so will enhance their influence in Washington, then Washington has to be willing to make at least a few concessions so that the junior partner can persuasively claim to have gained something for his (or her) efforts. For example, Britain under Blair took the lead role in negotiating with Libya over its responsibility for the bombing of Pan Am flight 103, "urging the United States along at critical junctures."[26] Similarly, Blair's entreaties reportedly influenced Bush's decision to take the Iraq issue to the UN Security Council, and Blair's influence may also have accelerated the release of several British citizens who were captured by the United States in Afghanistan and incarcerated (along with other suspected Taliban and al Qaeda members) at Guantanamo Bay.[27] And once Bush won reelection in November 2004, he rewarded Blair's loyalty by publicly pledging during the prime minister's visit to Washington that the United States would make a renewed effort to work for a Palestinian state.[28]

By itself, therefore, bonding will rarely produce significant influence over U.S. foreign policy. It can help at the margin, but it will not create substantial leverage over U.S. choices. States that want to have a more dramatic impact on U.S. behavior will have to establish more extensive and reliable means of control, as I shall now show.

Domestic Political Penetration

States that align with the United States do not do so passively. Instead, states that adopt a pro-American position often go to considerable lengths to ensure that U.S. power is used in ways that further their own interests. Instead of displaying a supine loyalty to Washington's wishes, their goal is to make sure that U.S. power is marshaled on their behalf.

Attempting to influence or manipulate the foreign policies of other states is one of the main tasks of traditional diplomacy. States send ambassadors abroad to represent their policies to foreign powers, and national leaders visit foreign countries and attend summit meetings in order to advance their countries' interests and persuade their counterparts. Trying to influence what other states will do is what diplomacy is all about, and America's size and power means that other states will naturally devote a lot of time and attention to cultivating U.S. officials.

Efforts to shape how the United States uses its power do not stop there, however. Foreign powers may also try to influence U.S. foreign policy indirectly, often by manipulating U.S. domestic politics. Such activities may include overt lobbying efforts on Capitol Hill— either to influence specific legislation or to create a powerful cadre of supporters in Congress. Alternatively, foreign states may try to influence public opinion through public outreach efforts, media campaigns, and other forms of propaganda. For example, Saudi Arabia launched a multimillion-dollar public-relations campaign in the United States after September 11, in order to counter the perception that the royal family was supporting terrorism. The Saudi government hired several prominent U.S. public-relations firms and professional lobbyists (including Qorvis Communications; Patton Boggs; and Akin, Gump, Strauss, Hauer and Feld) and began a much more overt effort to court U.S. opinion.[29] Foreign governments also join forces with sympathetic domestic interest groups—and especially ethnic diasporas—in order to encourage closer ties than might otherwise occur. Whatever the specific method, the goal is to ensure that alignment with the United States is amply rewarded, and that U.S. power is used in ways that the foreign government favors.

Domestic political penetration is not a new phenomenon. During World War I, England conducted an extensive propaganda campaign designed to persuade the United States to enter the war, a campaign that helped counter the opposition of Irish-Americans whose hostility to England led them to oppose U.S. involvement. During the Cold War, U.S. foreign policy was shaped—sometimes decisively— by foreign powers that managed to manipulate the U.S. political system, often in partnership with influential domestic interest groups. Prominent examples include the Greek, Armenian, Israeli, Taiwanese, and Korean lobbying efforts, although instances of transnational penetration are not confined to them.[30]

Penetration is likely to be even more important in the current era of U.S. primacy. The stronger the United States is relative to the rest of the world, the more latitude it has to define priorities for itself. Setting priorities is an intensely political activity, however, and domestic factors will exert relatively more impact when the external environment does not impinge very powerfully. During the Cold War, for instance, the Soviet Union was the obvious challenge, and other foreign-policy objectives were generally subordinated to that overarching concern. Foreign powers could gain influence at the margin (usually by portraying themselves as strategic assets in the struggle against Communism), but U.S. leaders were usually able to keep such distortions within bounds.

Today, however, a hierarchy of interests is less apparent. There is no clear and fixed enemy—even al Qaeda is too diffuse a threat to provide that focus—which means it is more difficult to identify a clear and fixed set of priorities. And when it is not obvious what the main task of U.S. foreign policy should be, then domestic forces will exert a greater impact on the definition of interests and the allocation of resources. Threats and commitments are not determined by the distribution of power or even by the location of particular threats; they are determined by whichever political groups—whether foreign or domestic—are able to persuade the American body politic that their priorities are the right ones.

Measuring the precise impact of foreign lobbying and domestic political manipulation is inherently difficult. Public testimony about such efforts can be unreliable, and lobbying efforts often take place in private venues or via other channels that are difficult to identify. Policymakers rarely admit when they have been influenced by political pressure, or admit to having adopted policies they felt were misguided because they were manipulated by a foreign government or influenced by a domestic lobby. Instead, policymakers often try to anticipate the wishes of important domestic interest groups, and they may alter their behavior in advance in order to avoid facing pressure from special-interest groups. Because no overt pressure can be observed in such cases, the actual impact of these groups may be understated.

When Does Penetration Work?

The ability of foreign powers to employ a strategy of penetration effectively depends on several factors.

First, as noted above, penetration will have more impact when the target state enjoys considerable latitude in identifying its foreign-policy priorities. In general, states that are strong and secure—and thus enjoy considerable freedom in formulating their foreign-policy goals—are more likely to have these choices shaped by foreign and/or domestic political manipulation. The wider the range of policy choices available, the more contested the decision process will be and the greater the potential impact of a foreign campaign of political persuasion. By contrast, states facing a clear and obvious threat are less likely to succumb to foreign manipulation that might divert their attention from the main task at hand.

Second, penetration is more likely to work in open societies where the political system is readily accessible to outside influences. When power is decentralized and public participation is encouraged, government officials and influential members of society will be more readily exposed to propaganda from abroad and more vulnerable to lobbying efforts at home. It follows that democracies will be more susceptible to penetration than dictatorships are, and a country like the United States—with a wide range of media outlets, a tradition of free speech and interest-group politics, and a divided system of government offering multiple channels of influence—is likely to be especially receptive to foreign manipulation. A foreign government that wants to shape U.S. foreign policy can do so in many different ways: by courting journalists, hiring public-relations firms, cultivating key legislators and congressional staffers, lobbying elected representatives directly, forging links with key members of the executive branch, and mobilizing sympathetic U.S. citizens. By contrast, trying to manipulate an authoritarian political system requires co-opting the top leaders, and such efforts will generally be more difficult and more vulnerable to sudden whims or leadership changes.

Third, penetration is more likely to work when there is a degree of cultural proximity between the target state and the country that is seeking to manipulate it. Cultural proximity encourages a sense of affinity between the basic values and institutions of the two societies and makes it more likely that representatives of the penetrating state will be able to communicate effectively with Americans. States that are culturally similar to the United States will have representatives who can speak English fluently and will understand how to make arguments that resonate with Americans. By contrast, states that are culturally distant will have more trouble relating to Americans, will find it harder to fashion arguments that Americans will find convincing, and will generally face an uphill battle for the American mind.

Fourth, transnational penetration will be easier and more effective when a foreign government can rely upon a sympathetic group of supporters within the target country. As we shall see, the most significant examples of successful penetration involve cooperation between foreign governments and indigenous ethnic lobbies, as suggested by the cases of Israel, Greece, Armenia, Ireland, and several others. The presence of a sympathetic population within the United States makes attempts to manipulate U.S. policy more legitimate, because their activities will be seen as "business as usual" in the interest-group–dominated world of U.S. domestic politics. If a foreign government tries to manipulate U.S. foreign policy by bribing U.S. officials or recruiting them as spies, for example, it runs the risk of a considerable backlash if its efforts are uncovered. But when Armenian Americans lobby to deny U.S. aid to Azerbaijan, or when Indian Americans press for closer ties between the United States and India, their actions are no different from the behavior of other special-interest groups. Even those who disagree with the policies that such groups advocate are likely to concede that their efforts are neither illegal nor inappropriate.

Penetration also works because it exploits the basic dynamics of interest-group politics. Special-interest groups of all types tend to enjoy disproportionate power when they are strongly committed to a particular issue, and when the bulk of the population is indifferent. Under these conditions, policymakers—and especially members of Congress—are more likely to accommodate those who care a lot about the issue in question (in hopes of gaining their support), knowing that the rest of the population will not penalize them for this concession. If one group cares a great deal and everyone else cares little, then the group that cares a lot will tend to get its way, even if its absolute numbers are small. Whether in farm subsidies or foreign policy, therefore, special-interest groups often wield political weight far exceeding their actual size.[31] And as long as U.S. power seems nearly limitless, U.S. leaders will be more inclined to give these groups what they want without worrying too much about the likely costs.

These features of interest-group politics also imply that penetration is more likely to work when a foreign power has the backing of a sympathetic domestic group, and when its opponents lack an equally powerful domestic constituency of their own. For example, although both Indian Americans and Pakistani Americans have created political-action committees and lobbying groups in order to shape U.S. policy toward South Asia, the pro-India groups are larger, better funded, and generally more effective, partly because the Indian-American population is larger and wealthier than its Pakistani-American counterpart is.[32]

Thus, in an era of U.S. primacy, we should expect other countries to devote considerable effort to ensuring that America's unmatched power is used to their benefit. We should also expect states that can exploit a sympathetic domestic constituency to be especially successful, while those that lack such resources are less likely to reap similar benefits. To show how this strategy can work, the remainder of this chapter looks at three salient examples: the Israel Lobby, the Indian Diaspora, and the Armenian Lobby. I focus in particular on the Israel Lobby because its activities have had the greatest impact on contemporary U.S. foreign policy.

Penetration in Practice: The U.S.–Israel "Strategic Partnership"

By virtually any measure, the most impressive example of successful transnational penetration is the strategic partnership between the United States and Israel. U.S. support for Israel has increased dramatically since the founding of the Jewish state in 1948, and U.S. foreign policy has become increasingly supportive of Israel over time. Although Israel remains heavily dependent on U.S. support, the U.S. government rarely uses its potential leverage to alter Israeli behavior. Indeed, U.S. support for Israel is rarely, if ever, questioned in the mainstream press, in the U.S. government, or in the traditional foreign-policy establishment.

Because U.S. support for Israel is so well established, we sometimes forget that it has not always been this way. Although the Truman administration played a key role in the establishment of a Jewish state, U.S. Middle East policy was not overwhelmingly pro-Israeli in the first two decades of Israel's existence. U.S. foreign aid to Israel was modest, and significant military assistance did not begin until the early 1960s.

U.S. support for Israel expanded dramatically after the Six-Day War in 1967 and has continued to rise ever since. Israel has been the largest annual recipient of U.S. foreign assistance since 1976 and is the largest cumulative recipient (at nearly $100 billion in direct aid) since World War II. Israel currently gets roughly $3 billion each year in direct military and economic assistance, along with a variety of loan guarantees, food grants, and other benefits.[33] In per capita terms, U.S. aid to Israel amounts to more than $500 per year for each Israeli citizen. Private contributions to Israel also receive special treatment: donations to other foreign countries are not tax-deductible, but donations to Israel are.[34] Israel's defense industry receives a variety of indirect subsidies (e.g., via "joint research and development projects" undertaken at Israel's behest) and is also linked to the U.S. military and intelligence establishments through a diverse array of formal agreements and informal links.[35]

In addition to this material assistance, the United States also provides Israel with consistent diplomatic support. Between 1972 and 2005, the United States vetoed thirty-eight UN Security Council resolutions that were critical of Israel, and U.S. representatives have repeatedly sought to deflect foreign opposition to Israel's policies. Although several U.S. administrations have criticized the expansion of Israeli settlements in the occupied territories, no U.S. president has offered serious resistance to these efforts or threatened to withhold direct U.S. aid if Israel did not stop. U.S. and Israeli diplomatic and foreign-policy objectives have also become closely aligned over time, with important consequences for the U.S. position in the region and the world.

The one-sided alignment between the United States and Israel is especially puzzling when one considers that the *objective* case for a close U.S.–Israel partnership is weaker today than it was in the past. In the 1950s, for example, U.S. backing could be justified on philanthropic grounds—as support for a weak state whose citizens were the victims of centuries of mistreatment and were surrounded by a sea of far more numerous enemies. Today, however, Israel is the dominant military power in the Middle East, more secure today than at any time in its history.[36] U.S. support for Israel was also justified by the claim that Israel was a "strategic asset" during the Cold War, but this rationale vanished when the Soviet Union collapsed.[37]

Israel and its supporters now argue that Israel is an indispensable partner in the war against terror and a valuable ally against rogue states like Saddam Hussein's Iraq, but this claim is also questionable. As we saw in chapter 2, the combination of U.S. support for Israel and Israel's treatment of the Palestinians is one of the main reasons why the United States is so unpopular in the Arab and Islamic world, and the United States would have less trouble with these societies (and face less danger from Islamic terrorists) were it to adopt a more evenhanded position.[38] Nor was Israel an asset in America's two wars against Saddam Hussein; its troops could not participate without disrupting the U.S.–led coalition, and the United States actually had to divert some of its forces to help protect Israel from Iraqi retaliation. In the war on terror, in short, Israel is more of a liability than an asset, which raises further questions about the strategic value of the U.S.–Israel partnership.

Close ties between the United States and Israel might also be justified by the claim that Israel is a fellow democracy. There is something to this argument, but it is not a sufficient explanation for the depth of U.S. support. After all, the United States does not provide any other democracy with the level of support it provides to Israel. Furthermore, Israel has become less democratic over time, given that it continues to deny full citizenship to its own Arab minority and denies political rights to the three million Palestinian Arabs in the West Bank and the Gaza Strip. The "shared democracy" explanation remains valid, but it is a less powerful justification than it used to be.

Given these trends, one would expect U.S. support for Israel to be declining over time. One might also expect U.S. policy in the Middle East to have shifted after September 11, as part of a broader effort to isolate al Qaeda and to "win hearts and minds" in the Arab and Islamic world. The puzzle, therefore, is to explain why U.S. support for Israel continues to increase, even though the positive case for close alignment has grown weaker and the cost of the U.S–Israeli connection has grown. What can account for this surprising pattern of behavior?

The Israel Lobby. The explanation for this anomaly is Israel's unmatched ability to manipulate the American political system for its own benefit. It is able to do so because the U.S. political system is unusually open to foreign manipulation and because Israel enjoys virtually all of the advantages described above. In particular, Israel is able to obtain U.S. support and influence U.S. policy because it receives sustained political support from the comparatively wealthy, well-educated, well-connected, and politically mobilized community of Jewish Americans, and from other social groups allied with them.

Jewish Americans form the core of the "Israel Lobby," though it is important to remember that not all Jewish Americans support Israel's policies, and many do not work actively on Israel's behalf.[39] Nonetheless, as Hyman Bookbinder, former head of the American Jewish Committee, puts it: "The essence of the Jewish lobby is an organized, committed, concerned Jewish community in America." American Jews are strongly committed to Israel as a symbol of Jewish pride and identity, and there is a strong norm against criticizing Israeli policy openly.[40] According to Bookbinder, "There is a feeling of guilt as to whether Jews should double-check the Israeli government. They automatically fall into line for that reason."[41] Moreover, when Jewish Americans do criticize Israel, they are likely to attract strong criticism from other members of the community.[42] Israeli officials and American Jewish leaders coordinate political positions carefully, to ensure that Israel's supporters in the United States can exert the maximum political effect. According to Edward Tivnan, in fact, by the 1970s, "total support for Israel had become a requirement of leadership in local Jewish communities throughout America."[43] Small wonder, then, that Israeli Prime Minister Ariel Sharon says that every Jew is "an ambassador for Israel," and that his Independence Day 2003 message to the diaspora communities declared, "The future of the Jewish people rests on our combined shoulders."

Israel's ability to influence U.S. policy is reinforced by the political power of sympathetic gentiles, and especially the so-called Christian Zionists. This group includes such public figures as Gary Bauer, Jerry Falwell, Ralph Reed, and Pat Robertson, as well as Richard Armey (R-TX) and Tom DeLay (R-TX), the former and present majority leaders of the U.S. House of Representatives.[44] As Speaker of the House, Armey told a *New York Times* reporter in 2003: "My number 1 priority in foreign policy is to protect Israel," and DeLay has described himself as "an Israeli at heart."[45] Prominent conservatives such as Vice President Dick Cheney, former UN Ambassador Jeane

Kirkpatrick, and former *Wall Street Journal* editor Robert Bartley have all been vocal defenders of Israel as well.

The pro-Israel attitudes of American Jewry and their gentile allies are mobilized and magnified by an interlocking web of lobbying organizations, think tanks, and pro-Israel publications. Such groups include the American Israel Public Affairs Committee (AIPAC), which is widely recognized as one of the most potent lobbying organizations in the United States; the Washington Institute for Near East Policy (WINEP); the Jewish Institute for National Security Affairs (JINSA); and the Conference of Presidents of Major American Jewish Organizations. Several prominent think tanks—including the American Enterprise Institute and the Heritage Foundation—are strongly pro-Israel as well, and the more mainstream Brookings Institution has moved in a more pro-Israel direction over time.[46]

How does the lobby work? In its general operations, the Israel lobby is no different from other organized special-interest groups. It tries to elect politicians who support its positions and tries to convert opponents or skeptics. It seeks to influence legislation in Congress and to shape policy within the executive branch as well. Like any lobby, it also tries to mold public perceptions on the issues it cares about. There is nothing illegitimate about this sort of conduct; it is how American politics works. What makes the Israel lobby unusual is not what it does, but rather how well it does it.

As with most special-interest groups, a key source of the lobby's power is its influence on campaign contributions. Over the past twenty years, AIPAC has repeatedly targeted members of Congress whom it deemed insufficiently friendly to Israel and helped drive them from office, often by channeling money to their opponents. To note one prominent example, in the late 1970s, incumbent Senator Charles Percy (R–IL) incurred AIPAC's wrath by declining to sign an AIPAC-sponsored letter protesting the Ford administration's "reassessment" of U.S.–Israel relations, and by observing that Palestinian leader Yasser Arafat was "relatively" more moderate than other

Palestinian extremists. When Percy was up for reelection in 1984, his opponents in the primary and general elections received large sums from pro-Israel political-action committees, and a pro-Israel businessman from California reportedly spent more than $1 million on anti-Percy advertising in Illinois.[47] As AIPAC head Thomas Dine boasted after Percy was defeated, "All the Jews in America, from coast to coast, gathered to oust Percy. And the American politicians—those who hold public positions now, and those who aspire—got the message."[48] The message, of course, is that criticizing Israel is politically risky. Most politicians have little to gain by doing so, and much to lose. Among other things, this helps explain why U.S. Middle East policy is never seriously debated on Capitol Hill, and why any serious presidential candidate goes out of the way to proclaim a strong commitment to the U.S.–Israel relationship.

AIPAC and its sister organizations also influence Congress directly, both by lobbying individual representatives and by providing information to guide legislation. As Douglas Bloomfield, a former AIPAC staff member, explains, "It is common for members of Congress and their staffs to turn to AIPAC first when they need information, before calling the Library of Congress, the Congressional Research Service, committee staff or administration experts." Indeed, he reports that AIPAC is "often called upon to draft speeches, work on legislation, advise on tactics, perform research, collect cosponsors and marshal votes."[49]

Another key avenue of influence is the presence of pro-Israel Americans in the executive branch, where they can shape U.S. policy directly. During the Clinton administration, for example, U.S. Middle East policy was in the hands of officials with close ties to Israel and to AIPAC, including Martin Indyk (former director of research at AIPAC and founder of WINEP), Dennis Ross (another former director of WINEP), and Aaron Miller. All three men supported the Oslo peace process and did not oppose creation of a Palestinian state, but only within the limits of what was acceptable to Israel.[50] This situation is even more pronounced in the Bush administration, whose foreign-policy team was filled with individuals whose pro-Israel credentials are well known.[51]

Finally, just as other lobbying groups engage in public-relations efforts to build broad support for their cause, pro-Israel organizations seek to shape public perceptions of Israel in order to convince other Americans to endorse continued U.S. support. Groups such as AIPAC and WINEP and the other pro-Israel think tanks offer a steady stream of analysis and commentary portraying Israel as a vital strategic partner for the United States and trying to discredit criticisms of Israeli policy. Their efforts are facilitated by the fact that many prominent newspapers and journals of opinion, including the *New York Times, Washington Post, Wall Street Journal, Weekly Standard, Commentary, New Republic,* and *The National Interest,* are staunchly pro-Israel, as are many prominent television and radio commentators. Indeed, as Eric Alterman has shown, the vast majority of American media figures are pro-Israel, to the extent that it is difficult to find a prominent columnist or political commentator who is willing to criticize Israel's actions in anything but the gentlest terms.[52] Nonetheless, pro-Israel groups like the Committee on Accurate Middle East Reporting in America (CAMERA) have also organized protests and financial boycotts of National Public Radio (which they regard as overly critical of Israel), and AIPAC has sought to enlist college students in identifying professors who are anti-Israel. Other prominent Israel supporters have also tried to blacklist scholars deemed critical of Israel, and have lobbied to cut U.S. government funding for area-studies programs focused on the Middle East.[53]

These various mechanisms underscore the degree to which Israel is well positioned to influence U.S. foreign policy. Because the U.S. political system is open, there are many avenues through which policy can be shaped and manipulated. If the executive branch is unresponsive, Congress may overrule. If the State Department is skeptical, then sympathetic Defense Department officials may be of assistance (or vice versa). If a politician is not sure how he or she should act, the potential impact on campaign contributions and critical swing votes in future elections may convince them that challenging U.S. support for Israel is not worth the risk. And if public opinion seems to be wavering, there are reports to issue and op-ed articles to write.

What makes these efforts especially effective is the fact that they rest primarily on the activities of American citizens who happen to be strongly committed to helping Israel. Efforts to mobilize political support for Israel do not look like foreign penetration; rather, they are consistent with the interest-group tradition in American politics.[54] Former AIPAC leader Morris Amitay emphasizes that "what is important is that none of this [activity] is untoward . . . you use the traditional tactics of the democracy." Or, as Hyman Bookbinder of the American Jewish Committee put it, American Jews "react viscerally to even the remotest suggestion that there is something 'unpatriotic' about their support for Israel," and are quick to challenge the charge of "dual loyalty."[55] The point is well taken, and it bears emphasizing that there is nothing inherently wrong or illegitimate when U.S. citizens lobby for increased support for Israel, even if their efforts do also provide the Israeli government considerable influence over U.S. policy in the region.

By contrast, Israel's opponents in the Middle East lack these advantages. Arab Americans are nearly as numerous as Jewish Americans, but they are neither as wealthy as a community nor as politically active. Equally significant, Arab Americans come from a variety of countries and backgrounds, and thus do not present a unified voice on many issues. Israel has also found it relatively easy to tap into support from Christian evangelicals, but Muslim societies cannot do so as easily. Corporate interest groups (including oil companies and defense contractors) have sometimes won concessions for particular Arab countries (as in the sale of advanced weaponry to Saudi Arabia), but these groups tend to focus their efforts on narrow issues and generally do not challenge the U.S. commitment to Israel or try to shape

U.S. policy toward the region as a whole. Pro-Arab forces—and especially professional lobbyists and public-relations efforts funded by wealthy Arab oil exporters—are also weakened by the lack of an indigenous domestic base and by the perception that they are simply the paid agents of a foreign power. In the struggle to manipulate U.S. foreign policy, therefore, Israel and its supporters are in an unusually favorable position.[56]

Indeed, were it not for the sustained efforts of numerous organizations whose declared purpose is to shape U.S. foreign policy on this issue, it is hard to imagine that the relationship between Israel and the United States would be anywhere near as intimate as it is today. No wonder Prime Minister Sharon once told an American audience, "If you want to help Israel, help AIPAC." Or, as former House Minority Leader Richard Gephardt told an AIPAC gathering, "Without your constant support . . . and all your fighting on a daily basis to strengthen [the U.S.–Israel] relationship, *it would not be*."[57]

Effects on U.S. foreign policy. In addition to making sure that the United States continues to provide generous economic and military aid, Israel also uses its influence on U.S. domestic politics to shape U.S. foreign policy more broadly, and especially U.S. policy in the Middle East. The Israel lobby is not the only factor shaping U.S. policy toward this critical region, but it is clearly an important one.

Since 2001, for example, the Bush administration has endorsed Prime Minister Ariel Sharon's basic approach to the Israeli–Palestinian conflict. In the words of the *Washington Post*, Bush and Sharon have been "nearly identical on Middle East policy," in large part due to the political influence of pro-Israel groups.[58] And on the rare occasions when disagreements did arise between Washington and Tel Aviv, domestic political pressure helped persuade Bush to back down.[59]

Israel's ability to influence U.S. foreign policy can also be seen in the decision to attack Iraq in March 2003. Israeli officials repeatedly pressed the Bush administration to remove Saddam Hussein from power, and former Israeli Prime Ministers Ehud Barak and Benjamin

Netanyahu published op-ed pieces calling for war in the *New York Times* and the *Wall Street Journal* in September 2002.[60] Israel's supporters in the United States echoed these sentiments, and the Jewish newspaper *Forward* reported that the most important Jewish organizations in the United States had "rallied as one" to support Bush's campaign to remove Saddam.[61] Within the Bush administration itself, the main driving force behind the war on Iraq was a small band of neoconservatives, most of them strongly pro-Israel and some with close ties to Israel's Likud Party.[62]

It would be a gross distortion, however, to blame the Iraq war on "Jewish influence." On the contrary, although the neoconservatives and the main pro-Israel lobbying groups were pushing for war, the broader American Jewish community was not. In fact, polls by the Pew Research Center showed that Jewish Americans were less supportive of the Iraq war than the population at large.[63] The path to war was smoothed not by "Jewish influence" but by the activities of pro-Israel *organizations*, whose efforts made it more likely that U.S. policy would evolve in the direction that Israel wanted.

Israel and its political allies in America have also encouraged the United States to go after Syria and Iran, although their efforts have yet to bear fruit because the occupation of Iraq proved to be more difficult than expected.[64] Israel's ability to manipulate the U.S. political system is certainly not the only reason the United States went to war with Iraq and has been drawn toward confrontation with Syria or Iran, but it has been a powerful force pressing successive U.S. administrations to take a hard-line approach to these countries, even when doing so might not be in the U.S. national interest.[65]

Summary. Israel is the "gold standard" by which transnational penetration should be judged. The Israeli case shows that small and relatively weak states can still gain considerable influence over U.S. foreign policy when circumstances are propitious. Israel enjoys unusual influence in part because Jewish Americans are strongly mobilized on its behalf, in part because they have forged effective alliances with other domestic special-interest groups, and in part because potential opponents lack similar access or advantages. The power of penetration is easiest to see simply by considering the counterfactual: What would U.S. Middle East policy be if AIPAC and other pro-Israeli organizations did not exist? Recall former Minority Leader Richard Gephardt's remark (quoted earlier): Were it not for the "constant support" of groups like AIPAC, the U.S.–Israel relationship "would not be."[66]

Were it not for Israel's capacity to manipulate U.S. domestic politics, the United States would not give Israel the same level of aid or the same amount of diplomatic backing, and would have been less likely to undertake an ambitious effort to remake the Middle East. Domestic political penetration is not the only reason why the United States has done these things, but it is far from a trivial element in shaping U.S. policy.

Israel may be the most successful case of a state manipulating the U.S. domestic political system for its own benefits, but it is hardly the only one. Indeed, the growing importance of penetration in an era of U.S. primacy can be observed by noting how other countries now seek to emulate the Israeli model. Consider two other examples: India and Armenia.

India

Over the past decade, the Indian-American diaspora has become an increasingly powerful force in shaping U.S. foreign policy in South Asia. There are roughly 1.5 million Indians in the United States, and, like American Jews, they are comparatively prosperous and well educated.[67] Indian Americans began forming political lobbying organizations in the late 1980s, including the Indian American Forum for Political Education (IAFPE), the U.S. India Political Action Committee (USINPAC), and the Indian American Center for Political Awareness (IACPA). The Congressional Indian Caucus grew from eight members in 1993 to nearly two hundred members by 2004, making it one of the largest ethnically oriented caucuses on Capitol Hill, and a parallel group in the Senate enrolled thirty-five members that same year. Prominent Indian-American leaders openly express their desire to emulate the success of AIPAC and the other elements of the Israel lobby, and they have forged close ties with key members of the American Jewish community. In July 2003, in fact, the USIN-PAC, the American Jewish Congress, and AIPAC jointly sponsored a Capitol Hill reception, providing tangible evidence of mutual support and emulation.[68] According to Amitabh Pal of *The Progressive,* "Indian officials have been bending over backwards to ingratiate themselves with the pro-Israel lobby in Washington in order to work Congress and to gain access to the neoconservatives who dominate the Bush administration's foreign policy."[69] As Israeli strategic analyst Efraim Inbar notes, "The two lobbies' relationship is excellent. They are working together on a number of domestic and foreign affairs issues, such as hate crimes, immigration, antiterrorism legislation, and backing pro-Israel and pro-India candidates."[70] This trend has been accompanied by a growing strategic partnership between the two countries, driven in part by their common links with Washington and in part by perceptions of a shared Muslim threat.[71]

The government of India has also recognized that its overseas population is becoming a potent political weapon, which helped lead it to grant dual citizenship to some of the roughly twenty million Indians living overseas.[72] An important objective of this act, of course, was to enhance India's influence in the host countries. As former Prime Minister Atal Bihari Vajpayee told a conference on the contributions of persons of Indian origin in February 2000: "We would like you to play the role of our unofficial ambassadors by communicating the reality of a new and resurgent India to the political, cultural, business, and intellectual establishments in your host countries. Whenever the need and the occasion arise, we would like you to strongly articulate India's case to the various constituencies in your adopted countries."[73]

India's nuclear tests in 1998 and the U.S. decision to impose economic sanctions proved to be a watershed for the India lobby. To protest the sanctions, Indian-American political groups arranged for a deluge of e-mails and letters that "flooded" congressional offices. Partly as a result of these efforts, the Clinton administration's sanctions were largely cosmetic (among other things, U.S. food exports were exempted), and Clinton soon became the first U.S. president to visit India since 1978.[74] The warming trend continued under the Bush administration, which lifted sanctions in September 2001 and initiated an unprecedented level of political and military cooperation between the United States and India.[75]

To be sure, the rapprochement between the United States and India is not due solely to the growing political clout of the Indian-American diaspora in the United States. The two countries are also drawn together by common fears of China's growing power and by a shared concern about the threat of global terrorism. Nor can the India lobby claim the same level of influence as the Israel lobby. Nonetheless, the emergence of a well-organized political movement of Indian Americans has enhanced New Delhi's influence in Washington and made it more likely that U.S. policy in South Asia will continue to evolve in a pro-India direction. Given the importance of shaping American conduct in an era of U.S. primacy, it is not surprising that Indian Americans are becoming more active.

Indeed, the Indian government is increasingly aware that a strategy of domestic penetration offers an ideal way to deal with the world's dominant power. In 2002, an official Indian government commission noted: "Indo-Americans have effectively mobilized on issues ranging from the nuclear test in 1998 to Kargil, have played a crucial role in generating a favourable climate of opinion in the [U.S.] Congress . . . and lobbied effectively on other issues of concern to the Indian community. . . . For the first time, India has a constituency in the United States with real influence and status. *The Indian community in the United States constitutes an invaluable asset in strengthening India's relationship with the world's only superpower.*"[76] Given the track record of other ethnic lobbies—a record that India knows well—it is hardly surprising that New Delhi is seeking to emulate them.

Armenia

The U.S. relationship with Armenia offers an even more striking example of the growing importance of domestic penetration. Armenia gained independence following the breakup of the Soviet Union in 1991 and soon became the largest recipient of U.S. foreign aid in the Caspian/Caucasus region.[77] When war broke out between Armenia and Azerbaijan over control of the disputed region of Nagorno-Karabakh, Armenian Americans successfully lobbied Congress to ban all U.S. aid to Azerbaijan, through a specific clause (Section 907) of the 1992 Freedom Support Act.[78] This ban remained in force for the next decade, despite Azerbaijan's importance as an oil producer and its own efforts to forge a new relationship with Washington. Azerbaijan's efforts finally bore fruit in 2002, when Congress approved a modification of Section 907 that made it easier for the president to waive the restrictions. This decision was partly a reward for Azerbaijan's willingness to grant the United States overflight rights and base access during the U.S. campaign in Afghanistan, but Armenia was also compensated by a grant of $4.6 million in military assistance and training. Although less one-sided than before, U.S. policy in the Caspian Basin remained heavily skewed toward Armenia.

What explains America's tilt toward Armenia, given that Azerbaijan is larger and possesses valuable energy resources, and given that neither country can boast a significantly stronger commitment to democracy or human rights? The answer, of course, is the far greater political weight of pro-Armenia forces in the United States. Although Armenian Americans are a small fraction of the U.S. population (with a total population of well under one million), they are concentrated in several historically important congressional districts. Many Armenian Americans also retain strong affinities for their homeland. As one writer in *Armenian International Magazine* put it, "We in the Armenian diaspora have a unique opportunity to exercise our dual allegiance to our host country and to Armenia. We should take advantage of our rights as citizens of the host country to gain its support of Armenia."[79] Like American Jews and Indian Americans, Armenian Americans are comparatively prosperous and have a long tradition of political action on behalf of their ethnic brethren. The history of Armenian-American political action has featured contentious struggles between groups representing diverging ideological and religious backgrounds, but the competition between these groups has also led to higher rates of political activity and greater overall impact.[80] The disproportionate importance of Armenian Americans is illustrated by the size of the Congressional Armenian Caucus, which now has well over one hundred members, and by the existence of several long-standing lobbying organizations.[81]

Prior to 1991, Armenian-American organizations focused on fostering greater awareness of the Armenian genocide during World War I, encouraging larger quotas for Armenian immigrants and challenging Soviet control of Armenia itself. Prominent Armenian organizations included the Armenian Revolutionary Front (ARF), the Armenian General Benevolence Union (AGBU), the Armenian Assembly of America, and the Armenian National Committee of America (ANCA), along with a number of smaller affiliated groups. By the end of the Cold War, the ANCA and the Armenian Assembly had emerged as the dominant lobbying organizations, but with rather different styles of operation and objectives. ANCA is a grassroots organization with more than forty chapters across the United States; the Armenian Assembly is a more centralized lobbying operation located primarily in Washington, DC. ANCA has focused on a broad range of federal, state, and local issues affecting Armenians (including foreign affairs); the Armenian Assembly has concentrated primarily on international issues and foreign policy. Both groups support associated research organizations and youth groups and maintain ties with other ethnic lobbies and various nongovernmental and international organizations (including the United Nations). The Armenian Assembly also maintains a small office within the Foreign Ministry in the Armenian capital, Yerevan.[82]

When Armenia gained independence in 1991, therefore, there were already well-organized pro-Armenia lobbying organizations in place in Washington. By contrast, Armenia's neighbors—and especially Azerbaijan—did not have comparable mechanisms for influencing U.S. policy.[83] Although President George H. W. Bush and President Clinton understood that the U.S. tilt toward Armenia might not be in the overall U.S. national interest, they found it politically difficult to adopt an evenhanded stance toward the entire Caspian region. Working singly and together, the Armenian-American organizations pressed for increased U.S. aid for Armenia, official U.S. recognition of the 1915 Armenian genocide, formal recognition of the independence of Nagorno-Karabakh from Azerbaijan, a ban on U.S. aid to Azerbaijan, the end of U.S. arms sales to Turkey, and the blocking of the Baku–Ceyhan oil pipeline project (because it bypasses Armenia on its route from Azerbaijan to Turkey). Although the Armenia lobby did not achieve all of these goals, it has managed to skew U.S. policy in a more pro-Armenia direction. For example, a 1999 attempt to reduce Armenia's annual foreign-aid allotment from $90 million to $75 million was defeated by the efforts of the Armenia lobby, a victory repeated in 2002 and 2003.[84]

Even in the aftermath of September 11—which led Congress to relax the provisions of Section 907 to permit the president to waive it, if doing so is "in the national security interest of the United States"—Armenia continued to occupy a special position among Caspian Basin countries. This favored position is due not to Armenia's strategic importance or even to particular political or cultural affinities. As one scholar notes, given Armenia's uneven human-rights record and erratic performance as a democracy, "it is hard to argue that Washington supports Armenia as a reward for its democracy and human rights practices."[85] Instead, it is due primarily to Armenia's ability to use its diasporic connection to leverage U.S. power.

Conclusion

For many countries, U.S. primacy is less a threat than an opportunity. Although all states have to be concerned with how the United States will use its power, there are still many ways to exploit America's dominant world position in order to advance one's own interests. States can align with Washington because they are scared (bandwagoning), although this response has been and is likely to remain rare. Instead, states that align with the United States are far more likely to do so in order to deal with local threats (regional balancing), just as they did during the Cold War.

States that align with the United States in order to balance a local threat will want to gain as much influence as possible over U.S. policy. One strategy is to *bond* with U.S. leaders, in effect accepting the role of junior partner in exchange for somewhat greater influence over U.S. policy decisions. This strategy can give weaker countries greater influence on world events than their raw-power position might otherwise provide, but it does require subordinating oneself to U.S. policy initiatives while trying to shape them at the margins.

A more ambitious strategy—when it works—is to engage in a deliberate effort to manipulate U.S. domestic politics. By shaping public perceptions and the electoral calculations of U.S. leaders, *domestic political penetration* seeks to ensure that U.S. power is used to advance the interests of a foreign power. Penetration works because the U.S. political system is remarkably permeable, because money plays a central role in U.S. elections, and because it is consistent with the interest-group traditions of American politics.

Penetration is also of relatively greater importance today because the United States does not face a clear and obvious adversary like the former Soviet Union. In this condition, efforts to define the "national interest" will be more hotly contested—because there is no overarching threat that is apparent to all—and policy debates will be more easily swayed by domestic special-interest groups (including those with strong attachments to foreign powers). This problem is itself a consequence of U.S. primacy: The stronger the United States is, the harder it is to maintain a clear sense of what its foreign policy should be. The danger, of course, is that the ability of other states to manipulate U.S. domestic politics will lead the United States to adopt policies that do not serve the broader U.S. national interest. If penetration leads to policies that leave the United States increasingly unpopular and isolated, or if it merely imposes costs on U.S. citizens that they would not otherwise choose to bear, then it is a serious problem for the conduct of U.S. foreign policy.

CHAPTERS 3 AND 4 have demonstrated, I hope, that other states have many ways of taming American power. The United States may be the strongest global power since Rome, but it does not exercise absolute hegemony over the international system and it cannot force every state to do what it wants. Even when states do choose to accommodate U.S. power, they will try to do so in ways that give them a voice in how U.S. power is used. The question, therefore, is whether the United States can conduct its foreign policy in ways that make its position of primacy acceptable to others, without granting them a veto over U.S. behavior and without allowing them to drag the United States into costly or dangerous excesses. In the next chapter, I offer a blueprint for how we can do just that.

CHAPTER 5

FOREIGN POLICY
IN THE NATIONAL INTEREST

I n the second debate of the 2000 presidential campaign, candidate George W. Bush declared that other nations would be attracted to the United States if it were strong but "humble." They would be repulsed, he warned, if the United States were to use its power in an "arrogant" fashion. Bush's instincts were correct, although his own decisions as president suggest that he did not really believe his own prescription. U.S. power is a potent source of attraction to others, and anyone who thinks the United States should try to halt the spread of weapons of mass destruction (WMD), promote human rights, advance the cause of democracy, or defend a particular ally must start by acknowledging that America's ability to do any or all of these things depends first and foremost upon its power.

Yet America's position of primacy also fosters fear and resistance when its power is misused. Because the United States is so strong and its impact on others is so pervasive, it inevitably generates suspicion by other states and finds it difficult to elicit their full and enthusiastic cooperation. Moreover, because the United States is wrestling with so many issues in so many places, it is prone to being manipulated or hoodwinked by states that wish to use U.S. power to advance their own interests. Given these constraints, how can the United States maximize the benefits that primacy brings and minimize the resistance that its power sometimes provokes?

Preserving Primacy

U.S. economic, military, and ideological power is the taproot of America's international influence and the ultimate guarantor of its security. It is also the main reason why U.S. support is valued and its opposition is feared. Trying to increase the U.S. lead might not be worth the effort (if only because the United States is already far ahead), but allowing other states to catch up would mean relinquishing the advantages that primacy now provides. For this reason alone, the central aim of U.S. grand strategy should be to preserve its current position for as long as possible.

Several obvious implications follow. First, U.S. leaders should take care not to squander U.S. power unnecessarily (e.g., by fighting unnecessary wars), or to mismanage the U.S. economy in ways that undermine its long-term vitality. Second, the United States should avoid giving other states additional incentives to build up their own power—either by acquiring new capabilities of their own or by joining forces with others—and encourage them to seek U.S. help when security problems arise in their own regions. In other words, we want to discourage balancing against the United States, and encourage regional balancing with us.

What grand strategy is most likely to achieve this result? One option is *global hegemony*, in which the United States tries to run the world more or less on its own.[1] In this strategy, the United States sets the agenda for world politics and uses its power to make sure that its preferences are followed. Specifically, the United States will decide what military forces and weapons other states will be allowed to possess, and will make it clear that liberal democracy is the only form of government that America deems acceptable and is prepared to support. Accordingly, U.S. power will be used to hasten the spread of democratic rule, to deny WMD to potential enemies, and to ensure that no countries are able to mount an effective challenge to the U.S. position.

This image of global dominance is undeniably appealing to some Americans, but the history of the past few years also demonstrates how infeasible it is. President George W. Bush has embraced many of the policies sketched above, but the rest of the world has not reacted positively. The Bush administration has been scornful of existing institutions and dismissive of other states' opinions, emphasizing instead the unilateral use of American power to "promote liberty" and preempt potential threats. The result? America's global standing has plummeted, and with it the U.S.'s ability to attract active support from many of its traditional allies. Instead, many of these states have been distancing themselves from the U.S. foreign-policy agenda and have begun looking for various ways to constrain the use of U.S. power. So-called rogue states like Iran and North Korea have become more resistant to U.S. pressure and more interested in acquiring the ability to deter U.S. military action. Efforts to "promote liberty" at the point of a gun have, if anything, strengthened the hands of authoritarian rulers in the Middle East, Central Asia, Russia, and elsewhere. To the extent that democratic reforms have occurred, they may have been primarily the result of indigenous developments within each of these countries and have arisen not in response to U.S. policy but in spite of it. The strategy of preventive war and the goal of regional transformation led the United States into a costly quagmire in Iraq, demonstrating once again the impossibility of empire in an era when nationalism is a profound social force. President Bush's overall approach to foreign policy demonstrates why global hegemony is beyond our reach, and even some supporters of this strategy have begun to recognize that fact.[2]

A second option is *selective engagement*.[3] In this strategy, the United States keeps large military forces deployed in Europe, Asia, and the Middle East/Persian Gulf, in the context of bilateral or multilateral alliances and for the purpose of dampening security competition in these regions. Selective engagement also emphasizes the need to control the spread of WMD, but it does not prescribe a policy of preventive war or call for costly "crusades" to spread democracy or other U.S. values.

Selective engagement corresponds closely to the strategies followed by Presidents George H. W. Bush and William J. Clinton, and their performance shows that U.S. primacy need not provoke widespread global resistance. U.S. power was committed in Europe, Asia, and the Middle East, but largely for defensive purposes. The use of U.S. military power was restrained, reluctant, and conducted largely through multilateral institutions. The United States did twist arms on occasion—in the 1991 Gulf War, the Bosnian settlement, and the Kosovo war—but it did not part company with its allies and was careful to acknowledge their concerns even as it pressured them to follow the U.S. lead. Although other states were concerned about the asymmetry of power in U.S. hands, and annoyed when U.S. officials praised their own indispensability too loudly, opposition to U.S. leadership was muted.

The chief problem with selective engagement, however, was that it was not selective enough. With Europe reliably democratic and the Soviet Union gone, there were fewer reasons for the United States to keep tens of thousands of its own troops tied down in Europe. In the Persian Gulf, the United States moved away from its traditional balance-of-power policy and adopted a policy of "dual containment" of both Iraq and Iran. This policy required the United States to deploy its own military forces in places like Saudi Arabia, thereby fueling the rise of al Qaeda. Unconditional backing for Israel, uncritical support for traditional Arab monarchies, and the failure to achieve a final peace settlement between Israel and the Palestinians contributed to growing anti-Americanism as well. And by declaring itself to be the "indispensable nation," the United States ended up taking responsibility for a vast array of global problems. Attempting to deal with all of them was too difficult and expensive, but failing to do so cast doubt on U.S. credibility and leadership.

A third and final option is *offshore balancing*, which has been America's traditional grand strategy.[4] In this strategy, the United States deploys its power abroad only when there are direct threats to vital U.S. interests. Offshore balancing assumes that only a few areas of the globe are of strategic importance to the United States (i.e., worth fighting and dying for). Specifically, the vital areas are the regions where there are substantial concentrations of power and wealth or critical natural resources: Europe, industrialized Asia, and the Persian Gulf. Offshore balancing further recognizes that the United States does not need to control these areas directly; it merely needs to ensure that they do not fall under the control of a hostile Great Power, and especially not under the control of a so-called peer competitor. To prevent rival Great Powers from doing this, offshore balancing prefers to rely primarily on local actors to uphold the regional balance of power. Under this strategy, the United States would intervene with its own forces only when regional powers were unable to uphold the balance of power on their own.

Most important, offshore balancing is not isolationist. The United States would still be actively engaged around the world, through multilateral institutions such as NATO, the United Nations, and the World Trade Organization and through close ties with specific regional allies. But it would no longer keep large numbers of U.S. troops overseas solely for the purpose of "maintaining stability" and would not try to use U.S. military power to impose democracy on other countries or to disarm potential proliferators. Offshore balancing does not preclude using U.S. power for purely humanitarian ends—i.e., to halt or prevent genocide or mass murder—but the United States would do so only when it was confident it could prevent these horrors at an acceptable cost.[5] The United States would still be prepared to use force when it was directly threatened—as it was when the Taliban allowed al Qaeda a safe haven in Afghanistan—

and would be prepared to help other governments deal with terrorists who also threaten the United States. Over time, a strategy of offshore balancing would make it less likely that the United States would face the hatred of radicals such as Osama bin Laden, and thus would make it less likely that the United States would have to intervene in far-flung places where it is not welcome.

Offshore balancing is the ideal grand strategy for an era of U.S. primacy. It husbands the power upon which U.S. primacy rests and minimizes the fear that U.S. power provokes. By setting clear priorities and emphasizing reliance on regional allies, it reduces the danger of being drawn into unnecessary conflicts and encourages other states to do more to help us. Equally important, it takes advantage of America's favorable geopolitical position and exploits the tendency for regional powers to worry more about each other than about the United States. But it is not a passive strategy, and it does not preclude using the full range of U.S. power to advance core American interests. What are the other steps that the United States could take to implement this strategy most effectively?

Mailed Fist, Velvet Glove

The rest of the world knows that the United States is the most powerful country on earth, and other states are understandably sensitive to the ways that America uses its power. If Americans want their power to attract others instead of repelling them, they must take care to use it judiciously. They should worry when generally pro–U.S. publications like *The Economist* describe the United States as "too easily excited; too easily distracted, too fond of throwing its weight around," or when knowledgeable and moderate foreign observers describe it as a "rogue superpower" or "trigger-happy sheriff."[6]

Two specific recommendations follow. First, the United States should use military force with forbearance: asking questions first and shooting later. U.S. power allows it to take a deliberate approach to many international dangers, and the world's most powerful country should never appear either overly eager to use force or indifferent to the human consequences of its own actions. In general, Americans should heed President Woodrow Wilson's wise advice to "exercise the self-restraint of a truly great nation, which realizes its own power and scorns to misuse it."[7]

In particular, the United States would do well to abandon the much-ballyhooed doctrine of "preemption" contained in the 2002 *National Security Strategy*, a policy that alarmed the rest of the world without conferring any concrete advantages on the United States. This new "Bush Doctrine" was not in fact a policy of preemption (i.e., a first strike intended to forestall an imminent attack). Rather, the new doctrine sought to justify a policy of "preventive war" (i.e., a war fought to forestall a shift in the balance of power, independent of whether or not the opponent was planning to attack). "Preemption" is a legitimate act in international law (provided there is a well-founded fear of imminent attack), but preventive war is not.

Supporters of this new doctrine argued that this preventive war might be needed to prevent "rogue states" from obtaining WMD, based on the fear that such regimes would give them to anti-American terrorists and thus expose the United States to the threat of surprise attack. Yet the danger that rogue regimes will give away WMD is extremely remote. After incurring all the costs and risks of obtaining these weapons, would any leader either give or sell them to terrorists, when he could not control how the terrorists might use them and could not be sure that the transfer would not be detected? Indeed, a rogue state that obtained WMD could not be sure that the United States would not retaliate if it merely *suspected* that they had transferred weapons to a terrorist group. For this reason, among others, new WMD states will go to great lengths to make sure that their arsenals do not find their way into terrorists' hands. No foreign government is going to give up the weapons they need for deterrence and allow them to be used in ways that would place their own survival at risk.

The invasion and occupation of Iraq offers abundant evidence of the inherent unworkability of a policy of preventive war. The failure to find any Iraqi WMD demonstrates that going to war merely on the basis of suspicions is fraught with peril—especially when leaders who want to go to war are able to distort the intelligence process to produce the "answers" that they want. Furthermore, when you invade a foreign country in order to disarm and oust a hostile regime, you end up owning the entire society and must therefore deal with all of its internal problems. As the United States has discovered in Iraq, trying to occupy and rebuild a divided and hostile society is costly and difficult. For both these reasons, preventive war will rarely (if ever) be a viable policy option.[8]

Equally important, making preventive war the centerpiece of U.S. national-security policy did considerable damage to America's international image. All nations retain the option of using force if their survival or vital interests are threatened, and America's enemies are well aware that the United States might use force first if its own security were at risk. But putting preventive war at the heart of U.S. national-security policy made the world's most powerful country seem eager to use force—at times and places of its own choosing— whether or not a genuine threat of attack was actually present. Not surprisingly, this policy was alarming to most countries, because no state could be entirely sure that they would not end up in America's crosshairs, or be confident that their interests would not be adversely affected by a unilateral U.S. decision for war. It also set a dangerous precedent: If preventive war made sense for the United States, then it could be equally legitimate for China, India, Pakistan, Syria, Russia, or any other country that concluded it could improve its strategic position by using force against a weaker adversary. In short, adopting a declaratory policy that emphasized preemption damaged America's global image without enhancing U.S. security, and repudiating this policy is the obvious first step in rebuilding America's reputation.[9]

Second, instead of emphasizing "preemption," the United States should strive to reassure its allies that it will use force with wisdom and restraint. In particular, the United States can reduce the fear created by its superior power by giving other states a voice in the circumstances in which it will use force. Although exceptions may arise from time to time, the United States should be willing to use a de facto "buddy system" to regulate the large-scale use of its military power—whether by NATO, the UN Security Council, or other international institutions. The point is not to cede control over U.S. foreign policy to foreign powers or to an international institution like the United Nations; the point is to use other states or existing institutions to *reassure* others about the ways the United States will use its power. Conservative critics of the UN and other multilateral institutions have mistakenly focused on the rather modest restrictions that these organizations might impose on the United States, and they have ignored the role these institutions could play in legitimating U.S. policy and reducing the risk of an anti-American backlash.

For the foreseeable future, the United States must think of this sort of "reassurance" as a continuous policy problem. During the Cold War, the United States took many steps—e.g., military exercises, visits by important officials, public declarations, etc.—to remind allies (and adversaries) that its commitments were credible. And it didn't just do these things once and consider the job over; rather, it reaffirmed these signals of commitment more or less constantly. Now that the Cold War is over and the United States is largely unchecked, U.S. leaders have to make similar efforts to convince other states of their goodwill, good judgment, and sense of restraint. U.S. leaders cannot simply assert these values once or twice and then act as they please— which is what George W. Bush's administration tried to do. Rather, reassuring gestures have to be repeated and reassuring statements have to be reiterated. And the more consistent the words and deeds are, the more effective such pledges will be.

The benefits of self-restraint can be demonstrated by considering how much the United States would have gained had it followed this approach toward Saddam Hussein's Iraq. Had the Bush administration rejected preventive war in Iraq in March 2003, and chosen instead to continue the UN–mandated inspections process that was then underway, it would have scored a resounding diplomatic victory. The Bush team could have claimed—correctly—that the *threat* of U.S. military action had forced Saddam Hussein to resume inspections under new and more intrusive procedures. The UN inspectors would have determined that Iraq didn't have any WMD after all. There was no reason for Bush and Company to rush to war, because Iraq's decaying military capabilities were already contained and Saddam was incapable of aggressive action as long as the inspectors were on Iraqi soil. If Saddam had balked after a few months, then international support for his ouster would have been much easier to obtain, and in the meantime, the United States would have shown the world that it preferred to use force only as a last resort. This course would have kept Iraq isolated, kept the rest of the world on America's side, undermined Osama bin Laden's claims that the United States sought to dominate the Islamic world—and, incidentally, allowed the United States to focus its energies and attention on defeating al Qaeda. Even more important, this policy of "self-restraint" would have avoided war, thereby saving billions of dollars and thousands of lives, and keeping the United States out of the quagmire in which it became engulfed. The Bush team had all these benefits in its hands and squandered them by rushing headlong into war. Instead of demonstrating that U.S. primacy would be used with wisdom and restraint, they gave the rest of the world ample reason to worry about the asymmetry of power in Washington's hands. Repairing the damage could take decades.

Don't Force Adversaries Together

As the world's number-one power, the United States has a vital interest in discouraging other states (or political movements) from joining forces against it. Accordingly, it should resist the widespread tendency to see potential enemies as part of a single unified monolith, and it should eschew policies that force different adversaries to overlook their differences and to make common cause against the United States. Lumping North Korea, Iraq, Iran, Libya, Syria, and other states together as a set of "rogue states," or announcing a global "crusade" against any political groups that employ "terrorist" methods, ignores the critical differences among these various parties, blinds us to the possibility of improving relations with some of them, and encourages them to cooperate with each other more actively. Even worse, labeling Iraq, Iran, and North Korea an "axis of evil"—as President Bush did in his 2002 State of the Union speech—made it less likely that these regimes would moderate their anti-American policies and made key U.S. allies question America's judgment. At a broader level, anticipating a looming "clash of civilizations" between the West and Islam, or between the United States and China, could easily lead U.S. leaders to act in ways that will aggravate existing differences and turn a valuable warning into a self-fulfilling prophecy.[10]

As Libya's decision to abandon its WMD program reveals, the United States will do much better if it pursues a strategy of "divide and conquer." Libya changed course because the United States employed carrots and sticks that were specifically tailored to Libya's particular aims, circumstances, and vulnerabilities. Indeed, the Libyan example provides a model for dealing with the most difficult and recalcitrant regimes, including such hard cases as Iran and North Korea. Viewing these states collectively as a single problem—even if only for rhetorical purposes—interferes with the adroit and effective use of U.S. power and should therefore be avoided, unless hostile states are really in cahoots. Even then, U.S. policymakers should still look for ways to drive wedges between them, instead of acting in ways that give them little choice but to cooperate with each other.[11]

The United States has many instruments of influence at its disposal, and other states (and movements) all have unique interests, goals, assets, and vulnerabilities. Instead of launching "crusades" against undifferentiated and abstract enemies (such as "international terrorism"), the United States should focus on the concrete foes that threaten key U.S. interests and then devise particular approaches to each one. Unless the United States has clear and compelling evidence that foreign states or terrorist groups are actively aiding each other, the proper strategy is to exacerbate and exploit the differences between them.

Defending the Legitimacy of U.S. Primacy

As discussed at length in chapter 3, U.S. power is most effective when it is seen as *legitimate*, and when other societies believe it is being used to serve their interests as well as those of the United States. America's enemies, in turn, will try to rally support by portraying the United States as a morally dubious society that pursues dangerous and immoral policies abroad.

In addition to engaging in the more familiar forms of geopolitical competition, therefore, the United States must also do more to defend the legitimacy of its position and its policies. This process must begin with the recognition of how America looks to others, and then the United States must devise clear, specific, and sustained initiatives for shaping these perceptions. The United States cannot expect to win over every heart and every mind, of course, because conflicts of interest will always arise, and sometimes the pursuit of the U.S. national interest will leave others angry and offended. But the United States can surely do better than it has done of late, both by adopting more sensible policy positions and by explaining them to others with greater care and respect. America will not be universally loved or admired, but it should get credit for the good that it does do, and it should not be blamed for misfortunes or evils that are not its fault.

Unfortunately, U.S. efforts at public diplomacy remain weak, half-hearted, and ineffective. A recent Council on Foreign Relations task force concluded: "Public diplomacy is all too often relegated to the margins of the policy process, making it effectively impotent." As a result, the task force discovered, "Anti-Americanism is on the rise throughout the world." Or, as former Ambassador to the United Nations Richard Holbrooke puts it: "How can a man in a cave [Osama bin Laden] out-communicate the world's leading communications society?"[12] The *9/11 Commission Report* offers a partial answer: al Qaeda and other anti-American groups take the struggle for legitimacy seriously. They know they are in a war for hearts and minds around the world, and they work hard at developing and disseminating a message that will place America in the worst possible light. In the commission's words: "Bin Laden's message . . . has attracted active support from thousands of disaffected young Muslims and resonates powerfully with a far larger number who do not actively support his methods."[13] As a result, the commission calls for the United States to "Engage the Struggle of Ideas" and recommends increased funding for and attention to media outreach, broadcasting, scholarships, and cultural exchange.

In particular, the commission emphasized the need for an improved capacity to communicate effectively in the Arab and Islamic world. The hatred that provoked the 9/11 attacks is partly a reaction to U.S. policy in the region (see below), but it is also fueled by myths and misperceptions promoted by anti-American groups and governments. To overcome them, the United States should launch a broad-based *and sustained* public-information campaign, using every instrument and channel at its disposal. In addition to preparing diplomats to engage on a regular basis with local media outlets such as *al-Jazeerah*, the United States must increase its own Arabic-language broadcasting and develop sophisticated and appealing Arabic websites to reach the growing population of Internet-savvy Arab youth. A major effort to train fluent Arabic speakers is also essential, so that we can engage Arabic and Islamic news agencies on an equal footing.[14]

The good news is that the United States possesses formidable assets in this sort of ideational competition. Not only is English increasingly the *lingua franca* of science, diplomacy, and international business, but the American university system remains a potent mechanism for socializing foreign elites.[15] Students studying in the United States become familiar with U.S. mores while simultaneously absorbing mainstream U.S. views on politics and economics.[16] To be sure, not all of them will have positive experiences or end up adopting favorable attitudes toward the United States, but most of them will. Among other things, this phenomenon means that the United States should not let its post–9/11 concern for homeland security interfere with the continued flow of foreign students to our colleges and universities.

To be effective, however, any public-diplomacy effort needs a good product to sell. Defending the legitimacy of U.S. primacy is not primarily a question of "spin," or propaganda, or even cultural exchange. If U.S. foreign policy is insensitive to the interests of others, and if it makes global problems worse rather than better, then no amount of "public diplomacy" is going to convince the rest of the world that the United States is really acting in the best interests of mankind.[17]

Imagine how the United States might appear had it behaved just a bit differently over the past few years. Suppose the second Bush administration had said that it was not going to submit the Kyoto Protocol for ratification (an announcement that would have surprised no one) but had immediately added that it recognized the dangers posed by global warming and was therefore ready to place on the table a new and fair-minded proposal that showed a sensitivity to the concerns of others as well as appropriate attention to particular U.S. interests. Suppose the United States had signed the landmines convention, had pressed hard for a small-arms treaty, and had not blocked the improved verification protocol for the Biological Weapons Convention. Suppose President Clinton had taken strong action to prevent the Rwandan genocide, and that President George W. Bush had actually delivered on his pledge to rebuild Afghanistan. As already discussed, imagine how the United States would look if President Bush had followed his father's policy of "multilateral containment" of

Iraq, instead of choosing preventive war and "regional transformation." And imagine how America's image might have been improved
had it placed the prisoners at Guantanamo Bay under the protections
of the Geneva Convention and had Secretary of Defense Rumsfeld
apologized and resigned in response to the torture scandal at Abu
Ghraib prison. Pursuing any or all of these policies would not have
eliminated all forms of anti-Americanism, but it would have made it
much harder to portray the United States as a "rogue superpower,"
and it would have given America's friends around the world far more
effective ammunition in the battle for world opinion. None of these
measures would have made America weaker, and none of them
would have given aid and comfort to America's enemies. On the
contrary, each would have made it easier to rally other countries to
America's side, and kept U.S. adversaries isolated.

A New Approach in the Middle East

Or imagine something even bolder: Suppose the Bush administration
had decided to invest the same level of energy, attention, and money
in rebuilding the U.S. relationship with the Arab and Islamic world
that it devoted to toppling Saddam Hussein. In particular, suppose it
had worked as hard to end the Israeli–Palestinian conflict as it worked
to engineer a war with Iraq. Instead of claiming that the road to
Jerusalem lay through Baghdad, what if Bush had realized that winning the war on terrorism requires ending the long-running conflict
between our main Middle East ally and the Palestinian people, as well
as eventually encouraging economic and political reform in the Arab
and Islamic world. Instead of embracing Ariel Sharon's rejection of
the peace process and Israel's own agenda of territorial expansion and
regional transformation, what if George Bush had made achieving a
just peace between Israel and Palestine the cornerstone of his foreign
policy after 9/11, and had been willing to commit the same amount of
time, political capital, and money (i.e., more than $160 billion and still
rising) that he committed to overthrowing Saddam?

Had the United States done any of these things, its position in the world today would be vastly improved. As the Pew Global Attitudes Survey concluded in 2003, "The bottom has fallen out of support for America in most of the Muslim world." The United States is hated and feared for a number of reasons, but a critical element in Arab and Islamic hatred is the combination of Israel's oppression of the Palestinians and America's increasingly one-sided support for Israel. U.S. support for autocratic Arab rulers plays a role as well, but it is clearly a lesser concern. These attitudes make it more difficult for Arab leaders to embrace any idea that seems to be "made in America." Equally important, U.S. Middle East policy is one of the main reasons why terrorists like Osama bin Laden want to attack the United States, and U.S. policy helps provide al Qaeda and its affiliates with a steady stream of new recruits. Even worse, America's tacit (and, at times, active) support for Israeli expansionism makes bin Laden and his ilk look like prophets and heroes rather than murderous criminals. If the United States wants to win the war on terrorism, it must find a way to reverse the steady deterioration of its standing in this critical part of the world.

To do this will require three steps:

First and foremost, the United States should use its considerable leverage to bring the Israeli–Palestinian conflict to an end. U.S. leaders have been actively engaged in virtually every aspect of the peace process, but they have never used the full leverage at their disposal. While reaffirming its commitment to Israel's security within its pre-1967 borders, the United States should make it clear that it is dead set against Israel's expansionist settlements policy (including the land-grabbing "security fence"), and that it believes this policy is not in either America's or Israel's long-term interest.[18] This approach means going beyond the Bush administration's moribund "road map" and laying out America's own vision for what a just peace would entail. Specifically, Israel should be expected to withdraw from virtually all territories it occupied in June 1967, in exchange for full peace.[19] The

United States has every right to pressure Israel in this way: so long as it is bankrolling Israel (and jeopardizing its own security by doing so), then it is entitled to say what it is willing to back and what it rejects. The "Clinton parameters" laid out in December 2000 contain the basic outlines of a settlement (and, contrary to the widespread myth that the late Palestinian leader Yasser Arafat "rejected" this offer, the reality is that the Palestinian and Israeli leaderships both accepted Clinton's guidelines, with both sides expressing extensive reservations).[20] And if an agreement can be reached, then the United States and the European Union should be willing to subsidize the new arrangements generously.[21]

If Israel remains unwilling to grant the Palestinians a viable state—or if it tries to impose an unjust solution unilaterally—then the United States should end its economic and military support. Consistent with the strategy of offshore balancing, the United States would pursue its own self-interest rather than adhere to a blind allegiance to an uncooperative ally. We can hope that it does not come to this, but U.S. leaders should be prepared to pursue the *American* national interest if it does. In effect, the United States would be giving Israel a choice: It can end its self-defeating occupation of the West Bank and the Gaza Strip and remain a cherished U.S. partner, or it can remain an occupying power on its own. In other words, the United States would be treating Israel the same way that it treats any other country. The United States would still support the continued existence of a Jewish state (the same way that we support a Norwegian state, a Thai state, a Polish state, etc.), and it would be prepared to help if Israel's survival were in jeopardy. But it would no longer treat Israel as though its interests and U.S. interests were identical, or behave as if Israel deserved generous U.S. support no matter what it did.

It might be argued that no change of course is needed, because the Sharon government is already planning to withdraw unilaterally from the Gaza Strip and has resumed talks with the Palestinians in the wake of Yasser Arafat's death and the election of the more moderate Abu Mazen. Unfortunately, there is still no clear sign that Sharon intends to offer the Palestinians a viable state, and considerable evidence suggests that he does not. As Sharon's close advisor and former chief of staff Dov Weisglas told *Ha'aretz* in October 2004, Sharon's withdrawal scheme "supplies the amount of formaldehyde that's necessary so that there will not be a political process with the Palestinians. . . . When you freeze that process you prevent the establishment of a Palestinian state. . . . Effectively, this whole package that is called the Palestinian state . . . has been removed from our agenda indefinitely."[22] Israeli settlements continue to expand on the West Bank, and there is little reason to expect a viable or just peace unless the United States uses its leverage to impose one.

This policy would undoubtedly be anathema to the different elements of the Israel lobby and would probably make some other Americans uneasy. Americans should recognize, however, that unconditional U.S. support for Israel has done great harm to the U.S. position in the Arab and Islamic world, and it continues to put the United States itself at risk. Indeed, if the United States fails to capitalize on the opportunity created by the passing of Yasser Arafat and the democratic election of Abu Mazen, it will confirm the Arab conviction that the United States is either unwilling or unable to play an evenhanded role in resolving the conflict.

Even worse, denying the Palestinians their legitimate political rights has not made Israel safer. On the contrary, those who have lobbied for unconditional U.S. backing for Israel have unwittingly nurtured Israeli extremists and inflicted unintended hardships on the very society they have sought to support. It is time to abandon this bankrupt policy and adopt a more evenhanded position. This shift will help the United States win its war on terrorism and encourage Israel to make the adjustments that can ensure a lasting peace. President Bush has said that he favors the creation of a "contiguous" Palestinian state; the question is whether he is willing to do what it takes to bring it about.

Second, the United States should reject the quasi-imperial role that neoconservatives in the Bush administration have tried to play in the Middle East and Persian Gulf. Instead of trying to impose democracy at the point of a gun—a project that has already gone seriously awry in Iraq—the United States should return to its earlier policy as an "offshore balancer" in this region. The United States does have important interests in the Middle East—including access to oil and the need to combat terrorism—but neither objective is well served by occupying the region with its own military forces. Because U.S. interests are served as long as no single state controls all (or even most) of the Persian Gulf oil, the United States can play the balancer's role: shifting its weight as needed to make sure that no one state is able to dominate the others. The United States pursued this policy successfully from 1945 to 1990 during the Cold War era, and it is still the right policy today. In fact, a balancing strategy will be much easier now, because we no longer have to protect Gulf oil resources from a Soviet invasion.

Taken together, these two steps would facilitate the long-range goal of helping various Arab and Islamic states make smooth transitions to more pluralist forms of government. At present, U.S. efforts to encourage democratic change in the Arab and Islamic world are undermined by America's one-sided support for Israel. Why should other Arabs believe the United States is committed to freedom when its money and its power are used to deny these rights to millions of Palestinians? History also warns that trying to run—let alone "transform"—the entire Middle East is a fool's errand: any leaders the United States might install will have little legitimacy, and a continued U.S. occupation will fuel anti-Americanism and make the terrorism problem worse. Neo-imperial pundits who call for the United States to rule a new empire (or, to put it more tactfully, a "U.S. protectorate") in the region ignore one of the central lessons of the twentieth century: Nationalism is the most powerful political ideology in the world, and trying to run large alien populations by force is a losing game. Nationalism and the desire for self-determination helped destroy the Austro-Hungarian, Ottoman, British, French, and Soviet empires, just as it defeated Israel's occupation of Lebanon and continues to bedevil the Indians in Kashmir and the Russians in Chechnya. Only a fool or a knave would send the United States down this path.

If the United States wants to play a positive role in the Middle East, then it must end the conflict between Israel and the Palestinians and use nonmilitary means to encourage progressive forces in the Arab and Islamic world. The United States should encourage the gradual transformation of Middle East monarchies and dictatorships, but not by imposing democracy through invasion and occupation.

A "Grand Bargain" on Nuclear Terrorism

As noted in chapter 3, among the most catastrophic threats to U.S. national security is the danger of nuclear terrorism. Conventional terrorism—including the 9/11 attacks—can be horrifying and tragic, but even an event as awful as September 11 does not threaten America's existence or way of life. Although the United States should take every reasonable step to prevent another terrorist attack, it could absorb a replay of September 11 once every ten years and continue to thrive as a society.

A terrorist attack involving WMD—and especially one involving a nuclear weapon—would be another matter entirely. If a nuclear bomb were to go off in any major U.S. city, hundreds of thousands of U.S. lives could be lost in an instant. The economic damage would be enormous and far-reaching. We could not know if additional attacks were coming, and we might have little idea how and where to retaliate. Such an event would probably have incalculable implications for U.S. security, prosperity, civil liberties, and foreign policy. Indeed, it could easily be the most significant single event in U.S. history.

Recognizing this fact, a number of analysts have called for renewed efforts to deny terrorists any possible access to the fissionable materials that would be needed to construct a nuclear device. Specifically, they call for: (1) redoubled efforts to secure loose nuclear materials in the former Soviet Union and elsewhere; (2) a global "clean-out" of nuclear research reactors and other unsecured materials; and (3) enhanced measures to block nuclear smuggling. Such measures are certainly worthwhile, and if implemented quickly and effectively, they could substantially reduce the risk that nuclear weapons or the materials to make them could fall into hostile hands.[23]

The risk of nuclear terrorism will also increase if more and more countries acquire nuclear weapons of their own. Accordingly, the United States should give states such as North Korea and Iran strong incentives to give up their nuclear-weapons programs, work to shut down black-market nuclear-technology networks, and take concrete steps to improve the global regime against the spread of nuclear arms. In particular, the United States should: (1) press for the revision of Article IV of the Nuclear Non-Proliferation Treaty (NPT), which currently gives all signatories access to the full nuclear-fuel cycle; (2) support a more ambitious "Proliferation Security Initiative" to intercept illegal shipments of nuclear materials and missile technology; and (3) make a coordinated, multilateral effort—using both carrots and sticks—to persuade Iran, North Korea, and other likely proliferators to abandon their nuclear ambitions.[24]

Unfortunately, getting other states to embrace these initiatives is going to require the United States to alter its own nuclear-weapons policies and its current approach to nuclear diplomacy. The United States wants to discourage other states from acquiring nuclear weapons or improving their existing arsenals, and hopes to enlist other nations in a broad set of antinuclear initiatives, yet it continues to maintain a nuclear arsenal that is far larger than it needs to deter any possible adversary. Indeed, the Bush administration insists that the United States should retain thousands of warheads in a nuclear reserve force and build a new generation of nuclear weapons in order to deal with a number of new threats—even though U.S. conventional forces dwarf those of any other state.[25] Thus, Mohamed El-Baradei, head of the International Atomic Energy Agency, likens the United States to "some who have . . . continued to dangle a cigarette from their mouth and tell everybody else not to smoke."[26] These policies send the clear message that despite what U.S. leaders say, they really believe that having lots of nuclear weapons is *very* desirable. If the United States thinks nuclear weapons are essential for *its* security, why is it so surprising that weaker and more vulnerable states have reached the same conclusion?

De-emphasizing U.S. nuclear-weapons programs is unlikely to alter the calculations of North Korea or Iran, whose nuclear ambitions are well advanced, but it would strengthen antinuclear advocates in countries where the nuclear option is still being debated. Equally important, U.S. nuclear-weapons policies make other states reluctant to embrace a more stringent nonproliferation regime—in large part because they believe the United States has yet to fulfill its own obligations under the existing Non-Proliferation Treaty.[27] Indeed, after both nuclear and nonnuclear states agreed on a thirteen-point program to implement the Article VI obligation at the 2000 NPT Review Conference, the Bush administration took office in early 2001 and either rejected or ignored virtually all of the thirteen points.[28] Trying to get other states to accept new constraints on their own conduct without offering parallel concessions in return is not likely to work.

To make matters worse, the United States continues to act in ways that increase other states' incentives to get nuclear weapons of their own. By putting North Korea and Iran in the "axis of evil," and by making it clear that the United States favors regime change in both countries, the Bush administration gave both regimes every reason to acquire some way to deter the United States from using its power to threaten their political survival. Given the overall asymmetry of power between the United States and these states, the only way to do this is by acquiring a potent deterrent of their own.

If the United States is serious about reducing the dangers of nuclear terrorism (and it should be), then it must offer the rest of the

world a "grand bargain." In exchange for a more reliable nonproliferation regime (accompanied by an aggressive effort to secure existing
stockpiles of loose nuclear materials), and the verifiable abandonment
of nuclear ambitions by countries like Iran and North Korea, the
United States would simultaneously agree to: (1) abandon current
plans to build a new generation of nuclear weapons; (2) significantly
reduce its own nuclear arsenal (while retaining a few hundred warheads as a deterrent against direct attacks on the United States itself);
and (3) take concrete steps to reduce the threat that it presents to
so-called rogue states, including a willingness to sign some sort of
non-aggression agreement with them.[29]

Some critics may see this proposal as a form of appeasement that
would undermine U.S. superiority and threaten its long-term
national security. This view is shortsighted. Unless it makes a series
of catastrophic blunders, the United States will be the strongest country on the planet for the next several decades, and its primacy will not
be altered whether it has five thousand nuclear warheads or only fifty.
Nor does this approach entail giving into threats; it is simply the
most obvious way to reduce other states' own incentives to take measures that are not in the U.S. national interest. This strategy would
also make the United States look much less hypocritical in the eyes of
others, and thus make it easier to line up other states behind a
tougher and broader nonproliferation regime.

In short, the grand bargain proposed here does involve making certain compromises, but it does so from a clear sense of national interest
and strategic priorities. Nuclear terrorism is the most worrisome danger that the world's only superpower now faces, and a grand strategy
centered on the U.S. national interest would focus on the biggest
problems and subordinate other goals in order to address them.

Playing Hard to Get

Key elements in the strategy of offshore balancing are reducing the
overall "footprint" of U.S. military power and beginning to play

"hard to get" when dealing with various regional powers. Instead of insisting that the United States be responsible for solving all global security problems, and instead of taking on the burden of running large areas of the world, offshore balancing seeks to take advantage of America's hegemonic position in the Western Hemisphere and its distance from the other key centers of world power. As discussed above, the United States would stand ready to deploy its power against specific threats to U.S. vital interests but would otherwise refrain from large-scale, quasi-permanent military engagements overseas.

What would this strategy mean in practice? First, the United States would remain a member of NATO but would drastically reduce its military presence in Europe. Most of Europe is now reliably democratic and faces no significant external military threats. Although far from united on matters of foreign policy, the EU countries have the political and economic wherewithal to deal with the modest security challenges that they are likely to face in the foreseeable future. Small U.S. contingents would remain in Europe for training purposes, and as a symbol of America's transatlantic commitments, but the United States would no longer play the leading security role there.

Second, the United States would maintain a significant military presence in Asia (primarily air and naval forces) and continue to build cooperative security partnerships with its current Asian allies. In addition to helping support counterterrorist operations against al Qaeda affiliates in several Asian countries, maintaining the U.S. military presence in Asia also lays the foundation for a future effort to contain China, in the event that China's rising power eventually leads to a more ambitious attempt to establish a hegemonic position in East Asia.[30]

Third, the United States would return to a balance-of-power policy toward the rest of the world, and especially the Middle East and the Persian Gulf. As discussed above, the United States has no need to occupy or dominate these regions; it just needs to ensure that no other state is able to do so. Trying to control other regions encourages anger and resentment, and it entangles the United States in events and processes that it cannot easily control. Instead, the United States should declare that it is committed to maintaining the territorial integrity of every state, and that it will oppose any acts of aggression that threaten to result in any one state exercising hegemony over any others. But it will do so in classic balance-of-power fashion: relying in the first instance on local allies, intervening only when absolutely necessary, and withdrawing once the threat has been thwarted.

Interestingly, the Bush administration has embraced several key elements of this approach without fully committing to its underlying logic or the policy implications. Although the Bush team has made many other errors, its members have recognized that the deployment patterns left over from the Cold War were no longer appropriate for dealing with the new array of global threats. As a result, they have begun to implement a far-reaching rearrangement of U.S. forces worldwide.[31] In particular, the new strategic environment requires less reliance on the semipermanent overseas deployments of large, heavy ground forces, and greater emphasis on more mobile and flexible forces that can go where they are needed and return home as soon as they are done. The Bush team seems also to be aware that the United States is more popular when it indicates a willingness to withdraw instead of insisting on staying, and that reducing America's overall military "footprint" might reduce some of the latent anti-Americanism that now exists.

There is a broader lesson here: As the world's only superpower, the United States has an incentive to play "hard to get." It also has the luxury of being able to do so. Given America's preponderance of power and favorable geographic position, the credibility of U.S. commitments is not our problem. On the contrary, whether U.S. pledges are credible is first and foremost a problem for those who are dependent on U.S. help. Instead of bending over backward to convince the rest of the world that the United States is 100 percent reliable, U.S. leaders should be encouraging other states to bend over backward to keep us in their corners. And other states are more likely to do so if they realize that U.S. support is conditional on cooperating with us. If other states were not entirely sure that the United States would come to their aid if asked, they would be willing to do much more to make sure that we would. America's Asian and Persian Gulf allies illustrate this dynamic perfectly: Whenever they begin to fear that the U.S. role might decline, they leap to offer Washington new facilities and access agreements and go to greater lengths to conform their foreign policy to ours.

To reiterate: Offshore balancing is not isolationist. The United States would not withdraw from world affairs under this strategy, and it will still retain potent power-projection capabilities. Playing "hard to get" simply means that the United States would only intervene when overt aggression occurred, and when U.S. vital interests were directly threatened. We would do so with the clear intention of coming home quickly—and with a clear strategy for doing so.

Reduce the Impact of Foreign Lobbies and Special Interests

If the United States does play "hard to get," then other states will work even harder to win its favor. As in any courtship, America's various suitors will use a variety of blandishments and deceptions in order to ensure that U.S. power is used in ways that advance their interests. Given the openness of the U.S. political system, and its tradition of interest-group politics, one of the most effective ways to do this is by organizing special-interest groups and lobbying organizations, often based on ethnic groups with strong attachments to foreign countries.

If Americans want a foreign policy that is truly in the U.S. national interest, then they must take steps to curb the influence of special-interest groups like the American Israel Public Affairs Committee, the Indian American Center for Political Awareness, the Armenian Assembly, and various other ethnic lobbies. The most effective way to do this would be campaign finance reform, which would help break the stranglehold that some of these groups now exert on the U.S. Congress. Barring such a far-reaching step (which is unlikely to occur anytime soon), the next best alternative would be for other U.S. citizens to challenge lobbyists and other special-interest groups to justify their positions in detail. In doing so, it should be entirely legitimate to criticize such groups for advocating policies that serve foreign interests but not those of the United States, and to have an open debate on the policies they are endorsing.

Americans must begin to talk more openly about the conflicts of interest that arise when key foreign-policy officials have strong affinities for particular foreign countries. The problem is not "dual loyalty": all U.S. citizens have many loyalties, and each of us has the right to hold particular attachments and to pursue these attachments within the limits of U.S. law.[32] The issue is more properly seen as a potential conflict of interest: is it in the best interests of the United States to place U.S. policy on key issues in the hands of individuals whose evenhandedness is not beyond question? In ordinary life, we routinely expect people to recuse themselves from issues in which their own interests or loyalties are involved. Stockbrokers are not supposed to recommend that clients invest in firms owned by their spouses; judges and jurors are excused from legal cases where they have ties to one of the parties; and even university administrators are expected to divulge relationships that might affect their objectivity or probity. Yet in the United States, it is commonplace for key foreign-policy officials to be given responsibility for conducting U.S. policy toward countries where they have very strong prior affinities and interests. Instead of insisting that our foreign policymakers be above reproach, it is more likely that anyone who questions this sort of relationship would be accused of slandering dedicated public servants.

Why does this matter? It matters because the United States cannot afford to lose sight of its own national interest, especially in an era where anti-Americanism is widespread and when terrorists are trying to gain access to weapons of mass destruction so that they can attack the United States directly. Under these conditions, the United States must take particular care that it not be enticed into conflicts that do not affect core U.S. interests, simply because some country was able to manipulate U.S. domestic politics. If the desire to placate domestic lobbies dominates the political calculations of U.S. leaders (both in Congress and in the executive branch), then the United States is in effect allowing its foreign policy to be determined in Taipei, Tel Aviv, Riyadh, New Delhi, Athens, Yerevan, and so on, rather than in Washington. It is one thing to pay a price for taking steps that are clearly in the U.S. national interest, but it is quite another matter to place U.S. security at risk doing something primarily on behalf of some other country.

Conclusion: A Mature Foreign Policy

The United States is the strongest and most influential Great Power in modern history. It also remains a remarkably immature Great Power—one whose rhetoric is frequently at odds with the reality of its own conduct and one that often treats the management of foreign affairs as an adjunct to domestic politics. Unlike Great Britain, whose empire was managed by a permanent civil service that could bring continuity and expertise to the conduct of foreign policy, the United States brings in a new team every time the White House switches parties. Americans remain remarkably ignorant of the world they believe it is their obligation and destiny to run, and the topic of foreign affairs captures public attention only when major mistakes have already been made.

If the United States wants to make its privileged position acceptable to others, then the American body politic must acquire a more serious and disciplined attitude toward the conduct of foreign policy. In the past, seemingly secure behind its nuclear deterrent and oceanic moats, and possessing unmatched economic and military

246 TAMING AMERICAN POWER

power, the United States allowed its foreign policy to be distorted by partisan sniping; hijacked by foreign lobbyists and narrow domestic special interests; blinded by lofty but unrealistic rhetoric; and held hostage by irresponsible and xenophobic members of Congress. Even after the dramatic wake-up call on September 11, 2001, efforts to reform U.S. intelligence services, to corral loose nuclear materials, and to improve U.S. homeland security have been halfhearted at best. And even though the country faced a new and very real enemy in al Qaeda, the Bush administration was able to persuade Congress and the American people that preventive war against a country that had nothing to do with 9/11 was still the best way to fight Osama bin Laden and his followers. Is this the way that a mature Great Power behaves?

The problem, alas, goes deeper than that. Despite its pretensions as the world's only superpower, the United States has starved its intelligence services, gutted its international-affairs budget, done little to attract the ablest members of its society to government service, neglected the study of foreign languages and cultures, and basically behaved as though it simply didn't matter whether U.S. foreign policy were run well or not.[33] This policy might have been sufficient in the past (though it is hard to be proud of it), but it will not serve us well in today's world.

What is needed, instead, is greater confidence in America's fundamental principles and institutions and greater wisdom in understanding what U.S. power can and cannot accomplish. America's core values of liberty and opportunity unleash the energy upon which our economic prosperity is built. That prosperity, in turn, provides the sinews of our military power and the hard core of our international influence. But the ability to defeat other armies and our influence over the world economy do not give the United States either the right or the ability to impose these principles on others, and it hardly gives 5 percent of the world's population the obligation, capacity, or right to govern vast areas of the world by force. Instead of telling the

world what to do and how to live—a temptation that both neoconservative empire-builders and liberal internationalists find hard to
resist—the United States should lead the world primarily by its
example. If we have faith in our core principles, we will expect to
win hearts and minds first and foremost because others will see how
we live, and see what we have, and they will want those things too.

Despite the missteps the United States has made in recent years, it
still retains enormous material power and considerable global influence. The question is whether its future choices will draw others
closer, drive them into sullen resentment, or provoke them into open
resistance. The United States can use its power and wealth to compel
others to do what it wants, but this strategy will surely fail in the long
run. In most circumstances, the key is not power but *persuasion*.

There is a lesson here. More than anything else, the United States
wants to retain its position of primacy for as long as it can. To do
this, it must persuade the rest of the world that U.S. primacy is
preferable to the likely alternatives. Achieving that goal will require a
level of wisdom and self-restraint that has often been lacking in U.S.
foreign policy—largely because it wasn't needed. But it is today.
Although geography, history, and good fortune have combined to
give the United States a remarkable array of advantages, it would still
be possible to squander them. And if the United States ends up has-
tening the demise of its existing partnerships and giving rise to new
arrangements whose main purpose is to contain *us*, we will have only
ourselves to blame.

NOTES

Introduction

1. On the different "schools of thought" in the history of U.S. foreign relations, see Felix Gilbert, *To the Farewell Address: Ideas of Early American Foreign Policy* (Princeton, NJ: Princeton University Press, 1961); Bradford Perkins, *The Creation of a Republican Empire, 1776–1865: Cambridge History of American Foreign Relations, Vol. I* (Cambridge: Cambridge University Press, 1993); Robert E. Osgood, *Ideals and Self-Interest in American Foreign Relations* (Chicago: University of Chicago Press, 1953); Walter Russell Mead, *Special Providence: American Foreign Policy and How It Changed the World* (New York: Alfred A. Knopf, 2002); Fareed Zakaria, *From Wealth to Power: The Unusual Origins of America's World Role* (Princeton: Princeton University Press, 1998); and Tony Smith, *America's Mission: The United States and the Worldwide Struggle for Democracy in the Twentieth Century* (Princeton: Princeton University Press, 1994).

2. For an early but still useful survey of the different options, see Barry R. Posen and Andrew L. Ross, "Competing Visions for U.S. Grand Strategy," *International Security* 21, no. 3 (Winter 1996–97).

3. Charles Krauthammer, "The Unipolar Moment," *Foreign Affairs* 70, no. 1 (1990–91); idem, "Democratic Realism: An American Foreign Policy for a Unipolar World," 2004 Irving Kristol Lecture, American Enterprise Institute, Washington, DC, February 10, 2004; William Kristol and Robert Kagan, "Toward a Neo-Reaganite Foreign Policy," *Foreign Affairs* 75, no. 4 (July/August 1996); idem, eds., *Present Dangers: Crisis and Opportunity in American Foreign and Defense Policy* (San Francisco: Encounter Books, 2000); and Zal-

may Khalilzad, "Losing the Moment?: The United States and the World after the Cold War," *Washington Quarterly* 18, no. 2 (Spring 1995).

4. Recommending the latter approach are Zbigniew Brzezinski, *The Choice: Global Domination or Global Leadership* (New York: Basic Books, 2004); and Joseph S. Nye, *The Paradox of American Power: Why the World's Only Superpower Cannot Go It Alone* (New York: Oxford, 2001).

5. This approach was especially evident in the first two years of the Clinton administration, and it played a prominent role in their early rhetoric. See William G. Hyland, *Clinton's World: Remaking American Foreign Policy* (New York: Praeger, 1999).

6. See Robert J. Art, "Geopolitics Updated: The Strategy of Selective Engagement," *International Security* 23, no. 3 (Winter 1998–99); idem, *A Grand Strategy for America* (Ithaca: Cornell University Press, 2003). This approach is also implicit in Henry Kissinger, *Does America Need a Foreign Policy? Toward a Diplomacy for the Twenty-first Century* (New York: Simon and Schuster, 2001).

7. On this version of grand strategy, see Christopher Layne, "From Preponderance to Offshore Balancing: America's Future Grand Strategy," *International Security* 22, no. 1 (Summer 1997); and John J. Mearsheimer, *The Tragedy of Great Power Politics* (New York: W. W. Norton, 2001), chap. 10.

8. See, for example, Hubert Vedrine with Dominique Moisi, *France in an Age of Globalization*, trans. Philip H. Gordon (Washington, DC: Brookings Institution Press, 2001).

9. See Stephen M. Walt, "The Enduring Relevance of the Realist Tradition," in Ira Katznelson and Helen Milner, eds., *Political Science: State of the Discipline III* (New York: W. W. Norton, 2003).

10. See Andrew Moravcsik, "Taking Preferences Seriously: A Liberal Theory of International Politics," *International Organization* 51, no. 4 (Autumn 1997), pp. 513–33.

11. Core works in the constructivist tradition include Alexander Wendt, *Social Theory of International Politics* (Cambridge: Cambridge University Press, 1999); John G. Ruggie, "What Makes the World Hang Together: Neo-Utilitarianism and the Social Constructivist Challenge," *International Organization* 52, no. 4 (Autumn 1998); and Martha Finnemore and Kathryn Sikkink, "International Norm Dynamics and Political Change," *International Organization* 52, no. 4 (Autumn 1998). A promising application to the history of U.S. foreign policy is Jeffrey W. Legro, *Ideas of Internationalism* (Ithaca: Cornell University Press, forthcoming).

12. David Vital, *The Survival of Small States: Studies in Small Power/Great Power Conflict* (London: Oxford University Press, 1971); Annette Baker Fox, *The Power of Small States: Diplomacy in World War II* (Chicago: University of Chicago Press,

1959); Marshall R. Singer, *Weak States in a World of Powers: The Dynamics of International Relationships* (New York: The Free Press, 1972); Michael I. Handel, *Weak States in the International System* (New York: Frank Cass, 1981).

13. See James C. Scott, *Domination and the Arts of Resistance: Hidden Transcripts* (New Haven: Yale University Press, 1992); idem, *Weapons of the Weak: Everyday Forms of Peasant Resistance* (New Haven: Yale University Press, 1985); Peter Blau, *Exchange and Power in Social Life* (New York: Transaction Publishers, 1986); Tzvetan Todorov, *Facing the Extreme: Moral Life in the Concentration Camps*, trans. Abigail Pollak and Arthur Denner (New York: Henry Holt, 1996); Antonio Gramsci, *Prison Notebooks*, trans. Quintin Hoare and Geoffrey Nowell Smith (New York: International Publishers, 1971); and Michel Foucault, *Discipline and Punish: The Birth of the Prison*, trans. Alan Sheridan (New York: Vintage Books, 1995).

14. In a wonderful scene in the movie *The Shawshank Redemption*, convicted murderer Andy Dufresne (a former banker) obtains a case of cold beer for the inmates on a work detail by giving tax advice to a brutal prison guard.

15. "Work-to-rule" tactics involve a group of workers insisting that the factory strictly conform to all the formal procedures of production (e.g., safety procedures, installation and assembly manuals, clothing regulations, etc.). In essence, they eliminate all the shortcuts normally adopted in order to increase production efficiency. The result is a drastic slowdown that cannot be punished, because the workers are, in fact, doing precisely what their job assignments *say* they should do.

16. These ideas are developed at length in Scott, *Domination and the Arts of Resistance*.

17. For example, a state can demand the extradition of a suspected criminal, but only in accordance with the prevailing extradition agreements.

18. The phrase is that of William C. Wohlforth, who argues that no state wants to face America's full wrath. See his "The Stability of a Unipolar World," *International Security* 24, no. 1 (Summer 1999). Since 1990, however, Serbia, the Taliban, and Iraq (twice) pursued policies that focused U.S. enmity upon them, although they overestimated their ability to resist U.S. pressure. In addition, Syria, Iran, and North Korea have deliberately acted in ways that increased the risk that they would face the full weight of U.S. power.

Chapter 1

1. See Richard N. Haass, "Defining U.S. Foreign Policy in a Post–Post–Cold War World," The 2002 Arthur Ross Lecture, Foreign Policy Association, April 22, 2002, available at www.state.gov/s/p/rem/9632.htm, accessed December 4, 2004.

2. On the definition of hegemony, see John J. Mearsheimer, *The Tragedy of Great Power Politics* (New York: W. W. Norton, 2001), pp. 40–42.

3. See Mearsheimer, *Tragedy of Great Power Politics*, p. 71.

4. The material bases of American primacy are described in William C. Wohlforth, "The Stability of a Unipolar World," *International Security* 24, no. 1 (Summer 1999); Stephen Brooks and William C. Wohlforth "American Primacy in Perspective," *Foreign Affairs* 81, no. 4 (July/August 2002); Barry R. Posen, "Command of the Commons: The Military Foundations of U.S. Hegemony," *International Security* 28, no. 1 (Summer 2003); and Niall Ferguson, *Colossus: The Price of America's Empire* (New York: Penguin, 2004).

5. This definition is from *The New Shorter Oxford English Dictionary*, vol. 2 (Oxford: Clarendon Press, 1993).

6. Based on data from The World Bank, "WDI Online," *World Development Indicators Database*, available at http://devdata.worldbank.org.ezp2.harvard.edu/dataonline, accessed June 29, 2004.

7. On the inherent adaptability of U.S. society, see Thomas Friedman, *The Lexus and the Olive Tree* (New York: Farrar, Straus and Giroux, 1998), chap. 15.

8. See "The *Technology Review* Patent Scorecard 2004," *MIT Technology Review*, available online at www.technologyreview/scorecards, 2004. See also U.S. Department of Commerce, Office of Technology Policy, *The New Innovators: Global Patenting Trends in Five Sectors* (Washington, DC: Office of Technology Policy, 1998).

9. China is often regarded as the most likely "peer competitor" for the United States, but it will take decades before China's economy can catch up to that of the United States. According to Richard Cooper, if China's economy grew by three percentage points more each year than the United States, it would take seventy-four years for China's GDP to exceed the U.S. total. See Richard Cooper, "Is 'Economic Power' a Useful and Operational Concept?" Working Paper, Weatherhead Center for International Affairs, Harvard University, September 2003, p. 22.

10. The three exceptions were Argentina, Brazil, and Japan. World Bank, "WDI Online," *World Development Indicators Database*, 2000.

11. Source: U.S. Census Bureau, at www.census.gov/foreign-trade/balance and The World Bank, at http://devdata.worldbank.org.

12. From least to greatest in terms of military spending, they were Israel, Turkey, Australia, South Korea, India, Saudi Arabia, Italy, Germany, United Kingdom, Japan, France, Russia, and China. See *The Military Balance: 2004–2005*, (London: International Institute for Strategic Studies, 2004), pp. 354–58.

13. The United States spent $48.7 billion on military research and development in 2002 and an estimated $56.8 billion in 2003. Total 2002 defense

spending for other major powers was: France, $38 billion; Germany, $31 billion; Russia, $48 billion; Japan, $37 billion; and China, $48.3 billion. It is hardly surprising, therefore, that the U.S. military is at least a generation ahead of the other major powers in the quality of its weaponry. See *The Military Balance 2003–2004* (London: International Institute for Strategic Studies, 2003).

14. Source: *Active Duty Military Personnel Strengths by Regional Area and by Country* (Washington, DC: U.S. Department of Defense, September 2003).

15. Chalmers Johnson, *The Sorrows of Empire: Militarism, Secrecy, and the End of the Republic* (New York: Henry Holt, 2004), p. 132.

16. Johnson estimates that the number of military facilities is at least 775, but this figure omits facilities whose existence and location are classified. See his *Sorrows of Empire*, chap. 6.

17. The United States possesses more than 7,000 operational nuclear warheads (including nearly 6,000 of intercontinental range). Russia has 5,400 strategic warheads, but their reliability is increasingly suspect. France, China, the United Kingdom, and Israel have several hundred warheads each; India and Pakistan are believed to have roughly forty, and North Korea may have between two and eight. See *The Military Balance 2003–2004* (London: International Institute for Strategic Studies, 2003), p. 229.

18. For example, U.S. pilots fly roughly two hundred training hours each year, compared with about ten hours for Russian pilots and fewer than a hundred hours for Chinese air-force personnel. For a summary of these advantages, see Cindy Williams, "Defense Policy for the 21st Century," in Robert J. Lieber, ed., *Eagle Rules? Foreign Policy and American Primacy in the Twenty-First Century* (Upper Saddle River, NJ: Prentice Hall, 2002), pp. 244–46.

19. Quoted in Stephen Fidler, "A Superpower Shows the World Its Calibre," *Financial Times*, December 8–9, 2001, p. 2.

20. One year after the invasion (March 2004), the United States had 18 percent of its regular army (11.33 percent of the Army plus Reserves and National Guard) stationed in Iraq. Of coalition member states, only Fiji (700 troops) and the United Kingdom (12,000 troops) deployed more than 10 percent of their active-duty strength. Omitting these two, the other members of the "coalition of the willing" contributed less than 1 percent of their combined active-duty strength. Sources: Congressional Research Service, and IISS, *The Military Balance* (various years).

21. Core works on the role of international institutions include Martha Finnemore and Michael Barnett, *Rules for the World: International Organizations in Global Politics* (Ithaca: Cornell University Press, 2004); Robert O. Keohane, *After Hegemony: Cooperation and Discord in the World Political Economy* (Princeton: Princeton University Press, 1984); Robert O. Keohane and Lisa L. Martin,

"Institutional Theory as a Research Program," in Colin Elman and Miriam Elman, eds., *Progress in International Relations Theory: Appraising the Field* (Cambridge: MIT Press, 2003); and Lisa L. Martin and Beth Simmons, "Theories and Empirical Studies of International Institutions," *International Organization* 52, no. 4 (Autumn 1998); More skeptical appraisals include Joseph Grieco, *Cooperation among Nations* (Ithaca: Cornell University Press, 1990); and John J. Mearsheimer, "The False Promise of International Institutions," *International Security* 19, no. 3 (Winter 1994–95).

22. See Guillaume Parmentier, "Redressing NATO's Imbalances," *Survival* 42, no. 2 (Summer 2000), p. 98.

23. See "U.S. Participation in the United Nations: U.S. Financial Contributions," Washington, DC. U.S. Department of State, Bureau of Public Affairs, September 9, 2003, available at www.state.gov/r/pa/ei/rls/24236.htm, accessed November 4, 2004.

24. Steven Erlanger, "U.S. Will Oppose Move to Re-Elect Top U.N. Official," *New York Times*, June 19, 1996.

25. See Ngaire Woods, "The United States and the International Financial Institutions: Power and Influence within the World Bank and the IMF," in Rosemary Foot, S. Neil MacFarlane, and Michael Mastanduno, eds., *U.S. Hegemony and International Organizations: The United States and Multilateral Institutions* (New York: Oxford University Press, 2003), pp. 98–99, 103.

26. The phrase *soft power* was coined by Joseph S. Nye in *Bound to Lead: The Changing Nature of American Power* (New York: Basic Books, 1990), and *The Paradox of American Power: Why the World's Only Superpower Cannot Go It Alone* (New York: Oxford, 2001). Nye initially suggested that America's "soft power" rested on enduring U.S. characteristics and was likely to be a durable source of influence. When America's international image declined rapidly during the second Bush administration, however, Nye began warning that neglecting U.S. "soft power" could cause the rapid erosion of America's international position. See his *Soft Power: The Means to Success in World Politics* (New York: Public Affairs Press, 2004).

27. According to the *New York Times*, 120 of the nearly two hundred member states of the United Nations have specified that official diplomatic correspondence should be in English, compared with forty nations listing French and twenty listing Spanish. See Barbara Crossette, "At the U.N., French Slips and English Stands Tall," *New York Times*, March 25, 2001, p. A9.

28. See *Open Doors 2003* (New York: Institute of International Education, 2004), summarized online at www.opendoors.iienetwork.org.

29. This tendency will be especially pronounced in U.S. business schools and public-policy programs, which tend to emphasize the U.S. commitment to free markets and liberal institutions.

30. Josef Joffe, "Gulliver Unbound: Can America Rule the World?" 12th Annual John Bonython Lecture, Centre for Independent Studies, Sydney, Australia, August 5, 2003.

31. According to the U.S. State Department's Advisory Group on Public Diplomacy for the Arab and Muslim World, "Education is an area where Americans and the peoples of the Arab and Muslim World have solid common ground. . . . Even today, when many Arabs and Muslims harbor an extremely negative opinion of the United States, they maintain a positive view of American education." See *Changing Minds, Winning Peace: A New Strategic Direction for U.S. Public Diplomacy in the Arab and Muslim World* (Washington, DC, 2003), pp. 32–33; and "Education, Still in Demand," *The Economist*, October 24, 2002.

32. See George Joffe, "Why Gaddafi Gave Up WMD," *BBC News World Edition*, December 21, 2003, available online at http://news.bbc.co.uk/2/hi/africa/3338713.stm, accessed December 20, 2004.

33. Based on data from www.worldwideboxoffice.com.

34. Quoted in Thomas A. Bailey, *A Diplomatic History of the American People*, 10th ed. (New York: Prentice Hall, 1980), p. 4.

35. Quoted in Michael Schaller, "The United States, Japan, and China at Fifty," in Akira Iriye and Robert A. Wampler, eds., *Partnership: The United States and Japan 1951–2001* (Tokyo: Kodansha, 2001), p. 52; and Robert J. Art, "Why Western Europe Needs the United States and NATO," *Political Science Quarterly* 111, no.1 (Spring 1996), p. 36.

36. Quoted in Michael Hirsh, *At War with Ourselves: Why America Is Squandering Its Chance to Build a Better World* (New York: Oxford University Press, 2003), p. 42.

37. See Mearsheimer, *Tragedy of Great Power Politics*, chap. 7; and Albert K. Weinberg, *Manifest Destiny: A Study of Nationalist Expansion in American History* (Chicago: Quadrangle Books, 1963).

38. Quoted in Melvyn J. Leffler, *A Preponderance of Power: National Security, the Truman Administration, and the Cold War* (Stanford: Stanford University Press, 1992), p. 19.

39. See Greg P. Mitrovich, *Undermining the Kremlin: America's Strategy to Subvert the Soviet Bloc, 1947–1956* (Ithaca: Cornell University Press, 2000). Undermining Soviet power was an explicit goal of the so-called Reagan Doctrine, which sought to overthrow Soviet clients in the developing world. See Thomas Bodenheimer and Robert Gould, *The Reagan Doctrine: Third World Rollback* (Boston: South End Press, 1999).

40. See George Shultz, *Turmoil and Triumph: My Years as Secretary of State* (New York: Charles Scribner's Sons, 1993), p. 894.

41. See George Bush and Brent Scowcroft, *A World Transformed* (New York: Alfred A. Knopf, 1998), pp. 542–43, 564.

42. The draft guidance was leaked to the *New York Times* and eventually repudiated by the administration, but it clearly revealed the basic goals of key administration personnel. See Patrick E. Tyler, "U.S. Strategy Plan Calls for Insuring No Rivals Develop," *New York Times*, March 8, 1992, p. A1. See also James Mann, *Rise of the Vulcans: The History of Bush's War Cabinet* (New York: Viking, 2004), pp. 208–15. Mann notes that a subsequent revision of the leaked and repudiated document "contained most of the same ideas as the original."

43. See *A National Security Strategy for a New Century* (Washington, DC: The White House, October 1998), p. 23. According to James Mann, "the Democrats' rhetoric and policies conformed in many respects to the ideas put forward by [the Bush administration] in 1992." See his *Rise of the Vulcans*, p. 214.

44. See *The National Security Strategy of the United States of America* (Falls Village, CT: Winterhouse edition, 2002), Section 8, p. 5, and Section 9, p. 3.

45. As Secretary of Defense Les Aspin stated in 1993, "Today, the United States is the biggest kid on the block when it comes to conventional military forces and it is our potential adversaries who may attain nuclear weapons. So nuclear weapons may still be the great equalizer; the problem is the United States may now be the equalizee." See Secretary of Defense Les Aspin, "The Defense Department's New Counterproliferation Initiative," Address to National Academy of Sciences Committee on International Security and Arms Control, Washington, DC, December 7, 1993.

46. See Ashton B. Carter, John M. Deutch, and Philip D. Zelikow. "Catastrophic Terrorism: Elements of a National Policy," *Preventive Defense Project Occasional Papers* 1, no. 6 (Stanford and Cambridge: Stanford University/Harvard University, 1998).

47. On these various efforts, see Howard Baker and Lloyd Cutler, *A Report Card on the Department of Energy's Nonproliferation Programs with Russia* (Washington, DC: U.S. Department of Energy, Secretary of Energy Advisory Board, January 2001); and Jason D. Ellis, *Defense by Other Means: The Politics of U.S. NIS Threat Reduction and Nuclear Security Cooperation* (Westport, CT: Praeger, 2001).

48. Although the treaty remains an imperfect barrier to WMD acquisition, it has slowed the spread of these technologies and thus helped maintain the imbalance of WMD capabilities in America's favor. See "Status of the Nuclear Non-Proliferation Treaty: Interim Report," *Bipartisan Security Group Policy Brief* (Washington, DC: Global Security Institute, June 2003).

49. See Dinshaw Mistry, *Containing Missile Proliferation: Strategic Technology, Security Regimes, and International Cooperation in Arms Control* (Seattle: University of Washington Press, 2003).

50. See "Nuclear Posture Review: Excerpts," at www.globalsecurity.org/wmd/library/policy/dod/npr.htm. The one-sided nature of U.S. policy is

emphasized by Daryl Kimball, "U.S. Nuclear Weapons Policy: Present and Future," Remarks Prepared for a Breakfast Briefing to Governmental Delegates Organized by the Friends Committee on National Legislation, Arms Control Association, May 5, 2004.

51. See Daryl G. Press and Keir Lieber, "The Unspoken Dimension of American Primacy, or The End of Mutual Assured Destruction," Paper Presented at the Annual Meeting of the American Political Science Association, Chicago, September 2, 2004.

52. See Scott Elliott, "Teets: America Must Reach for Space Dominance," *Air Force Link*, September 15, 2004, available at www.af.mil/news/story.asp?storyID=123008652, accessed December 20, 2004.

53. See Ronald Asmus, *Opening NATO's Door: How the Alliance Remade Itself for a New Era* (New York: Columbia University Press, 2002); and James M. Goldgeier, *Not Whether But When: The U.S. Decision to Enlarge NATO* (Washington, DC: Brookings Institution Press, 1999).

54. See Ronald Tiersky, "French Military Reform and NATO Restructuring," *Joint Force Quarterly* 15 (Spring 1997).

55. On these disputes, see Ivo H. Daalder, *Getting to Dayton: The Making of America's Bosnia Policy* (Washington, DC: Brookings Institution Press, 1999); Ivo H. Daalder and Michael O'Hanlon, *Winning Ugly: NATO's War to Save Kosovo* (Washington, DC: Brookings Institution Press, 2000); and David Halberstam, *War in a Time of Peace: Bush, Clinton and the Generals* (New York: Scribners, 2001).

56. In addition to clarifying the controversial "status of forces agreement" governing the U.S. military presence in Japan, the new defense guidelines committed the two states to cooperate in the event of a crisis "surrounding Japan" and to jointly develop a theater missile defense system. For background, see Michael Green and Patrick Cronin, eds., *The U.S.-Japan Alliance: Past, Present, and Future* (New York: Council on Foreign Relations, 1999). See also G. John Ikenberry and Takashi Inoguchi, *Reinventing the Alliance: U.S.-Japan Security Partnership in an Era of Change* (New York: Palgrave/Macmillan, 2003).

57. Toward this end, Taiwan President Lee Teng Hui was permitted to make an "unofficial" visit to the United States in 1995 and the United States sent two aircraft carriers to the Taiwan Straits following a series of belligerent Chinese missile tests in 1996. See Michael Laris, "China Protests Taiwan Leader's Visit to US: Beijing Warns Washington of Damaged Relations," *Washington Post*, May 24, 1995; Mark Mueller, "China Threatens 'Sea of Fire'; U.S. Navy Warned to Keep Its Distance," *Boston Herald*, March 22, 1996.

58. George W. Bush, "A Distinctly American Internationalism," Speech at the Ronald Reagan Presidential Library, Simi Valley, California, November 19, 1999. Several prominent members of the Bush foreign-policy team had

expressed deep concerns about a potential threat from China and had openly advocated closer U.S. ties with Taiwan. See Mann, *Rise of the Vulcans*, pp. 113–16, 232–33, 284–86.

59. *National Security Strategy* (2002), section 8.

60. See Bruce W. Jentleson, *With Friends Like These: Reagan, Bush and Saddam, 1982–1990* (New York: W. W. Norton, 1994).

61. There have been a handful of minor exceptions to this observation: The United States sent troops to Lebanon in 1958 to avert what was seen (incorrectly) as a potential communist takeover, and U.S. naval forces were deployed in the Eastern Mediterranean to deter possible Soviet intervention during the 1967 and 1973 Arab–Israeli wars. The United States also conducted an aerial resupply of Israel's army during the October War in 1973. The United States provided troops for international peacekeeping operations in the Sinai and in Lebanon, and U.S. naval forces escorted Kuwaiti vessels during the latter stages of the Iran–Iraq War. The United States also created a Rapid Deployment Force after the Iranian revolution, largely to deter a Soviet invasion of the Gulf, but it never had to use this force for its intended purpose. Until 1990–91, in fact, U.S. military forces had not engaged in large-scale combat operations anywhere in the Middle East or Persian Gulf regions since World War II.

62. There were only 421 U.S. military personnel in Saudi Arabia in 1989, but the United States kept several thousand troops in Saudi Arabia and Kuwait from 1991 to 2003, along with prepositioned equipment for additional reinforcements.

63. In October 1992, President George H. W. Bush signed the Iran–Iraq Arms Nonproliferation Act, which prohibited the transfer of goods or technology that might contribute to the development of destabilizing weapons; this act was subsequently amended to include WMD technologies as well. On overall U.S. policy toward these two states, see Robert S. Litwak, *Rogue States and U.S. Foreign Policy: Containment after the Cold War* (Washington, DC: Woodrow Wilson Center Press, 2000), chaps. 4–5.

64. See Barry Buzan, "Economic Structure and International Security: The Limits of the Liberal Case," *International Organization* 38, no. 4 (1984); and Dale C. Copeland, "Economic Interdependence and War: A Theory of Trade Expectations," *International Security* 20, no. 4 (Spring 1996). For a thorough survey of the current "state of the art," see Edward D. Mansfield and Brian Pollins, eds., *Economic Interdependence and International Conflict: New Perspectives on an Enduring Debate* (Ann Arbor: University of Michigan Press, 2003).

65. Or, as Thomas Friedman has written, "without America on duty, there will be no America Online." See his *Lexus and the Olive Tree*, p. 376.

66. According to U.S. Trade Representative Charlene Barshefsky, the United

States negotiated more than three hundred separate trade agreements during the Clinton administration. But as Jagdish Bhagwati reminds us, not all agreements are equal, and some of them may have had trade-limiting features. See their respective comments on Robert Lawrence, "International Trade Policy in the 1990s," in Jeffrey A. Frankel and Peter Orszag, eds., *U.S. Economic Policy in the 1990s* (Cambridge: MIT Press, 2002).

67. World Bank, "WDI Online," *World Development Indicators Database*, available at http://devdata.worldbank.org.ezp2.harvard.edu/dataonline, accessed August 17, 2004.

68. The ability of powerful actors to "go it alone," and thus exert greater leverage over the terms of international institutions, is ably documented in Lloyd Gruber, *Ruling the World: Power Politics and the Rise of Supranational Institutions* (Princeton: Princeton University Press, 2000).

69. Since 1990, the United States has pursued or completed bilateral free-trade treaties with the Dominican Republic, Costa Rica, El Salvador, Guatemala, Honduras, Nicaragua, Singapore, Chile, Israel, and Jordan.

70. For example, bilateral trade agreements normally contain complex "rules of origin" provisions that establish which products are in fact eligible for the lower tariff rates. As written, these rules can encourage weaker parties to divert trade toward the stronger partner. For example, current rules of origin encourage foreign clothing manufacturers to rely on U.S. cloth (even when it is not the cheapest or best), because using cloth from a third party would make the item of clothing ineligible for lower tariffs.

71. See Robert Zoellick, "Free Trade and Competition," *Wall Street Journal*, July 10, 2003; and *Economic Report of the President 2003* (Washington, DC: U.S. Government Printing Office, 2003), p. 246.

72. According to the Bank of International Settlements, foreign-exchange trading rose 42 percent from 1989 to 1992, another 48 percent between 1992 and 1995, and 25 percent by 1998. See J. Bradford DeLong and Barry Eichengreen, "Between Meltdown and Moral Hazard: The International Monetary and Financial Policies of the Clinton Administration," in Frankel and Orszag, *U.S. Economic Policy in the 1990s*.

73. *Economic Report of the President 2003* (Washington, DC: U.S. Government Printing Office, 2003), pp. 214, 253–54.

74. Ibid., pp. 241, 248–52.

75. See in particular Tony Smith, *America's Mission: The United States and the Worldwide Struggle for Democracy in the Twentieth Century* (Princeton: Princeton University Press, 1994).

76. A *National Security Strategy of Engagement and Enlargement* (Washington, DC: The White House, 1995).

77. *National Security Strategy*, 2002, p. 1; George W. Bush, "The Inaugural Address," *New York Times*, January 22, 2005, pp. A16–17.

78. There is considerable empirical evidence showing that established democracies have better human-rights records and more productive economies, and are less prone to internal violence. See Rudolph Rummel, *Power Kills: Democracy as a Method of Nonviolence* (New Brunswick, NJ: Transaction Books, 1997); Christian Davenport and David A. Armstrong II, "Democracy and the Violation of Human Rights: A Statistical Analysis from 1976 to 1996," *American Journal of Political Science* 48, no. 3 (July 2004).

79. *A National Security Strategy of Engagement and Enlargement*, p. 2, and see also p. 22.

80. A brief survey of these efforts is Larry Diamond, *Promoting Democracy in the 1990s: Actors and Instruments, Issues and Imperatives* (Washington, DC: Carnegie Commission on Preventing Deadly Conflict, 1995). See also Thomas Carothers, *Aiding Democracy Abroad: The Learning Curve* (Washington, DC: Carnegie Endowment for International Peace, 1999).

81. U.S. support for certain democratizing leaders (such as Boris Yeltsin in Russia) made it easier for them to ward off authoritarian opponents and keep their countries on a pro-democracy trajectory. In particular, President Clinton's open support for Yeltsin helped him defeat several reactionary challengers in the 1996 Russian elections.

82. See "Military Expenditures, Armed Forces, GNP, CGE, Population, and Their Ratios, By Group and Country, 1989–1999," *World Military Expenditures and Arms Transfers* (Washington, DC: U.S. Department of State, 2003); and Curt Tarnoff and Larry Nowels, "Foreign Aid: An Introductory Overview of U.S. Programs and Policy," Congressional Research Service Report for Congress (Order Code 98-916, April 15, 2004), p. 33.

83. On this failure, and on the generally tepid U.S. response to previous genocides, see Samantha Power, *"A Problem from Hell": America and the Age of Genocide* (New York: Basic Books, 2002).

84. Quoted on the Global Security website at www.globalsecurity.org/military/systems/ship/sealift.htm.

85. As President George H. W. Bush and former National Security Advisor Brent Scowcroft recalled, "most of the world trusts and asks for our involvement. The United States is mostly perceived as benign, without territorial ambitions, uncomfortable with exercising our considerable power." See their *A World Transformed*, p. 566. The main exception to this claim is the emergence of al Qaeda, which was inspired in large part by U.S. policies in the Middle East and Persian Gulf.

86. An immediate sign of this direction was incoming Secretary of Defense

Donald Rumsfeld's emphasis on the need to "transform" the U.S. military: shifting it from large, fixed, and semipermanent deployments in Europe and Asia and toward a more flexible, mobile approach that would rely on advanced technology and "revolutionary" military tactics to bring U.S. power to bear wherever it might be needed. See "Rumsfeld Aides Seek Deep Personnel Cuts in Armed Forces to Pay for New Weaponry," *Wall Street Journal*, August 8, 2001, p. A3.

87. Condoleezza Rice, "Promoting the National Interest," *Foreign Affairs* 79, no. 1 (January/February 2000), p. 46. Useful surveys of the ideas of the Bush foreign-policy team are Ivo H. Daalder and James M. Lindsay, *America Unbound: The Bush Revolution in Foreign Policy* (Washington, DC: Brookings Institution Press, 2003); and Mann, *Rise of the Vulcans*.

88. "Stop the World, I Want to Get Off," *The Economist*, July 28, 2001.

89. George W. Bush, "Statement by the President in His Address to the Nation," Washington, DC, September 11, 2001; and "Address to a Joint Session of Congress and the American People," Washington, DC, September 20, 2001, both downloaded from www.whitehouse.gov.

90. A *preemptive* war is an attempt to get in the first blow when one side thinks the other is about to attack; a *preventive* war is fought when one side wants to prevent a potential enemy from becoming stronger (e.g., by acquiring WMD), even if there is no sign of an imminent attack.

Chapter 2

1. See "President Holds Primetime News Conference," Washington, DC, October 22, 2001, available at www.whitehouse.gov/news/releases/2001/10/20011011-7.html.

2. William J. Clinton, *A National Security Strategy of Engagement and Enlargement* (Washington, DC: The White House, 1995), pp. i, iii.

3. See Samuel P. Huntington, "Why International Primacy Matters," *International Security* 17, no. 4 (Spring 1993), p. 83. Similarly, Dartmouth political scientist William C. Wohlforth argues that U.S. primacy will be both "durable and peaceful" because it will prevent hegemonic wars among the major powers and discourage regional conflict among minor ones. Americans should welcome being number one, therefore, and so should everyone else. See William C. Wohlforth, "The Stability of a Unipolar World," *International Security* 24, no. 1 (Summer 1999); also Stephen Brooks and William C. Wohlforth, "American Primacy in Perspective," *Foreign Affairs* 81, no. 4 (July/August 2002).

4. Charles Krauthammer, "The Unipolar Moment Revisited," *The National Interest* 70 (Winter 2002/03); and idem, "Democratic Realism: An American

Foreign Policy for a Unipolar World," 2004 Irving Kristol Lecture, American Enterprise Institute, Washington, DC, February 10, 2004; Niall Ferguson, "A World Without Power," *Foreign Policy* 143 (July/August 2004). In the same spirit, William Kristol and Robert Kagan describe U.S. primacy as "the only reliable defense against the breakdown of peace and international order." William Kristol and Robert Kagan, "Toward a Neo-Reaganite Foreign Policy," *Foreign Affairs* 75, no. 4 (July/August 1996).

5. Cited in Minxin Pei, "The Paradoxes of American Nationalism," *Foreign Policy* 136 (May/June 2003), p. 32; "What the World Thinks in 2002: How Global Publics View Their Lives, Their Countries, The World, America" (Washington, DC: Pew Global Attitudes Project, December 2002), p. 6. Americans also rate highest in "national pride," as measured by the National Opinion Research Center at the University of Chicago. See Tom W. Smith and Lars Jarkko,"National Pride: A Cross-National Analysis," General Social Survey Report No. 19 (Chicago: National Opinion Research Center, May 1998).

6. See "What the World Thinks in 2002," Topline Survey, p. 53. "Little Support for Expanding War on Terrorism," Online Report, Pew Global Attitudes Project, December 19, 2001. A subsequent Pew survey in July 2004 found that 45 percent of Americans thought the United States "plays a more important and powerful role as world leader than it did 10 years ago—the largest percentage expressing that opinion in the three decades that this question has been asked." See "Foreign Policy Attitudes Now Driven by 9/11 and Iraq," Online Report, Pew Global Attitudes Project, August 18, 2004. These surveys are all available at www.people-press.org.

7. "Little Support for Expanding War on Terrorism," especially p. 2.

8. "Little Support for Expanding War on Terrorism," Survey Methodology, p. 3.

9. See "Mistrust of America in Europe Ever Higher, Muslim Anger Persists," Pew Global Attitudes Survey, March 16, 2004, pp. 18–19, at www.people-press.org.

10. In 2002, only Venezuela, the Philippines, and Vietnam reported percentages declaring that the United States took the interests of others into account that were equal or greater than the U.S. figures. See "What the World Thinks in 2002," pp. 58, 70, including the Final Topline Survey, p. T-49.

11. See *Transatlantic Trends 2003*, A Project of the German Marshall Fund of the United States, Washington, DC, June 2003, p. 5.

12. See "A Year after Iraq War: Mistrust of America in Europe Ever Higher, Muslim Anger Persists."

13. See "Zogby International Survey of Iraq," August 22, 2003 (Washington, DC: Zogby International), pp. 4, 6; and "Progress or Peril: Measuring Iraq's

Reconstruction," Post-Conflict Reconstruction Project, Center for Strategic and International Studies, Washington, DC, November 2004, pp. 7, 13.

14. For prescient analyses of foreign concerns about the U.S. role, see Hubert Vedrine with Dominique Moisi, *France in an Age of Globalization*, trans. Philip H. Gordon (Washington, DC: Brookings Institution Press, 2001); Martin Walker, "What Europeans Think of America," *World Policy Journal* 17, no. 2 (Summer 2000), pp. 26–38; François Heisbourg, "American Hegemony? Perceptions of the U.S. Abroad," *Survival* 41, no. 4 (Winter 1999–2000); Peter W. Rodman, "Drifting Apart? Trends in U.S.–European Relations," (Washington, DC: The Nixon Center, June 1999); and idem, *Uneasy Giant: The Challenges to American Predominance* (Washington, DC: The Nixon Center, 2000).

15. See "The Writer at War," *Far Eastern Economic Review*, November 15, 2001; John le Carré, "The United States of America Has Gone Mad," *The Times* (London), January 15, 2003; Angelique Chrisafis and Imogen Tilden, "Pinter Blasts 'Nazi America' and 'Deluded Idiot' Blair," *The Guardian*, June 11, 2003. Pinter's full statement read: "The US is really beyond reason now. . . . There is really only one comparison: Nazi Germany. Nazi Germany wanted total domination of Europe and they nearly did it. The United States wants total domination of the world and is about to consolidate that."

16. Günter Grass, quoted in Alan Riding, "Still Intrigued by History's Shadows: Günter Grass Worries about the Effects of War, Then and Now," *New York Times*, April 8, 2003; Nigel Morris, "Livingstone Says Bush Is Greatest Threat to Life on Planet," *Financial Times*, November 18, 2003; and Tim Elfrink, "Hawking Decries Iraq War at London Protest," *Associated Press*, November 2, 2004.

17. In each of these categories, the percentage with an "unfavorable" view of U.S. policy ranged from a low of 75 percent (in Jordan, on the subject of U.S. terrorism) to a high of 98 percent (in Morocco, on the subject of U.S. policy toward Iraq). See "Impressions of America 2004: How Arabs View America, How Arabs Learn About America," Washington, DC, Zogby International, June 2004, p. 3.

18. See "Impressions of America 2004," p. 5. In this open-ended question, the percentages answering "unfair foreign policy" were: Morocco, 12.5 percent; Saudi Arabia, 39.5 percent; Jordan, 21.5 percent; Lebanon, 20.5 percent; the UAE, 33.5 percent; and Egypt, 32 percent.

19. "How Deep Is the Rift?" *The Economist*, February 15, 2003, p. 11.

20. See *Standard Eurobarometer*, November 2003, available at http://europa.eu.int/public_opinion/archives. A majority of Europeans also saw the U.S. role as negative on the environment (56 percent) and the fight against poverty (52 percent), and "positive" appraisals exceeded "negative" appraisals only with respect to the "fight against terrorism" (by a margin of six percentage points).

21. See George W. Bush, "Statement by the President in His Address to the Nation," September 11, 2001, at www.september11news.com/PresidentBush .htm. Other U.S. officials have echoed these comments. See: "National Security Advisor Condoleezza Rice's Remarks to Veterans of Foreign Wars," August 25, 2003, at www.whitehouse.gov; "Secretary Rumsfeld's Veterans Day Message," November 11, 2003, www.defenselink.mil; and "Chairman of the Joint Chiefs of Staff Veterans Day Message," November 11, 2003, www.defenselink.mil.

22. Or, as Bush remarked on the anniversary of his declaration of war on Iraq: "No concession will appease [the terrorists'] hatred. No accommodation will satisfy their endless demands." From "Remarks by the President at the United States Air Force Academy Graduation Ceremony," June 2, 2004, from www.whitehouse.gov; and Richard W. Stevenson, "President, Marking Anniversary of War, Urges World to Unite to Combat Terrorism," *New York Times*, March 20, 2004.

23. Susan Sontag, "Reflections on September 11," *The New Yorker*, September 24, 2001, p. 32.

24. Representative examples of this view include Chalmers Johnson, *Blowback: The Costs and Consequences of American Empire* (New York: Henry Holt, 2000); Clyde Prestowitz, *Rogue Nation: American Unilateralism and the Failure of Good Intentions* (New York: Basic Books, 2003); Ivan Eland, *The Empire Has No Clothes: U.S. Foreign Policy Exposed* (Oakland: Independent Institute, 2004).

25. Among scholars of international relations, this perspective is commonly associated with the realist tradition. See Stephen M. Walt, "The Enduring Relevance of the Realist Tradition," in Ira Katznelson and Helen Milner, eds., *Political Science: State of the Discipline III* (New York: W. W. Norton, 2003).

26. Winston S. Churchill, *The Second World War, Vol. I: The Gathering Storm* (Boston: Houghton Mifflin, 1946), pp. 207–8.

27. On this general point, see John J. Mearsheimer, *The Tragedy of Great Power Politics* (New York: W. W. Norton, 2001), chap. 7.

28. See "Russia's National Security Concept," *Arms Control Today* 30, no. 1 (January/February 2000), p. 15 [emphasis added].

29. Quoted in "We're Not Children!" *The Economist*, May 17, 2003, p. 45.

30. Krauthammer, "Democratic Realism," p. 5.

31. Michael Hirsh, *At War with Ourselves: Why America Is Squandering Its Chance to Build a Better World* (New York: Oxford University Press, 2003), pp. 39–40, 254.

32. See George W. Bush, "A Distinctly American Internationalism," Speech at the Ronald Reagan Presidential Library, Simi Valley, California, November 19, 1999.

33. See Eric Eckholm, "China Says U.S. Missile Shield Could Force a

Nuclear Buildup," *New York Times*, May 11, 2000, pp. A1, A6; and Timothy Garton Ash, "The Peril of Too Much Power," *New York Times*, April 9, 2002.

34. See John M. Owen IV, *Liberal Peace, Liberal War* (Ithaca: Cornell University Press, 2000); and Ido Oren, *Our Enemies and US: America's Rivalries and the Making of Political Science* (Ithaca: Cornell University Press, 2003). Spencer Weart also notes that liberal republics like the United States have been willing to use covert action against a number of democratic states, especially if it judged them to be less than perfectly republican. See his *Never at War: Why Democracies Will Not Fight One Another* (New Haven: Yale University Press, 1998).

35. See Hugh Thomas, *Suez* (New York: Harper and Row, 1966), pp. 130, 146–49; and Richard Neustadt, *Alliance Politics* (New York: Columbia University Press, 1970), chap. 2.

36. See James D. Fearon, "Domestic Audience Costs and the Escalation of International Disputes," *American Political Science Review* 88, no. 3 (1994); and Charles Lipson, *Reliable Partners: How Democracies Have Made a Separate Peace* (Princeton: Princeton University Press, 2003).

37. See especially G. John Ikenberry, *After Victory: Institutions, Strategic Restraint, and the Rebuilding of Order after Major War* (Princeton: Princeton University Press, 2001); and "Democracy, Institutions, and American Restraint," in Ikenberry, ed., *America Unrivaled: The Future of the Balance of Power* (Ithaca: Cornell University Press, 2002).

38. This general phenomenon is ably analyzed in Robert Jervis, *System Effects* (New York: Basic Books, 1997).

39. Pierre Elliott Trudeau, "On Relations with the U.S.," Address to the National Press Club, Ottawa, Canada, March 26, 1969.

40. Sayyid Qutb, quoted in David Benjamin and Steven Simon, *The Age of Sacred Terror: Radical Islam's War Against America* (New York: Random House, 2003), p. 64. Given that Qutb's hostility was based on his experiences in the 1940s, one can only imagine what he would think of U.S. culture today.

41. See Osama bin Laden, "Letter to the American People," November 2, 2002, from *Observer Worldview*, November 24, 2002, available at http://observer. guardian.co.uk/worldview/0,11581845725,00.html.

42. See Jessica Stern, *Terror in the Name of God: Why Religious Militants Kill* (New York: HarperCollins, 2003), chap. 1.

43. See Denis Lacorne, "The Barbaric Americans," *Wilson Quarterly* 25 (Spring 2001), p. 53.

44. See *Views of a Changing World 2003* (Washington, DC: Pew Research Center for the People and the Press, June 2003), pp. 71–85; and *What the World Thinks in 2002*, p. 63.

45. See George H. W. Bush, "Outlines of a New World of Freedom,"

Address to the UN General Assembly, September 25, 1989. Department of State *Bulletin* (November 1989); idem, "America Must Remain Engaged," Speech at Texas A & M University, U.S. Department of State *Dispatch* 3, no. 51, December 21, 1992.

46. *National Security Strategy of the United States* (2002).

47. Most revolutionary ideologies (liberalism, Marxism-Leninism, religious fundamentalism, etc.) portray themselves as having universal validity, which helps explain why revolutionary states usually find themselves in conflict with other powers. See Stephen M. Walt, *Revolution and War* (Ithaca: Cornell University Press, 1996), especially chap. 2.

48. For brief discussions of this phenomenon, see Stephen M. Walt, "Fads, Fevers and Firestorms: Understanding Political Contagion," *Foreign Policy* 121 (November/December 1999); and Daniel W. Drezner, "Globalization and Policy Convergence," *Mershon International Studies Review* 3, no. 1 (Spring 2001).

49. Writing in 1821, Adams declared, "Wherever the standard of freedom and independence has been or shall be unfurled, there will [America's] heart . . . be. But she goes not abroad in search of monsters to destroy. She is the well wisher to the freedom and independence of all. She is the champion and vindicator only of her own." Quoted in David Armstrong, *Revolution and World Order: The Revolutionary State in International Society* (Oxford: Clarendon Press, 1993), p. 52. The universalism expressed by Adams remains a key element in American political ideology; what has changed is the willingness to export these ideals and the power available for doing so.

50. See especially Tony Smith, *America's Mission: The United States and the Worldwide Struggle for Democracy in the Twentieth Century* (Princeton, NJ: Princeton University Press, 1994).

51. See John M. Owen IV, "The Foreign Imposition of Domestic Institutions," *International Organization* 56, no. 2 (Spring 2002).

52. *National Security Strategy* (2002), p. 1.

53. See Michael McFaul, "The Liberty Doctrine," *Policy Review* 112 (April–May 2002).

54. See Anna Dean and Mary Demeri, *Europeans and Anti-Americanism: Fact vs. Fiction* (Washington, DC: U.S. Department of State, Office of Research, September 2002), pp. 26–27.

55. See *Eurobarometer*, Spring 2003. On the many "varieties of capitalism," see David Soskice and Peter Hall, eds., *Varieties of Capitalism: The Institutional Foundations of Comparative Advantage* (New York: Oxford University Press, 2001).

56. George W. Bush, "The Inaugural Address," *New York Times*, January 21, 2005, pp. A16–17. Although the Bush administration has proclaimed these ideological objectives in especially stark and self-congratulatory terms, the same

basic goal was also a centerpiece of the Clinton administration. Clinton's own *National Security Strategy* statements referred explicitly to the goal of "enlarging" the sphere of democratic rule, and the 1997 version of this document stated that one of the "core objectives" of U.S. national security strategy was "to promote democracy and human rights." See William J. Clinton, *A National Security Strategy for the 21st Century* (Washington, DC: The White House, 1997).

57. See "President Bush Speaks at AEI's Annual Dinner," February 28, 2003, available online at www.aei.org/news/newsID.16197/news_detail.asp.

58. See Marina Ottaway and Thomas Carothers, "The Greater Middle East Initiative: Off to a False Start," *Policy Brief 29* (Washington, DC: Carnegie Endowment for International Peace, March 2004).

59. *The National Defense Strategy of the United States of America* (Washington, DC: Department of Defense, March 2005), p. 5; and Max Boot, "Power: Resentment Comes with the Territory," *Washington Post*, March 3, 2003.

60. Kagan and Kristol continue: "Those who suggest that these international resentments could somehow be eliminated by a more restrained American foreign policy are engaging in pleasant delusions. Even a United States that never intervened in a place like Kosovo or never expressed disapproval of China's human rights practices would still find itself the target of jealousy, resentment, and in some cases even fear." See "The Present Danger," *The National Interest* 59 (Spring 2000), p. 67.

61. See Bernard Lewis, "The Roots of Muslim Rage," *Atlantic Monthly* (September 1990); idem, *What Went Wrong? Western Impact and Middle East Response* (New York: Oxford University Press, 2001); and Fareed Zakaria, "Why Do They Hate Us?" *Newsweek*, October 15, 2001.

62. Ajami also declared, "No great apologies ought to be made for America's 'unilateralism,'" and he predicted that a successful war in Iraq would "embolden those who wish for the Arab world deliverance from retrogression and political decay." See his "Iraq and the Arab Future," *Foreign Affairs* 82, no. 1 (January/February 2003), pp. 2–4.

63. There is some evidence that certain terrorists—including Islamist terrorists—are motivated in part by feelings of inferiority and humiliation. See in particular Stern, *Terror in the Name of God*, chap. 2. But the question remains: Are such attitudes simply a response to perceptions of weakness *independent* of the specific actions that the United States (or other states) have taken, or are they a reaction to more powerful societies imposing their will upon them?

64. Robert Kagan, *Of Paradise and Power: America and Europe in the New World Order* (New York: Alfred A. Knopf, 2003); and Charles Krauthammer, "The Axis of Petulance," *Washington Post*, March 1, 2002, p. A25.

65. See Benjamin J. Cohen, "Containing Backlash: Foreign Economic Policy in an Age of Globalization," in Robert J. Lieber, ed., *Eagle Rules? Foreign Policy and American Primacy in the Twenty-First Century* (Upper Saddle River, NJ: Prentice Hall, 2002), p. 300.

66. Henry Kissinger and George C. Marshall were the other two U.S. recipients of this award.

67. See "Jihad against Jews and Crusaders," *World Islamic Front Statement*, February 23, 1998; "Transcript of Osama bin Laden's March 20, 1997, Interview with Peter Arnett," *CNN News*, May 10, 1997; and National Commission on Terrorist Attacks Upon the United States (The 9/11 Commission), "Outline of the 9/11 Plot," Staff Statement No. 16, June 16, 2004.

68. See in particular Osama bin Laden, "Declaration of War Against the Americans Occupying the Land of the Two Holy Places [Saudi Arabia]," first published in *Al-Quds al-'Arabi*, February 23, 1998; and "Excerpts: Bin Laden Video," *BBC News World Edition*, October 29, 2004, available at http://news .bbc.co.uk/2/hi/middle_east/3966817.stm, accessed January 15, 2005. For background, see Benjamin and Simon, *Age of Sacred Terror*, especially pp. 106, 117, 121.

69. The same report noted: "In nearly every country surveyed, at least a plurality blames differences their country has with the United States on policy disputes rather than on fundamental differences over values." *What the World Thinks in 2002*, pp. 61, 69. An earlier Pew survey of foreign "opinion leaders" reached a similar conclusion, saying that the leaders surveyed felt that "positive feelings toward the United States are strongly attributable to what America *stands for,* not what America does in the world." See "America Admired, Yet Its New Vulnerability Seen as Good Thing, Say Opinion Leaders," Pew Global Attitudes Project, December 19, 2001, p. 2.

70. See *Report of the Defense Science Board Task Force on Strategic Communication* (Washington, DC: Office of the Undersecretary of Defense for Acquisition, Technology, and Logistics, U.S. Department of Defense, September 2004), p. 40, available at www.acq.osd.mil/dsb/reports/2004-09-Strategic_Communica tion.pdf; also Thom Shanker, "U.S. Fails to Explain Policies to Muslim World, Panel Says," *New York Times*, November 24, 2002, p. 1.

71. See *Changing Minds, Winning Peace*, p. 24.

72. When asked what America should do to improve its image in the Arab world, most responders recommended changes in specific aspects of U.S. policy, such as "stop supporting Israel," "get out of Iraq," "change Middle East policy," etc. See "Impressions of America 2004," pp. 4, 8; and Shibley Telhami, "Arab Attitudes Towards Political and Social Issues, Foreign Policy, and the Media," A Public Opinion Poll by the Anwar Sadat Chair of Peace and Development,

University of Maryland, and Zogby International, at www.bsos.umd.edu/sadat.pub.

73. Erekat continued: "Americans perceive themselves as supporters of freedom and justice and the rule of law, but the image that American foreign policy projects to the Arab world is often the exact opposite. It is an image of a pseudo-colonialist power applying double standards and supporting illegitimate regimes . . . all in an effort to advance its own economic and political interests." See Saeb Erekat, "U.S. Policy 'Alienating' Arabs," *BBC News*, June 17, 2003, at www.news.bbc.co.uk/go/pr/fr/-/hi/programmes/wtwta/2956974.stm.

74. Or, as UN Special Envoy Lakhdar Brahimi (who was enlisted by the Bush administration to arrange the transfer of power in Iraq) put it: "The problems are linked. The big poison in the region is the Israeli policy of domination and the suffering imposed on the Palestinians." See "Egyptian Prez: Arabs Hate US," available at www.cbsnews.com/stories/2004/04/20/world/printable612831.shtml; and "Brahimi's Israel comments draw Annan, Israeli Fire," *Ha'aretz*, April 23, 2004, at www.haaretzdaily.com.

75. See *The Defense Science Board 1997 Summer Study Task Force on DoD Responses to Transnational Threats*, Vol. I (Washington, DC: U.S. Department of Defense, October 1997), p. 15.

76. The connection between U.S. activities and terrorist attacks appears to hold in every part of the world. Thus, the Libyan bombing of Pan Am flight 103 was an act of retaliation for the 1986 U.S. bombing raids; al Qaeda's attack on the USS *Cole* in 1999 was a response to the continued U.S. military presence in Saudi Arabia; and a July 1991 rocket attack on a U.S. military base in Japan was inspired by opposition to the U.S. military presence there. For these and many other examples, see Ivan Eland, "Protecting the Homeland: The Best Defense Is to Give No Offense," *Policy Analysis 306* (Washington, DC: Cato Institute, May 1998).

77. Domestic terrorists also react to specific policies. The FBI siege of the Branch Davidian Compound in Waco, Texas, reportedly inspired Timothy McVeigh's bombing of the federal building in Oklahoma City, and attacks on abortion providers remain the most common form of domestic terrorism.

78. See, for example, Charles Krauthammer's attack on the Sontag essay cited earlier: "Voices of Moral Obtuseness," *Washington Post*, September 21, 2001.

79. For a provocative but careful argument suggesting that the costs exceed the benefits, see Ivan Eland, *The Empire Has No Clothes*.

80. Krauthammer, "The Unipolar Moment Revisited."

81. Josef Joffe, "Who's Afraid of Mr. Big?" *The National Interest* 64 (Summer 2001).

82. It is worth remembering that the United States started out as a weak band of thirteen colonies, clinging to one shore of North America. Over the next century, the fledgling nation exterminated most of the native population (aided greatly by disease), and either bought or conquered its way to the Pacific Ocean. As its power increased, it worked to expel other Great Powers from the Western Hemisphere and took an increasingly proprietary attitude toward its own "backyard." See John J. Mearsheimer, *The Tragedy of Great Power Politics* (New York: W. W. Norton, 2001), chap. 7; Albert K. Weinberg, *Manifest Destiny: A Study of Nationalist Expansionism in American History* (Chicago: Quadrangle Books, 1935); and Lars W. Schoultz, *Beneath the United States: A History of U.S. Policy Toward Latin America* (Cambridge: Harvard University Press, 1998).

83. Democratic governments overthrown with the help of the United States include Iran (1953), Guatemala (1954), British Guiana (1953/64), Indonesia (1957), Ecuador (1963), Brazil (1964), Dominican Republic (1965), Costa Rica (1950s), and Chile (1973). See Stephen Van Evera, "Why Europe Matters; Why the Third World Doesn't," *Journal of Strategic Studies* 13, no. 2 (June 1990).

84. See David M. Edelstein, "Managing Uncertainty: Beliefs about Intentions and the Rise of Great Powers," *Security Studies* 12, no. 1 (Autumn 2002).

85. See Stuart Kaufman, *Modern Hatreds: The Symbolic Politics of Ethnic Violence* (Ithaca: Cornell University Press, 2003).

86. See Neta Crawford, "The Passion of World Politics: Propositions on Emotion and Emotional Relationships," *International Security* 24, no. 4 (Spring 2000), pp. 150–53; and Stern, *Terror in the Name of God.*

87. See James A. Bill, *The Eagle and the Lion: The Tragedy of American-Iranian Relations* (New Haven: Yale University Press, 1988), p. 277; Ervand Abrahamian, *Khomeinism: Essays on the Islamic Republic* (Berkeley: University of California Press, 1993); Richard Cottam, "Inside Revolutionary Iran," in R. K. Ramazani, ed., *Iran's Revolution: The Search for Consensus* (Bloomington: Indiana University Press, 1990); and Gary Sick, *All Fall Down: America's Tragic Encounter with Iran* (New York: Random House, 1985).

88. See, among many others, Schoultz, *Beneath the United States;* Walter LaFeber, *Inevitable Revolutions: The United States in Central America* (New York: W. W. Norton, 1984); and Cole Blasier, *The Hovering Giant: U.S. Responses to Revolutionary Change in Latin America* (Pittsburgh: University of Pittsburgh Press, 1976).

89. On Japan, see especially John Dower, *Embracing Defeat: Japan in the Wake of World War II* (New York: W. W. Norton, 1999). Postwar reconciliation was also fueled by geopolitics, insofar as Germany and Japan both wanted U.S. protection against the Soviet Union.

90. See Benny Morris, *The Birth of the Palestinian Refugee Problem Revisited*

(New York: Cambridge University Press, 2004); idem, *Righteous Victims: A History of the Zionist-Arab Conflict, 1881–2001* (New York: Vintage, 2001), pp. 198–99, 207–10, 252–58; Norman G. Finkelstein, *Image and Reality of the Israel-Palestine Conflict* (New York: Verso, 2001), chap. 3; and Eugene L. Rogan and Avi Shlaim, eds., *The War for Palestine: Rewriting the History of 1948* (New York: Cambridge University Press, 2001).

91. As David Ben-Gurion once remarked to Zionist leader Nahum Goldmann, "If I were an Arab leader I would never make terms with Israel. That is natural: we have taken their country. . . . There has been antisemitism, the Nazis, Hitler, Auschwitz, but was that their fault? They only see one thing: we have come here and stolen their country. Why should they accept that?" Quoted in Nahum Goldmann, *The Jewish Paradox*, trans. Steve Cox (New York: Grosset & Dunlap, 1978), p. 99.

92. Quoted in "Overheard," *Newsweek*, August 15, 1988.

93. Quoted in Shanker, "U.S. Fails to Explain Policies to Muslim World, Panel Says."

94. See "Young Egyptians Speak Up," transcript from *NOW with Bill Moyers*, July 12, 2002, available at www.pbs.org/now/transcript/transcript 126_full.html, accessed January 14, 2005. For other Arab reactions, see Saeed Shihabi, "War with Iraq, Peace with Israel," *Islam Online*, March 18, 2002; available at www.muslimwakeup.com/mainarchive/000659.php; Tariq a Al-Maeena, "The 51st State," October 2003, www.aljazeerahinfo.com; "Ariel Sharon and the Execution of Sheik Yassin," www.muslimwakeup.com/mainarchive/000659.php; and Joshua Hammer, Richard Wolffe, and Christopher Dickey, "The Wars Through Arab Eyes," *Newsweek*, May 31, 2004.

95. In bin Laden's words, "Had [Bush] been truthful about his claim for peace, he would not describe the person who ripped open pregnant women in Sabra and Shatila . . . as a man of peace." See "Bin Laden Threatens Revenge on Israel, U.S., Offers Truce with Europe," from www.why-war.com, April 15, 2004.

96. In the "just war" tradition, one criterion for assessing whether the use of force is justified is the principle of "proportionality": the benefits of using force must be greater than the damage inflicted.

97. See Trevor N. Dupuy, *Elusive Victory: The Arab-Israeli Wars, 1947–1974* (New York: Harper and Row, 1978), p. 265; and Wangui Kanina, "Nobel Laureate Defends Her Suggestion That AIDS Stems from Plot," *Boston Globe*, October 10, 2004.

98. A useful survey of U.S. unilateralism is David Malone and Yuen Foong Khong, eds., *Unilateralism and U.S. Foreign Policy: International Perspectives* (Boulder, CO: Lynne Rienner, 2003).

99. See Jim Lobe, "US Economy Comes First, Says Bush," *InterPress Service*, March 31, 2001.

100. See Nicholas Lemann, "How It Came to War: When Did Bush Decide That He Had to Fight Saddam?" *The New Yorker*, March 31, 2003, p. 36.

101. *The Military Balance 2003–2004* (London: International Institute for Strategic Studies, 2003), pp. 214–15.

102. Geoffrey Perret, *Winged Victory: Army Air Forces in World War II* (New York: Random House, 1997); and Ronald Schaffer, *Wings of Judgment: American Bombing in World War II* (New York: Oxford University Press, 1985).

103. See bin Laden's "Letter to America."

104. See "George Bush's Travels: Putting the World Back Together Again," *The Economist*, June 7, 2003, p. 22. According to Steven E. Miller of Harvard, "The Bush administration simply could not believe . . . that some of its close NATO allies were not supporting Washington against Saddam Hussein." See his "Primacy or Order: American Power and the Global System after Iraq," Workshop on the Future of Transatlantic Relations, Bertelsmann Foundation Transatlantic Strategy Group, Frankfurt, Germany, July 17–18, 2003.

105. *The 2001 Chart of Armed Conflict* (London: International Institute for Strategic Studies, 2001).

106. See Bruce W. Jentleson, *American Foreign Policy: The Dynamics of Choice in the 21st Century*, 2d ed. (New York: W. W. Norton, 2003).

107. See Johnson, *Blowback: The Costs and Consequences of American Empire*, pp. 8–11.

108. See Craig S. Smith, "The Intimidating Face of America," *New York Times*, October 13, 2004, p. A4.

109. As Secretary of State Dean Acheson later asserted, "No possible shred of evidence could have existed in the mind of the Chinese Communist authorities about the [peaceful] intentions of the United Nations," yet we now know the Chinese were deeply worried and went to war to counter what they saw as an imminent threat. Quoted in Richard Ned Lebow, *Between Peace and War: The Nature of International Crisis* (Baltimore: Johns Hopkins University Press, 1981), pp. 205–16.

110. On this general phenomenon, see Stephen Van Evera, *More Causes of War: Misperception and the Roots of Conflict* (Ithaca: Cornell University Press, forthcoming). See also Frances Fitzgerald, *America Revised: History Textbooks in the 20th Century* (Boston: Little, Brown, 1979); James Loewen, *Lies My Teacher Told Me: Everything Your American History Textbook Got Wrong* (New York: Touchstone, 1996); and E. H. Dance, *History the Betrayer: A Study in Bias* (London: Hutchinson, 1960).

111. See Andrew Sullivan, "Unbound: Liberation's New World Order," at www.andrewsullivan.com, April 14, 2003.

112. See Niall Ferguson, *Colossus: The Price of America's Empire* (New York: Penguin, 2004), p. 29, also p. 302.

113. Paul Wolfowitz, "Remembering the Future," *The National Interest* 59 (Spring 2000), p. 41.

114. Quoted in Ivo H. Daalder and James Lindsay, *America Unbound: The Bush Revolution in Foreign Policy* (Washington, DC: Brookings Institution Press, 2003), p. 86.

Chapter 3

1. Interview available at www.pbs.org/wgbh.pages/frontline/shows/kosovo/interview.short.html. For background, see Ivo H. Daalder and Michael O'Hanlon, *Winning Ugly: NATO's War to Save Kosovo* (Washington, DC: Brookings Institution Press, 2000).

2. Vladimir Putin, "Putin Comments on Current Events, Iraq, Chechnya in French TV Interview," Moscow ITAR-TASS, in Foreign Broadcast Information Service, February 9, 2003. See also Craig R. Whitney, "NATO at 50: Is It a Misalliance?" *New York Times*, February 15, 1999, p. A7. More recently, *Le Monde* editor Jean-Marie Colombani noted that differences between the United States and Europe reflected a fundamental concern over basic principles of international legitimacy. "At stake," he wrote, "is the way in which the new 'United States of America' intends to lead the world." See "America's Challenge: Moving Beyond Opposition," *Le Monde*, February 6, 2003.

3. See David Murphy, "Best Friends," *Far Eastern Economic Review* 167, no. 18 (May 6, 2004), p. 30; and Samuel P. Huntington, "The Lonely Superpower," *Foreign Affairs* 78, no. 2 (March/April 1999), p. 43.

4. See Daniel Drezner, *The Sanctions Paradox: Economic Sanctions and International Relations* (Cambridge: Cambridge University Press, 1999). On the relatively modest impact of economic sanctions more generally, see Robert Pape, "Why Economic Sanctions Do Not Work," *International Security* 22, no. 2 (Autumn 1997); and Richard N. Haass, *Economic Sanctions and American Diplomacy* (New York: Council on Foreign Relations Press, 1998).

5. The possibility that states will "design around" a deterrent warning is emphasized by Alexander George and Richard Smoke in *Deterrence in American Foreign Policy: Theory and Practice* (New York: Columbia University Press, 1974).

6. See Schelling's discussion in *Arms and Influence* (New Haven: Yale University Press, 1966), pp. 66–67.

7. For insightful discussions of the credibility issue in international politics, see Robert Jervis, *The Logic of Images in International Relations* (Princeton: Princeton University Press, 1970); Jonathan Mercer, *Reputation and International*

Politics (Ithaca: Cornell University Press, 1996); and Paul K. Huth, "Reputations and Deterrence," *Security Studies* 7, no. 1 (Autumn 1997).

8. On U.S. efforts against al Qaeda before September 11, see Daniel Benjamin and Steven Simon, *The Age of Sacred Terror: Radical Islam's War against America* (New York: Random House, 2003), especially chap. 7; and Richard A. Clarke, *Against All Enemies: Inside America's War on Terror* (New York: Free Press, 2004).

9. The U.S. war on "global terrorism" has achieved some important successes, but it would be premature to conclude that the attacks themselves were a total failure or that the "war" has been won. Indeed, one might argue that bin Laden's strategic objectives are being realized: (1) the United States is now bogged down in Iraq, thereby confirming his claim that the United States is fundamentally hostile to Arabs and Muslims; (2) the Bush administration has moved closer to the Likud government in Israel, thereby vindicating bin Laden's accusations about U.S. support for the repression of the Palestinians, and (3) the United States has removed most of its forces from Saudi Arabia, thereby acceding to one of bin Laden's original demands. We may be winning battles, but al Qaeda may be winning the war.

10. On Saddam's motivations, see Ephraim Karsh and Inari Rautsi, "Why Saddam Hussein Invaded Kuwait," *Survival* 33, no. 1 (Spring 1991); and Lawrence Freedman and Ephraim Karsh, *The Gulf Conflict, 1990–91: Diplomacy and War in the New World Order* (Princeton: Princeton University Press, 1993).

11. See "Iran Says It Will Not Give Up Uranium Enrichment Program," *New York Times*, August 1, 2004, p. A8; and Paul Reynolds, "Iran: The Next Crisis?" *BBC World News Service*, at http://news.bbc.co.uk/2/hi/middle_east/3929369.stm.

12. In November 2004, a protracted diplomatic effort by the EU convinced Iran to suspend uranium enrichment for six months, but Iran remained unwilling to end its nuclear activities permanently. The text of the EU–Iran agreement is at www.albawaba.com/news/index.php3?sid=288927&lang=e&dir=news.

13. Kenneth N. Waltz, "Structural Realism after the Cold War," *International Security* 25, no. 1 (Summer 2000).

14. See Stephen M. Walt, "The Ties That Fray: Why Europe and America Are Approaching a Parting of the Ways," *The National Interest* 54 (Winter 1998/99); Peter W. Rodman, *Drifting Apart? Trends in U.S.–European Relations* (Washington, DC: The Nixon Center, 1999); and Jeffrey Gedmin, "Continental Drift: A Europe United in Spirit against the United States," *The New Republic*, June 28, 1999. For an especially pessimistic view, see Charles A. Kupchan, *The End of the American Era: U.S. Foreign Policy and the Geopolitics of the 21st Century* (New York: Vintage, 2003).

15. Quoted in Craig R. Whitney, "NATO at 50: With Nations at Odds, Is

It a Misalliance?" *New York Times*, February 15, 1999, p. A7. Or, as a French academic stated in 2000: "[The United States] does what it wants. Through NATO it directs European affairs. Before we could say we were on America's side. Not now. There is no counterbalance." Michel Winock, quoted in "More Vehemently than Ever: Europeans are Scorning the United States," *New York Times*, April 9, 2000, pp. A1, A8.

16. As a Council on Foreign Relations task force concluded in 2004, "The transatlantic relationship is under greater strain today than at any point in at least a generation." See *Renewing the Atlantic Partnership*, Report of an Independent Task Force (New York: Council on Foreign Relations, 2004), p. 1.

17. See "Russia and China Sign 'Friendship Pact,' " *New York Times*, July 17, 2001, pp. A1, A8; "India a Great Power: Putin," *Times of India*, October 2, 2000; and "A Man with Big Ideas, a Small Country . . . and Oil," *New York Times*, September 24, 2000, p. 4:3.

18. Iran's defense minister visited Damascus in February 2004, and the two countries established a joint committee to review additional ways to cooperate in military affairs. See "Iran, Syria Set up Panel for Defense Cooperation," at www.menewsline.com/stories/2004March/03_01_2.html.

19. See "Europe Seeks Unity on New Bush Term," *New York Times*, November 6, 2004, p. A8; and "European Leaders Remain Split over Bush Election and Future Diplomacy," *Financial Times*, November 6, 2004, p. 4.

20. See Scott MacMillan, "Yankees Go Home—and Europe Will Miss Them: The International Press Weighs the Impact of Bush's Troop Withdrawals," *Slate*, August 19, 2004; available online at http://slate.msn.com/id/2105375, accessed December 16, 2004; and Robert Marquand, "U.S. Redeployments Afoot in Asia," *Christian Science Monitor*, November 18, 2003, available online at http://csmonitor.com/2003/1118/p06s01-woap.html, accessed December 16, 2004.

21. In 1998, these states possessed a combined GNP of $165 billion (which is substantially smaller than the U.S. defense budget alone and less than 2 percent of U.S. GNP). Similarly, their combined defense spending in 1999 was only $11 billion, compared to roughly $260 billion for the United States. See *The Military Balance 1999–2000* (London: International Institute for Strategic Studies, 2000). This group of states was never a cohesive alliance and is even weaker today, now that Saddam Hussein has been toppled and Libyan leader Muammar Ghaddafi has chosen to accommodate with the West.

22. For a complete discussion of balance-of-threat theory, see Stephen M. Walt, *The Origins of Alliances* (Ithaca: Cornell University Press, 1987). For an application to America's global position in the 21st century, see idem, "Keeping the World 'Off-Balance': Self-Restraint and U.S. Foreign Policy," in G. John

Ikenberry, ed., *America Unrivaled: The Future of the Balance of Power* (Ithaca: Cornell University Press, 2002).

23. Earlier Great Powers did establish large overseas empires, but they did so before nationalism became a powerful social force around the world. In the twentieth century, trying to govern large numbers of alien peoples became excessively costly, and nationalist resistance eventually destroyed the British, French, Ottoman, Austro-Hungarian, and Soviet empires.

24. See Thomas J. Christensen, "China, the U.S.–Japan Alliance and the Security Dilemma in East Asia," *International Security* 23, no. 4 (Spring 1999).

25. See John J. Mearsheimer, *The Tragedy of Great Power Politics* (New York: W. W. Norton, 2001), chap. 7.

26. Thus, William Wohlforth is partly correct to say, "The raw power advantage of the United States means that . . . second-tier states face incentives to bandwagon with the unipolar power." As discussed in chapter 4, however, Wohlforth overstates the magnitude of these incentives. See Wohlforth, "The Stability of a Unipolar World," *International Security* 24, no. 1 (Summer 1999), pp. 7–8.

27. For an insightful discussion of "soft balancing" that makes many of the same points, see Robert A. Pape, "Soft Balancing: How States Pursue Security in a Unipolar World," *International Security* 30, no. 1 (Summer 2005); and see also T. V. Paul, "Introduction: The Enduring Axioms of Balance of Power Theory and Their Contemporary Relevance," in T. V. Paul, James J. Wirtz, and Michel Fortmann, eds., *Balance of Power: Theory and Practice in the 21st Century* (Stanford: Stanford University Press, 2004), pp. 3, 13–17.

28. As a Pentagon spokesman put it: "These are two countries, both subject to attack by forces within NATO. They both have primarily Soviet-built or -purchased air-defense systems, and they are both subject to international embargoes. So they obviously might look for ways to work together." See Philip Shenon, "Crisis in the Balkans: The Iraqi Connection," *New York Times*, April 1, 1999, p. A16.

29. See "North Korea Exported Nuclear Materials to Iran," *Dong-A Ilbo*, November 7, 2004, at http://english.donga.com, downloaded November 10, 2004.

30. According to the *New York Times*, Amorim was "a star of the negotiations," whose "influence came from his role as spokesman for a powerful new bloc of countries and from the lawsuits Brazil has brought to World Trade Organization tribunals against the United States and the European Union. See Elizabeth Becker, "Trade Group Close to Deal on New Rules," *New York Times*, August 1, 2004, p. A8; and Elizabeth Becker, "Interim Trade Triumph Short on Hard Details," *New York Times*, August 2, 2004, p. C1.

31. See "Third World Alliance Hits at Rich Nations' Trade Rules," *Financial Times*, September 11, 2003, p. 7.

32. See Vladimir Isachenkov, "Russia and China to Hold Joint Maneuvers," *Associated Press*, December 27, 2004, available at www.allheadlinenews.com/articles/1104156933; and Ali A. Jalali, "The Strategic Partnership of Russia and Iran," *Parameters* 31 (Winter 2001–2002).

33. See David Shambaugh, "China and Europe: The Emerging Axis," *Current History* 103, no. 670 (September 2004).

34. See Robert J. Art, "Europe Hedges Its Security Bets," in Paul, Wirtz, and Fortmann, eds., *Balance of Power*, pp. 179–214.

35. When a sufficiently large number of states is committed to some form of "soft balancing," however, uncommitted states may be more likely to free-ride. States may share a desire to check U.S. power (even if only modestly), but they may also want to avoid the costs and risks of open opposition. The more confident they are that others will publicly oppose the United States, the greater the temptation to remain aloof.

36. A former U.S. official, Stephen Sestanovich, later commented, "The anti-American stance is a familiar French thing. . . . After they'd been French for awhile, they'd stop being French. People thought they understood the limits of the game and it would be over at a certain point. And then it wasn't. And it turned out that the Russians were prepared to be French, *as long as the French were being French.*" Quoted in Nicholas Lemann, "How It Came to War," *The New Yorker*, March 31, 2003 [emphasis added].

37. See Richard Bernstein, "Poland Upstages, and Irks, European Powerhouses," *New York Times*, May 13, 2003, p. A3; and Ian Fisher, "Romania, Wooed by U.S., Looks to a Big NATO Role," *New York Times*, October 23, 2002, p. A3.

38. "Bush Backs Diplomacy with Tehran," *BBC News World Edition*, March 12, 2005, available at http://news.bbc.co.uk/2/hi/middle_east/4340453.stm.

39. From this perspective, it was neither surprising nor necessarily wrong for the Bush administration to "punish" France and Germany for their actions over Iraq—just as it made sense to "reward" states that joined the "coalition of the willing." See Elisabeth Bumiller, "U.S., Angry at French Stance on War, Considers Punishment," *New York Times*, April 24, 2003.

40. *The National Defense Strategy of the United States of America* (Washington, DC: Department of Defense, March 2005), p. 2. See also "Strategic Assessment 1998" (Washington, DC: Institute for National Security Studies/National Defense University, 1998), chap. 11; Jonathan Tucker, "Asymmetric Warfare," *Forum for Applied Research and Public Policy* (Summer 1999); and Bruce W. Bennett, Christopher P. Twomey, and Gregory Treverton, "What are Asymmetric Strategies?" *Designated Briefing 246* (Santa Monica: RAND, 1999).

41. *National Defense Strategy*, p. 3. Other core works on asymmetric conflict include Andrew Mack, "Why Big Nations Lose Small Wars: The Politics of Asymmetric Conflict," *World Politics* 27, no. 2 (January 1975); and Ivan Arreguin-Toft, *How the Weak Win Wars: A Theory of Asymmetric Conflict* (Cambridge: Cambridge University Press, 2005).

42. See, for example, Mao Tse-tung, "The Present Situation and Our Tasks," in *Selected Works of Mao Tse-Tung*, vol. 4 (Beijing: Foreign Languages Press, 1961), pp. 160–61.

43. See Barry R. Posen, "Command of the Commons: The Military Foundation of U.S. Hegemony," *International Security* 28, no. 1 (Summer 2003).

44. During the first Gulf War in 1991, for example, the AEGIS missile cruiser USS *Princeton* was put out of action by a relatively crude Iraqi mine. See Tucker, "Asymmetric Warfare," p. 33.

45. This is a central theme in Roger W. Barnett, *Asymmetrical Warfare: Today's Challenge to U.S. Military Power* (Washington, DC: Brassey's, 2003), although he greatly exaggerates U.S. vulnerability to any of these constraints.

46. See Barry R. Posen, "The War for Kosovo: Serbia's Political–Military Strategy, *International Security* 24, no. 4 (Spring 2000).

47. See Ryan Welch, "Operation Anaconda: The Battle for Shah-i-Kot Valley," *Armor* (Nov.–Dec., 2003); Stephen Biddle, *Afghanistan and the Future of Warfare: Implications for Army and Defense Policy* (Strategic Studies Institute, U.S. Army War College, Carlisle, PA, 2002).

48. Among other things, Chinese military spending increased by more than 11 percent in 2004. See "China to Increase Defense Spending by 11.6% in 2004," *Xinhua News Agency*, March 7, 2004, downloaded from www.bjreview.com/cn/npc2004/0308–03.htm on November 6, 2004.

49. See "China Ponders New Rules of 'Unrestricted War,'" *Washington Post*, August 8, 1999, p. A1; Qiao Liang and Wang Xiangsui, *Unrestricted War: China's Master Plan to Destroy America* (Panama City: Pan American Publishing, 2002).

50. See Thomas J. Christensen, "Posing Problems without Catching Up: China's Rise and Challenges for U.S. Security Policy," *International Security* 25, no. 4 (Spring 2001), p. 9.

51. It is not surprising, therefore, that open societies facing a severe terrorist challenge usually respond by compromising various civil liberties. Great Britain conducted unauthorized assassinations of IRA officials; Israel has detained Palestinian suspects for years without trial; and the United States has cut corners handling detainees from the Afghan War. These examples all involve significant departures from cherished democratic ideals. On these general points, see Philip Heymann, *Terrorism and America* (Cambridge: MIT Press/BCSIA, 2000);

and idem, *Terrorism, Freedom, and Security: Winning Without War* (Cambridge: MIT Press/BCSIA, 2004).

52. Bin Laden has been at least partly successful, insofar as the Bush administration has withdrawn U.S. forces from Saudi Arabia in an attempt to reduce anti-U.S. sentiment within Saudi society.

53. See especially Robert A. Pape, "The Strategic Logic of Suicide Terrorism," *American Political Science Review* 97, no. 3 (August 2003).

54. According to the Carnegie Endowment for International Peace, there are at present at least four and perhaps as many as eight nations with active nuclear, chemical, or biological weapons development programs: Egypt, India, Iran, Israel, North Korea, Pakistan, Sudan, and Syria. This list excludes the other nuclear powers (the United States, Russia, China, France, and Great Britain). See George Perkovich et al., *Universal Compliance: A Strategy for Nuclear Security* (Washington, DC: Carnegie Endowment for International Peace, 2004); and also "Nuclear Weapon Status 2004," "Chemical Weapon Status 2004," and "Bio-weapon Status 2004," available online at www.ceip.org/files/non prolif/default.asp, accessed December 20, 2004.

55. The motivations for nuclear weapons acquisition are examined in Bradley A. Thayer, "The Causes of Nuclear Proliferation and the Utility of the Nuclear Nonproliferation Regime," *Security Studies* 4, no. 3 (Spring 1995); and Zachary S. Davis and Benjamin Frankel, eds., "The Proliferation Puzzle: Why Nuclear Weapons Spread (and What Results)," *Security Studies* 2, nos. 3–4 (Spring 1993).

56. As Kenneth Waltz notes, "If weak countries have some [WMD] it will cramp our style. Militarily punishing small countries for behavior we dislike would become much more perilous." See Kenneth N. Waltz and Scott D. Sagan, *The Spread of Nuclear Weapons: A Debate* (New York: W. W. Norton, 1995), p. 111.

57. Quoted in Ray Takeyh, "Iran's Nuclear Calculations," *World Policy Journal* 20, no. 2 (Summer 2003). Takeyh concludes: "Iran's nuclear calculations are not derived from an irrational ideology, but rather from a judicious attempt to craft a viable deterrent capability against an evolving range of threats. . . . Iran's leadership clearly sees itself as being in Washington's cross hairs, and it is precisely this perception that is driving its accelerated nuclear program."

58. See "Status of the Nuclear Non-Proliferation Treaty," *Bipartisan Security Group of the Global Security Institute,* June 2003.

59. The dangers of nuclear terrorism and the need for a comprehensive strategy to prevent it are presented most vividly in Graham T. Allison, *Nuclear Terrorism: The Ultimate Preventable Catastrophe* (New York: Henry Holt, 2004).

60. I am indebted to Seyom Brown for suggesting the term "balking," and for encouraging me to include it as a separate strategy.

61. The seminal analysis is Mancur Olson and Richard Zeckhauser, "An Economic Theory of Alliances," *Review of Economics and Statistics* 48, no. 3 (1966).

62. This point is nicely made by John Ikenberry in "Strategic Reactions to American Preeminence: Great Power Politics in the Age of Unipolarity," Report to the National Intelligence Council, July 28, 2003, available at www.cia.gov/nic/confreports_stratreact.html.

63. For the orthodox view of international institutions, see Robert Keohane, *After Hegemony: Cooperation and Discord in the World Political Economy* (Princeton: Princeton University Press, 1984); and Lisa L. Martin and Beth Simmons, "Theories and Empirical Studies of International Institutions," *International Organization* 52, no. 4 (Autumn 1998), pp. 729–57. For a pointed critique, see John J. Mearsheimer, "The False Promise of International Institutions," *International Security* 19, no. 3 (Winter, 1994–95).

64. See Michael Hirsh, *At War with Ourselves: Why America Is Squandering Its Chance to Build a Better World* (New York: Oxford University Press, 2003), pp. 8–9.

65. According to John Ikenberry, the "Western order has a structure of institutions and open polities that bind major states together, thereby mitigating the implications of power asymmetries and reducing the opportunities of the United States to abandon or dominate other states. . . . A cooperative order is built around a basic bargain: the hegemonic state gets commitments by secondary states to participate within the postwar order, and in return the hegemon places limits on the exercise of its power." See G. John Ikenberry, "Democracy, Institutions, and American Restraint," in Ikenberry, ed., *America Unrivaled*, pp. 214–15; and also his *After Victory: Institutions, Strategic Restraint, and the Rebuilding of Order after Major Wars* (Princeton: Princeton University Press, 2001).

66. Charles Krauthammer, "Democratic Realism: An American Foreign Policy for a Unipolar World," 2004 Irving Kristol Lecture, American Enterprise Institute, Washington, DC, February 10, 2004, p. 3.

67. Jean-Marie Colombani, "America's Challenge: Moving Beyond Opposition," *Le Monde*, February 6, 2003.

68. *The National Security Strategy of the United States* (Washington, DC: The White House, September 2002).

69. On this point, see John G. Ruggie, "American Exceptionalism, Exemptionalism, and Global Governance," in Michael Ignatieff, ed., *American Exceptionalism and Human Rights* (Princeton: Princeton University Press, 2004).

70. See Nico Krisch, "Weak as Constraint, Strong as Tool: The Place of International Law in U.S. Foreign Policy," in David Malone and Yuen Foong

Khong, eds., *Unilateralism and U.S. Foreign Policy: International Perspectives* (Boulder, CO: Lynne Rienner, 2003).

71. Quoted in Elaine Sciolino and Steven Lee Myers, "Bush Says 'Time Is Running Out'; U.S. Plans to Act Largely Alone," *New York Times*, October 7, 2001, p. 1A.

72. See Ikenberry, "Democracy, Institutions, and American Restraint," p. 221.

73. As Ikenberry admits, "The United States may be willing to reduce its policy autonomy in trade and other 'low politics' realms through commitments to the World Trade Organization (WTO) and other multilateral economic regimes, but it is more reluctant to cede any real autonomy in the areas of arms control and the use of force." See "Strategic Reactions to American Preeminence," p. 16.

74. See Rosemary Foot, S. Neil MacFarlane, and Michael Mastanduno, "Conclusion," in *U.S. Hegemony and International Organizations* (New York: Oxford University Press, 2003), p. 266.

75. See Robert B. Zoellick, "America Will Not Wait for the Won't-Do Countries," *Financial Times*, September 22, 2003, p. 23.

76. See Per Magnus Wijkman, "U.S. Trade Policy: Alternative Tacks or Parallel Tracks?" in Malone and Khong, eds., *Unilateralism and U.S. Foreign Policy*, pp. 271–72, 278. As of April 2001, the United States had been involved in 106 formal WTO disputes (57 as plaintiff and 44 as defendant). As plaintiff, the United States won 29 of 34 cases in which the full settlement procedure was employed. As defendant, the United States lost 13 of the 14 cases where the full dispute settlement process had been completed.

77. See Cherif A. Bassiouni, "Negotiating the Treaty of Rome on the Establishment of an International Criminal Court," *Cornell International Law Journal* 32, no. 3 (1999), p. 457.

78. One observer notes regarding the ICC: "Its significance extends beyond the institutionalization of international criminal responsibility for individuals: it touches on the kind of world order that is perceived to exist." And by opposing the ICC, "The United States has proclaimed its intention to pursue a different type of world order . . . that leaves more room for unilateralism." See Georg Nolte, "The United States and the International Criminal Court," in Malone and Khong, eds., *Unilateralism and U.S. Foreign Policy*, p. 72.

79. The classic analysis remains Daniel Ellsberg, "The Theory and Practice of Blackmail" (Santa Monica: RAND Corporation, 1968); and see also Robert Jervis, "Bargaining and Bargaining Tactics," in J. Roland Pennock and John W. Chapman, eds., *Coercion* (Chicago: Aldine-Atherton, 1972).

80. A threat that would harm both blackmailer and victim can still exert

some leverage, if the blackmailer can convince the target that it is more willing to bear the costs of executing the threat. If the blackmailer seems highly resolved and the target fears the consequences more than the blackmailer does, then a seemingly "irrational" threat might still work.

81. The price of paying off a blackmailer includes both the immediate costs of meeting the demand and the potential damage to one's reputation. If a state is worried that giving in to blackmail will encourage others to issue threats of their own, it might decide to reject the demand (and pay the larger price) in order to deter future attempts at extortion.

82. See Michael O'Hanlon, "Stopping a North Korean Invasion: Why Defending South Korea is Easier than the Pentagon Thinks," *International Security* 22, no. 4 (Spring 1998).

83. In 2003, for example, U.S. GDP was nearly five hundred times larger than North Korea's, and U.S. defense spending was more than two hundred times larger.

84. Useful analyses of the negotiations between the United States and North Korea include Lee V. Sigal, *Disarming Strangers: Nuclear Diplomacy with North Korea* (Princeton: Princeton University Press, 1998); and Joel S. Wit, Daniel B. Poneman, and Robert L. Gallucci, *Going Critical: The First North Korean Nuclear Crisis* (Washington, DC: Brookings Institution Press, 2004).

85. North Korea seized a U.S. reconnaissance ship (the USS *Pueblo*) in 1968; its agents assassinated four members of the South Korean cabinet in 1983; and its soldiers brutally beat to death a U.S. infantryman along the demilitarized zone (DMZ) in 1976. North Korea has also been willing to sell missile technology to a variety of countries. As a result, U.S. leaders have been especially concerned about its possible conduct should it acquire nuclear weaponry.

86. See Jonathan D. Pollock, "The United States, North Korea, and the Agreed Framework," *Naval War College Review* 56, no. 3 (Summer 2003).

87. Quoted in Pollock, p. 24.

88. In August 2002, President Bush told reporter Bob Woodward, "I loathe Kim Jong Il. I've got a visceral reaction to this guy because he is starving his people. They tell me, we don't need to move too fast [against Kim] because the financial burdens on people will be so immense if we try to—if this guy were to topple. I just don't buy that." Quoted in Bob Woodward, *Bush at War* (New York: Simon & Schuster, 2002), p. 340.

89. It is worth noting that Assistant Secretary of State James Kelly was given very limited latitude at the first meeting with the North Korean representatives, "other than informing DPRK officials and rebuking them for the North's evident attempt to circumvent the Agreed Framework." As Gary Samore notes, the Bush administration's initial approach to North Korea "demanded more

and offered less." See Gary Samore, "The Korean Nuclear Crisis," *Survival* 45, no. 1 (Spring 2003), p. 11.

90. See Mohamed Heikal, *The Road to Ramadan* (New York: Ballantine Books, 1976), pp. 84–91; and Leslie H. Gelb with Richard K. Betts, *The Irony of Vietnam: The System Worked* (Washington, DC: Brookings Institution Press, 1979), pp. 82–84.

91. Readers will recall that the claim that Iraq was close to obtaining nuclear weapons and that it would use these weapons to "blackmail" the world was a key element in the Bush administration's case for preventive war.

92. See Richard K. Betts, *Nuclear Blackmail and Nuclear Balance* (Washington, DC: Brookings Institution, 1987).

93. Ironically, some of the officials who invoked the fear of blackmail in order to justify preventive war against Iraq used to recognize that these weapons could not be used in this way. In the January/February 2000 issue of *Foreign Affairs*, for example, Bush National Security Advisor (and now Secretary of State) Condoleezza Rice described how the United States should react if Iraq were to obtain WMD. "The first line of defense," she wrote, "should be a clear and classical statement of deterrence—if they do acquire WMD, their weapons will be unusable *because any attempt to use them will bring national obliteration."* See Condoleezza Rice, "Preserving the National Interest," *Foreign Affairs* 79, no. 1 (January/February 2000), p. 61 [emphasis added].

94. On the inherently defensive nature of nuclear weapons, see Robert Jervis, *The Meaning of the Nuclear Revolution: Statecraft and the Prospect of Armageddon* (Ithaca: Cornell University Press, 1989), and *The Illogic of U.S. Nuclear Strategy* (Ithaca: Cornell University Press, 1984); and Kenneth N. Waltz, "Nuclear Myths and Political Realities," *American Political Science Review* 84, no. 3 (Summer 1990).

95. See Barry R. Posen, "What if Iraq Had Nuclear Weapons?" and Stephen M. Walt, "Containing Rogues and Renegades: Coalition Strategies and Counterproliferation," in Victor R. Utgoff, ed., *The Coming Crisis: Nuclear Proliferation, U.S. Interests, and World Order* (Cambridge: MIT Press, 2000).

96. For an intriguing study of delegitimation within a traditional political order, see Don Herzog, *Poisoning the Minds of the Lower Orders* (Princeton: Princeton University Press, 1998).

97. Thus, many people believed the 2000 presidential election in the United States undermined George W. Bush's legitimacy, for he seemed (to some Americans, at least) to have gained the White House through electoral chicanery.

98. Secretary-General Kofi Annan, "Address to the General Assembly," September 23, 2003, available at www.un.org/webcast/ga/58/statements/sg2eng 030923.htm.

99. See John G. Ruggie, *Winning the Peace: America and World Order in the New Era* (New York: Columbia University Press, 1996).

100. Thus, when U.S. negotiators forced the collapse of an international conference on measures to strengthen the Biological Weapons Convention in 2001, EU diplomats told reporters that the U.S. delegation "had treated us like dirt . . . it was insulting." See Frances Williams, "U.S. Scuppers Germ Warfare Talks," *Financial Times*, December 8–9, 2001, p. 4.

101. This argument places the strategy of "binding" in a somewhat different light. Institutions and procedures cannot bind a country as powerful as the United States—at least not on most issues—but forcing the United States to operate outside the norms developed by others is another way to undermine the legitimacy of U.S. power. Institutions cannot force the United States to act as others might wish, but they establish standards of behavior that can be used to judge whether a powerful actor is behaving "properly" or not. The UN Security Council could not prevent the United States from attacking Iraq, for example, but the fact that there was an accepted procedure for authorizing the use of force meant that the U.S. decision to invade would be seen as an illegitimate act. The United States got what it wanted—regime change in Iraq—but it paid a higher price.

102. For various statements of this position, see Wohlforth, "The Stability of a Unipolar World"; Stephen M. Walt, "American Primacy: Its Prospects and Pitfalls," *Naval War College Review* 55, no. 2 (Spring 2002); Samuel P. Huntington, "Why International Primacy Matters," *International Security* 17, no. 4 (Spring 1993); and Niall Ferguson, "A World Without Power," *Foreign Policy* 143 (July/August 2004).

103. "President Speaks to the United Nations General Assembly," September 21, 2004, available at http://www.whitehouse.gov/news/releases/2004/09/20040921-3.html.

104. NATO's intervention in Kosovo is defended primarily on similar grounds by former Deputy National Security Advisor James Steinberg in "A Perfect Polemic: Blind to Reality in Kosovo," *Foreign Affairs* 78, no. 6 (November/December 1999).

105. See Osama bin Laden, "Letter to the American People," as printed in *Observer Worldview*, November 24, 2002, available at http://observer.guardian.co.uk/worldview/story/0,11581845725,00.html, viewed on January 15, 2005.

106. "Why We Fight America: Al-Qa'ida Spokesman Explains September 11 and Declares Intentions to Kill 4 Million Americans with Weapons of Mass Destruction," *Middle East Media Research Institute*, Special Dispatch no. 388, June 12, 2002, available at http://memri.org/bin/opener.cgi?Page-archives8ID=SP3880Z.

107. As French President Jacques Chirac put it, "I have no doubt whatsoever that the multipolar vision of the world that I have defended for some time is certainly supported by a large majority of countries throughout the world." See Grant R. Mainland, "American Primacy Is a Lesser Evil," *San Diego Union-Tribune*, July 23, 2003; and Howard LaFranchi, "Real Message Sent at G-8 Summit," *Christian Science Monitor*, June 3, 2003.

108. I am indebted to Frances Kamm for suggesting this line of argument to me.

109. Ironically, primacy also means the United States has to do more for others in order to get credit for acting in a disinterested or altruistic fashion. Bill Gates would be seen as niggardly if he gave only $10,000 each year for charitable purposes, but someone who made only $50,000 a year would be seen as exceptionally generous if he or she gave the same amount. Because the United States can make large sacrifices without jeopardizing its own well-being, it has to do more than others in order to meet its "fiduciary" responsibilities. This point also means that any failure to act on behalf of others hurts America's image more than it hurts the image of weaker or poorer states. No one blames Bolivia or Togo for failing to stop a genocide, but they do blame the United States.

110. Gwen Robinson, "Alarm Grows among U.S. Allies over Afghan War Detainees," *Financial Times*, January 17, 2002, p. 5; Philip Stephens, "Losing Ground at Camp X-Ray," *Financial Times*, January 18, 2002, p. 11; and William Glaberson, "Critics' Attack on Tribunals Turns to Law Among Nations," *New York Times*, December 26, 2001.

111. For a summary of what occurred, see James Schlesinger et al., *Final Report of the Independent Panel to Review DoD Detention Operations* (Washington, DC: Department of Defense, August 2004); and Douglas Jehl, "Pentagon Will Not Try 17 GIs Implicated in Prisoners' Deaths," *New York Times*, March 26, 2005, p. A1.

112. See Sarah Boxer, "Torture Incarnate, and Propped on a Pedestal," *New York Times*, June 13, 2004.

113. "German TV: U.S. Soldiers Abused Kids," *The Metro: Boston Edition*, July 7, 2004; "US-Soldaten sollen inhaftierte Kinder misshandelt haben," *Spiegel* magazine, July 4, 2004; "Norway Reacts to Alleged American Child Abuse in Iraq," *The Norway Post*, July 8, 2004, at www.norwaypost.no.

114. These quotations are drawn from "Bush on Arab TV: 'Crisis Management,' not a 'Confession of Guilt,' " *Foreign Media Reaction*, Office of Research, International Information Programs, U.S. Department of State (Washington, DC, May 11, 2004), available at http://usinfo.state.gov.

115. As a French scholar warns, "What should be of most concern to Amer-

icans is the perception that their country is a violent, uncivilized society, incapable even of assimilating its own immigrants properly." See Denis Lacorne, "The Barbaric Americans," *Wilson Quarterly* 25 (Spring 2001), pp. 53–54. Lacorne points out that roughly 38 out of every 100,000 U.S. males between 25 and 34 commit a murder each year, compared with fewer than 2 out of 100,000 in Germany and 1 out of 100,000 in France. Similarly, 650 out of 100,000 Americans were imprisoned in 1997, compared with 90 per 100,000 in France and Germany and 120 out of 100,000 in the United Kingdom.

116. See Raymond Bonner, "Veteran U.S. Envoys Seek End to Executions of Retarded," *New York Times*, June 10, 2001, p. 3. Thus, the chairman of the French National Assembly, Raymond Forni, described U.S. reliance on the death penalty as "savagery," and a prominent French jurist condemned the United States for joining "the head pack of homicidal states, together with China, Iran, the Congo, and Saudi Arabia." Quoted in Lacorne, "Barbaric Americans," p. 54.

117. See Information Office, State Council, People's Republic of China, "The Human Rights Record of the United States in 2004," available at http://english.people.com.cn/200503/03/eng20050303_175406.html; and Peter Edidin, "China Gives America a D," *New York Times*, March 27, 2005, p. 4:7.

118. See Osama bin Laden, "Letter to America." He charges the United States with having "used your force to destroy mankind more than any other nation in history," including the dropping of nuclear bombs on Japan.

119. Barbara Crossette, "US Is Voted Off Rights Panel of the UN For the First Time," *New York Times*, May 4, 2001; and "Vote in U.N. Against U.S. Embargo Against Cuba," *Reuters*, November 27, 2001.

120. See Allison Sparks, "A View of Rome from the Provinces," *Wilson Quarterly* 25 (Spring 2001), p. 48.

121. Quoted in Wang Jisi, "Beauty—and Beast," *Wilson Quarterly* 25 (Spring 2001), p. 61. Or consider the following editorial from the Greek daily newspaper *Eleftherotypia*: "Americans are, yet again, flaunting their arrogance and their contempt for global values. Everything they do is the best, everything they say is the wisest . . . they alone have the right to apply measures that are in their best interest . . . leaving everyone else to obey and follow and perhaps worship." *Foreign Media Reaction*, Office of Research, International Information Programs, U.S. Department of State, August 3, 2001, at http://usinfo.state.gov.

122. See Les Roberts et al., "Mortality before and after the 2003 invasion of Iraq: cluster sample survey," *The Lancet* 364, no. 9448 (2003) published online October 29, 2004, available at www.thelancet.com/extras/04art10342.web.pdf. The authors were faculty members from the Bloomberg School of Public Health at Johns Hopkins University, the College of Medicine at Al-Mustansiriya University in Iraq, and the School of Nursing at Columbia University.

123. See Sam Tanenhaus, "Bush's Brain Trust," *Vanity Fair*, no. 515 (July 2003).

124. See Thomas Borstelmann, *The Cold War and the Color Line: American Race Relations in the Global Arena* (Cambridge: Harvard University Press, 2001).

125. Ahmad's remarks were made at the opening session of the U.S.–Islamic World Forum in Doha, Qatar, on January 10, 2004. He referred explicitly to U.S. support for authoritarian regimes, unilateral sanctions, trade embargoes, and a "hostile approach" to regional conflicts. See "JI Ameer Accuses United States of Hypocrisy," at www.jamaat.org/news/pr011104.html.

126. Quoted in Takeyh, "Iran's Nuclear Calculations."

127. Editorial in *an-Nahar*, excerpted in "Abu Ghreib Scandal: Media Say Rumsfeld's 'Only Option' Is to Resign," *Foreign Media Reaction*, Office of Research, International Information Programs (Washington, DC: U.S. Department of State), May 12, 2004, available at http://usinfo.state.gov.

128. Secretary Albright annoyed her foreign counterparts by declaring that the United States was the "indispensable nation . . ." which "stands taller and hence sees further than other nations," and Secretary Rumsfeld irritated NATO allies by drawing an invidious distinction between "old Europe" (which was skeptical of the Iraq war) and "new Europe" (which was more supportive). He also angered Germans by comparing their country to Libya and Cuba.

129. As Charles Krauthammer put it in 1990, "Why it should matter to Americans that their actions get a Security Council nod from, say, Deng Xiaoping and the butchers of Tiananmen Square is beyond me." Or, as he later wrote: "[B]y what logic is [the UN Security Council] a repository of international morality? How does the approval of France and Russia, acting clearly and rationally in pursuit of their own interests in Iraq (largely oil and investment) confer legitimacy on an invasion?" See "The Unipolar Moment Revisited," *The National Interest* 70 (Winter 2002/03), pp. 11, 17; and also his "Democratic Realism."

130. A Council on Foreign Relations task force observed in 2002: "In the past, foreign policy was often the sole prerogative of nation-states, and it was formed through interaction between heads of state and government ministers. Today, people have far more access to information, more 'soft power' to influence global affairs directly. . . . The information age has democratized communication by providing freedom of access to information, the ability to voice opinions, and the opportunity to enter debate. Therefore, no foreign policy can succeed without a sustained, coordinated capability to understand, inform, and influence people and private organizations, as well as governments." See *Public Diplomacy: A Strategy for Reform* (New York: Council on Foreign Relations, 2002).

131. See Dan Roberts, "Tarnished Image: Is the World Falling Out of Love with U.S. Brands?" *Financial Times*, December 20, 2004, p. 7.

132. As Karzai told the Senate Foreign Relations Committee in February 2003: "If you leave the whole thing for us to fight again, it will be repeating the mistakes that the United States made during the Soviet occupation of Afghanistan." See Kathleen T. Rhem, " 'Don't Forget Afghanistan,' Karzai Cautions U.S. Congress," *American Forces Press Service*, February 26, 2003, available at www.dod.gov/news/Feb2003/n02262003_20.

Chapter 4

1. See Yuen Foong Khong, "Coping with Strategic Uncertainty: The Role of Institutions and Soft Balancing in Southeast Asia's Post–Cold War Strategy," in Allen Carlson, Peter Katzenstein, and J. J. Suh, eds., *Rethinking Security in East Asia: Identity, Power, and Efficiency* (Stanford: Stanford University Press, 2004).

2. For detailed discussions of bandwagoning behavior, see Stephen M. Walt, *The Origins of Alliances* (Ithaca: Cornell University Press, 1987), chaps. 2 and 5; and John J. Mearsheimer, *The Tragedy of Great Power Politics* (New York: W. W. Norton, 2001), pp. 162–64. A slightly different conception can be found in Randall K. Schweller, "Bandwagoning for Profit: Bringing the Revisionist State Back In," *International Security* 19, no. 1 (Summer 1994).

3. Quoted in James Mann, *Rise of the Vulcans: The History of Bush's War Cabinet* (New York: Viking, 2004), p. 237.

4. See Richard Perle, "Should Iraq Be Next?" *San Diego Union-Tribune*, December 16, 2001; and "Those Dictator Dominoes," *Wall Street Journal*, April 15, 2003.

5. See Seymour Hersh, "The Syrian Bet," *The New Yorker*, July 28, 2003.

6. See Gary Samore, "The Korean Nuclear Crisis," *Survival* 45, no. 1 (Spring 2003).

7. See Kamal Nazer Yasin, "U.S. Hard-line Policies Helped Bring About Reformists' Demise in Iran," *Eurasia Insight*, March 8, 2004, available at www.eurasianet.org.

8. Barbara Slavin, "Libya's Rehabilitation in the Works Since the Early '90s," *USA Today*, April 27, 2004.

9. See Ronald Bruce St. John, "Libya Is Not Iraq: Preemptive Strikes, WMD, and Diplomacy," *Middle East Journal* 58, no. 3 (Summer 2004); Flynt Leverett, "Why Libya Gave Up on the Bomb," *New York Times*, January 23, 2004; and Martin Indyk, "The Iraq War Did Not Force Gadaffi's Hand," *Financial Times*, March 9, 2004.

10. According to the International Atomic Energy Agency, Libya had only

managed to produce a few grams of plutonium. See "UN: Libya Converted Small Amount of Plutonium," *Associated Press*, February 20, 2004.

11. Libyans clearly saw long-term benefits to associating with the West. As Ghaddafi's son put it, "If you have the backing of the West and the United States, you will be able to achieve in a few years what you could not achieve in 50." See "Qadhafi's Son Says Libya Was Promised Economic, Military Gains for WMD Disarmament," *Global Security Newswire*, March 10, 2004, at www.nti .org/d_newswire/issues/2004/3/10.

12. See Robert J. Art, "Why Western Europe Needs the United States and NATO," *Political Science Quarterly* 111, no. 1 (Spring 1996); and Christoph Bertram, *Europe in the Balance: Securing the Peace Won in the Cold War* (Washington, DC: Carnegie Endowment for International Peace, 1995).

13. Quoted in Richard Bernstein, "Poland Upstages, and Irks, European Powerhouses," *New York Times*, May 13, 2003; and Ian Fisher, "The U.S. and Its Leader Are Popular with Poles," *New York Times*, June 16, 2001, p. A8.

14. Lee also said, "If the Americans are not around, [the Japanese] cannot be sure who will protect their oil tankers. So they have to do something themselves. That will trigger the Koreans, who fear the Japanese, then the Chinese. Will India then come down to our seas with two aircraft carriers?" To avoid a regional competition, Lee wanted to "stick with what has worked so far"—the U.S. military presence—which he regarded as "*essential* for the continuation of international law and order in East Asia." Quoted in Khong, "Coping with Strategic Uncertainty."

15. Quoted in Amitav Acharya, "Containment, Engagement, or Counter-dominance? Malaysia's Response to the Rise of China," in Alastair Iain Johnston and Robert Ross, eds., *Engaging China: The Management of an Emerging Power* (London: Routledge, 1999), p. 140.

16. Walker adds: "This [trend] started some time ago and Qatar led the way. . . . It capitalised on this to set up a counterforce with other small countries because everyone had suffered under the shadow of the big boys." Adds Saudi political analyst Jamal Khashoggi: "They're all trying to score points with the U.S. at the expense of Saudi Arabia." Quoted in Roula Khalaf, "Arab Minnows Make Waves by Defying Big Neighbours," *Financial Times*, April 5, 2004, p. 5. See also Craig S. Smith, "A Tiny Gulf Kingdom Bets Its Stability on Support for U.S.," *New York Times*, October 24, 2002, p. A14.

17. See Nicholas Wood, "A Fake Macedonian Terror Tale That Led to Deaths," *New York Times*, May 17, 2004; and Juliette Terzief, "A War Against Terror That Went Very Wrong: Fabricating Terrorism to Win U.S. Approval," *San Francisco Chronicle*, June 20, 2004.

18. The term *bonding* was coined by John Ikenberry, in "Strategic Reactions to American Preeminence: Great Power Politics in the Age of Unipolarity,"

Report to the National Intelligence Council, July 28, 2003, available at www.cia.gov/nic.confreports.stratreact.html.

19. See Bradford Perkins, *The Great Rapprochement: England and the United States 1895–1914* (New York: Atheneum, 1968); and Stephen Rock, *Why Peace Breaks Out: Great Power Rapprochement in Historical Perspective* (Chapel Hill: University of North Carolina Press, 1989).

20. See John Dumbrell, *A Special Relationship: Anglo-American Relations in the Cold War and After* (London: Palgrave/Macmillan, 2000).

21. "Text of PM Blair's Speech," available at www.clinton.warwick.ac.uk/blairspch.com.

22. Blair's strategy is carefully documented in Peter Riddell, *Hug Them Close: Blair, Clinton, Bush and the Special Relationship* (London: Politico's Publishing, 2003).

23. Paul Harris, Kamal Ahmed, and Martin Bright, "Seeing Eye to Eye," *The Guardian*, November 16, 2003.

24. Quoted in David Cannadine, "A Special Relationship, or an Abusive One?" *New York Times*, November, 22, 2003.

25. As a close associate of Blair put it (anonymously): "If Tony had gone off and done a Schroeder, we'd have had no influence." Quoted in David Coates and Joel Krieger, *Blair's War* (Cambridge: Polity Press, 2004), pp. 51–53; and see also Cannadine, "A Special Relationship, or an Abusive One?"

26. Michele Dunne, "Libya: Security Is Not Enough," *Policy Brief 32* (Carnegie Endowment for International Peace, Washington, DC), October 2004, p. 2.

27. It is not clear how large Blair's influence really was. He did travel to Camp David in September 2002 to persuade Bush to go to the United Nations, but Philip Gordon and Jeremy Shapiro argue that Bush had already decided to take this step and that Blair was therefore "pushing on an open door." See Philip H. Gordon and Jeremy Shapiro, *Allies at War: America, Europe, and the Crisis over Iraq* (New York: McGraw-Hill, 2004), p. 107; and Brian Groom, "Caught in the Middle," *Financial Times*, February 6, 2002, p. 12.

28. See Patrick E. Tyler, "Blair's Prize Is President's Commitment," *New York Times*, November 13, 2004, p. A6; and Richard Stevenson and Steven R. Weisman, "Bush Says U.S. Will Push Hard for Peace Plan," *New York Times*, November 13, 2004, pp. A1, A6.

29. See "Saudi Arabia Tries to Improve Its Image among Americans," *Alexander's Gas and Oil Connections* 7, no. 18 (September 19, 2002), available at www.gasandoil.com/goc/news/ntn2382/htm.

30. See Horace C. Peterson, *Propaganda for War: The British Campaign against American Neutrality, 1914–1918* (Norman: University of Oklahoma Press,

1939); Ross Y. Koen, *The China Lobby in American Politics* (New York: Harper and Row, 1974); Charles Mathias, "Ethnic Groups and Foreign Policy," *Foreign Affairs* 59, no. 5 (1981); Paul Arthur, "Diasporan Intervention in International Affairs: Irish America as a Case Study," *Diaspora* 1, no. 2 (Fall 1991); and Tony Smith, *Foreign Attachments: The Power of Ethnic Groups in the Making of American Foreign Policy* (Cambridge: Harvard University Press, 2000).

31. Elhanan Helpman and Gene M. Grossman, *Special Interest Politics* (Cambridge: MIT Press, 2002).

32. According to the 2000 Census, there are 1.67 million Indian Americans in the United States, compared with only 153,533 Pakistani Americans. The median household income for Indian Americans in 1999 was $67,669, but the figure for Pakistani Americans was only $47,241. See Jessica S. Barnes and Claudette E. Bennet, "The Asian Population 2000," *Census 2000 Brief* (Washington, DC: Bureau of the Census, 2002); and data generated by Stephen Smith from Census 2000, U.S. Bureau of the Census, using American FactFinder Data Sets, available at http://factfinder.census.gov, accessed November 30, 2004.

33. See Clyde R. Mark, *Israel: U.S. Foreign Assistance*, Issue Brief 85066 (Washington, DC: Congressional Research Service, October 17, 2002); Shirl McArthur, "A Conservative Total for U.S. Aid to Israel: $91 Billion—and Counting," *Washington Report on Middle East Affairs* (January/February 2001), pp. 15–16, from www.washington-report.org/backissues/010201/0101015 .html.

34. This largesse is especially striking when one considers that Israel is not a poor country like Botswana or Bangladesh; in fact, its per capita income is double that of Hungary or the Czech Republic and substantially higher than that of Portugal, New Zealand, or South Korea.

35. A short summary of these arrangements can be found on the AIPAC website, under the heading "United Defense." See www.aipac.org/docu ments/unitedefforts.html, downloaded November 7, 2004.

36. As Israeli military historian Martin Van Creveld notes, "Relative to their enemies, [Israeli] forces are now infinitely more powerful than they were 30 years ago." Martin Van Creveld, "Opportunity Beckons," *Jerusalem Post*, May 15, 2003. See also the appraisal in *The Middle East Strategic Balance 2002–2003* (Tel Aviv: Jaffee Center for Strategic Studies, 2003).

37. See A. F. K. Organski, *The $36 Billion Bargain: Strategy and Politics in U.S. Assistance to Israel* (New York: Columbia University Press, 1991). Even this justification is debatable, however, insofar as U.S. support for Israel also helped drive these states into Moscow's arms.

38. U.S. support for Israel is not the only source of anti-Americanism in the

Arab and Islamic world, nor is it the only motivation for anti-American terrorism. But as the *9/11 Commission Report* noted, "America's policy choices have
consequences. Right or wrong, it is simply a fact that American policy regarding the Israeli-Palestinian conflict and American actions in Iraq are dominant
staples of popular commentary across the Arab and Muslim world." *The 9/11
Commission Report* (New York: W. W. Norton, 2004), p. 376.

39. A 2002 survey of American Jews found that nearly 28 percent were "not
very" or "not at all" attached to Israel, and fewer than half of all American Jews
made contributions to Israel-related charities. American Jews also hold varying
attitudes toward specific Israeli policies—for example, some supported the Oslo
peace process while others opposed it, just as some favor an Israeli withdrawal
from the occupied territories while others favor annexation. See Steven M.
Cohen, *2002 National Survey of American Jews* (New York: Florence G.
Heller/JCCA Research Center, January 2003); and also idem, "An Ambivalent
Loyalty," *Ha'aretz*, January 24, 2003.

40. When a dissenting group of Jewish-Americans formed a pro-peace
group known as *Breira* ("Choice" in Hebrew) in the 1970s, they were condemned by mainstream Jewish organizations and accused of undermining U.S.
support for Israel. The Conference of Presidents of Major American Jewish
Organizations and the National Jewish Community Relations Advisory Council met with Israeli Ambassador Simcha Dinitz to develop guidelines for the
American Jewish community. The first two principles were that Israel alone
should determine its policies, and that American Jews must stand publicly
united with Israel. See J. J. Goldberg, *Jewish Power: Inside the American Jewish
Establishment* (Reading, MA: Addison-Wesley, 1996), p. 208.

41. Quoted in Congressional Quarterly, Inc., *The Middle East*, p. 64; and
Wolf Blitzer, *Between Washington and Jerusalem*, pp. 147–48.

42. For example, when Tony Judt, an American Jew and professor of history
at New York University, wrote an article in the *New York Review of Books* that
described Zionism as an "anachronism" and called for the creation of a bina-
tional state in Palestine, his essay sparked a firestorm of criticism from American
Jews. He was also removed from the masthead of the pro-Israel *New Republic*,
where he had previously been listed as a contributing editor. Similarly, when
Clinton administration aide Robert Malley published an account of the Camp
David talks that blamed their failure more or less equally on all three sides, he
was promptly condemned by a host of Jewish leaders. See Marc Perelman,
"Clinton Aide Attacked for Offering 'Revisionist' Take on Camp David," *For-
ward*, August 3, 2001.

43. Edward Tivnan, *The Lobby: Jewish Political Power and American Foreign Policy* (New York: Simon and Schuster, 1987), p. 76.

44. See Victoria Clark, "The Christian Zionists," *Prospect* (July 2003); Jeff Jacoby, "Israel's Unshakeable Allies," *Boston Globe*, May 15, 2003, p. A15; and Donald Wagner, "The Evangelical-Jewish Alliance," *The Christian Century*, June 28, 2003, pp. 20–24.

45. See "Questions for Dick Armey: Retiring, but not Shy," *New York Times Magazine*, September 1, 2002; and James Bennet, "DeLay Says Palestinians Bear Burden for Achieving Peace," *New York Times*, July 30, 2003. One would think that the number-one priority for the Speaker of the House would be to "protect America," but that is not what Armey said.

46. For many years, the senior Brookings staff member on Middle East issues was William B. Quandt, a distinguished academic and former U.S. government official. Quandt's books and articles focused primarily on U.S. interests and favored neither the Israeli nor the Arab side. Today, policy analysis on Middle East issues at Brookings is conducted through its Saban Center for Middle East Policy, which is named for and financed by Haim Saban, a wealthy Israeli-American businessman who has said, "I'm a one-issue guy, and my issue is Israel." The director of the Saban Center is Martin Indyk, former research director of AIPAC, founder of WINEP, and former U.S. ambassador to Israel. Thus, what was once an evenhanded policy institute has moved in a decidedly pro-Israel direction. For a revealing profile of Saban, see "Schlepping to Moguldom," *New York Times*, September 5, 2004.

47. The businessman, Michael Goland, had been a board member of a political action committee run by Morris Amitay, the former head of AIPAC, who later conceded that he had "given Goland legal advice and put him in touch with a direct mail firm specializing in Jewish donors." See Tivnan, *The Lobby*, p. 191.

48. Quoted in Tivnan, *The Lobby*, p. 191. Other examples of politicians defeated in part due to AIPAC's efforts include Cynthia McKinney (D-GA), Earl Hilliard (D-AL), Paul Findley, (R-IL), J. William Fulbright (D-AR), Roger Jepsen (R-IA), and Pete McCloskey (R-CA).

49. Quoted in Camille A. Mansour, *Beyond Alliance: Israel in U.S. Foreign Policy* (New York: Columbia University Press, 1994), p. 242. As former AIPAC head Morris Amitay remarked some years ago, "There are now a lot of guys at the working level up here [on Capitol Hill] . . . who happen to be Jewish, who are willing . . . to look at certain issues in terms of their Jewishness. . . . These are all guys who are in a position to make the decision in these areas for these senators. . . . You can get an awful lot done just at the staff level." Quoted in Stephen Isaacs, *Jews and American Politics* (New York: Doubleday, 1974), pp. 255–57.

50. As a member of the U.S. negotiating team at Camp David later admitted, Israeli proposals "were presented generally as US concepts, not Israeli

ones." See Hussein Agha and Robert Malley, "Camp David: The Tragedy of Errors," *New York Review of Books*, August 9, 2001. This is the same tactic that led a Palestinian negotiator at the talks on Hebron to observe: "We are negotiating with two Israeli teams—one displaying an Israeli flag, and one an American flag." Quoted in Laura Blumenfeld, "Three Peace Suits; For These Passionate American Diplomats, A Middle East Settlement Is the Goal of a Lifetime," *Washington Post*, February 24, 1997.

51. These individuals include Deputy Secretary of Defense Paul Wolfowitz, Undersecretary of Defense Douglas Feith, Vice Presidential Chief of Staff Lewis Libby, Assistant Secretary of State John Bolton, National Security Council staffer Elliott Abrams, Vice Presidential advisor David Wurmser, and the former head of the Defense Policy Board, Richard Perle.

52. See Eric Alterman, "Intractable Foes, Warring Narratives," MSNBC. com, April 2, 2002, downloaded from www.alternet.org/story.html?StoryID= 12769.

53. In 2002, the pro-Israel group Campus Watch established a website listing U.S. academics suspected of being anti-Israel and encouraging students to report professors making anti-Israel statements. See Kristine McNeill, "The War on Academic Freedom," *The Nation*, November 11, 2003; and Will Rasmussen, "Middle East Courses Plant a Flag in U.S. College Classrooms," *The Daily Star*, July 1, 2004.

54. See Mathias, "Ethnic Groups and Foreign Policy," pp. 975–77.

55. Quoted in Isaacs, *Jews and American Politics*, pp. 255–57, and Congressional Quarterly, Inc., *The Middle East*, 5th ed. (Washington, DC: Congressional Quarterly, 1981), p. 68.

56. On the weak impact of the "Arab lobby," see Ali A. Mazrui, "Between the Crescent and the Star-Spangled Banner: American Muslims and U.S. Foreign Policy," *International Affairs* 72, no. 3 (July 1996), pp. 493–506; Nabeel A. Khoury, "The Arab Lobby: Problems and Prospects," *Middle East Journal* 41, no. 3 (Summer 1987), pp. 379–96; and Andrea Barron, "Jewish and Arab Diasporas in the United States and Their Impact on U.S. Middle East Policy," in Yehuda Lukacs and Abdalla M. Battah, eds., *The Arab-Israeli Conflict: Two Decades of Change* (London: Westview, 1988), pp. 238–59.

57. Downloaded from the AIPAC website, www.aipac.org [emphasis added].

58. See Robert G. Kaiser, "Bush and Sharon Nearly Identical on Mideast Policy," *Washington Post*, February 9, 2003.

59. On these incidents, see James Bennet, "Sharon Invokes Munich in Warning U.S. on 'Appeasement,'" *New York Times*, October 5, 2001; Alan Sipress and Lee Hockstader, "Sharon Speech Riles U.S.," *Washington Post*, October 6, 2001; Jane Perlez and Katharine Q. Seelye, "U.S. Strongly Rebukes Sharon for Criticism of Bush, Calling It 'Unacceptable'," *New York Times*, Octo-

ber 6, 2001; Elaine Sciolino, "Senators Urge Bush Not To Hamper Israel," *New York Times*, November 17, 2001; Dana Milbank, "Bush Spokesman Gentle on Israeli Assault," *Washington Post*, December 3, 2001; David Sanger, "U.S. Walks a Tightrope on Terrorism in Israel," *New York Times*, December 4, 2001; Fareed Zakaria, "Colin Powell's Humiliation: Bush Should Clearly Support His Secretary of State," *Newsweek*, April 29, 2002; and Arieh O'Sullivan, "Visiting Congressmen Advise Israel to Resist Administration Pressure to Deal with Arafat," *Jerusalem Post*, May 6, 2002.

60. See Ehud Barak, "Taking Apart Iraq's Nuclear Threat," *New York Times*, September 4, 2002; Benjamin Netanyahu, "The Case for Toppling Saddam," *Wall Street Journal*, September 20, 2002. The Israeli newspaper *Ha'aretz* reported on August 16, 2002, that "Israel is pressing the United States not to defer action aimed at toppling Saddam Hussein's regime in Iraq," and a related article published the same day quoted one of Sharon's aides as saying that putting off the attack "will only give him [Saddam] more of an opportunity to accelerate his program of weapons of mass destruction." In February 2003, *Ha'aretz* reported that Israel's military and political leadership "yearns for war in Iraq." See Aluf Benn, "PM Urging U.S. Not to Delay Strike against Iraq," *Ha'aretz*, August 16, 2002; idem, "PM Aide: Delay in U.S. Attack Lets Iraq Speed Up Arms Program," *Ha'aretz*, August 16, 2002; Jason Keyser, "Israel Urges U.S. to Attack," *Washington Post*, August 16, 2002; "Enthusiastic IDF Awaits War in Iraq," *Ha'aretz*, February 17, 2003; and also James Bennet, "Israel Says War on Iraq Would Benefit the Region," *New York Times*, February 27, 2003; and "Jerusalem Frets as U.S. Battles Iraq War Delays," *Forward*, March 7, 2003.

61. See "An Unseemly Silence," *Forward*, May 7, 2004; and also Gary Rosenblatt, "Hussein Asylum," *Jewish Week*, August 23, 2002; idem, "The Case for War against Saddam," *Jewish Week*, December 13, 2002. The president of the Conference of Presidents of Major American Jewish Organizations, Mortimer B. Zuckerman, was also a staunch advocate of war. See his "No Time for Equivocation," *U.S. News & World Report*, August 26/September 2, 2002; idem, "Clear and Compelling Proof," *U.S. News & World Report*, February 10, 2003; idem, "The High Price of Waiting," *U.S. News & World Report*, March 10, 2003.

62. The main advocates of war included Deputy Secretary of Defense Paul Wolfowitz and Undersecretary of Defense Douglas Feith, who had coauthored (with fellow neoconservative Richard Perle) a study for then–Prime Minister Benjamin Netanyahu in 1996, calling for a "clean break" from the Oslo peace process and active efforts to depose or intimidate the Syrian, Iraqi, and Iranian governments. See *A Clean Break: A New Strategy for Securing the Realm*, Institute for Advanced Strategic and Political Studies, Jerusalem (June 1996). On the campaign for war within the administration, see Susan Page, "Showdown with

Saddam: The Decision to Act," *USA Today*, September 11, 2002; Michael Elliott, "First Stop: Iraq," *Time*, March 21, 2003; Greg Miller, "Spy Unit Skirted CIA on Iraq," *Los Angeles Times*, March 10, 2004; Julian Borger, "The Spies Who Pushed for War," *The Guardian*, July 17, 2003; Jim Lobe, "Pentagon Office Home to Neo-Con Network," *Inter Press Service*, August 7, 2003; and Karen Kwiatkowski, "The New Pentagon Papers," *salon.com*, March 10, 2004.

63. See Samuel G. Freedman, "Don't Blame Jews for This War," *USA Today*, April 2, 2003.

64. On these efforts, see Bennet, "Israel Says War on Iraq Would Benefit the Region"; Robert S. Greenberger and Karby Leggett, "President's Dream: Changing Not Just Regime but a Region: A Pro-U.S., Democratic Area Is a Goal that Has Israeli and Neo-Conservative Roots," *Wall Street Journal*, March 21, 2003; George Packer, "Dreaming of Democracy," *New York Times Magazine*, March 2, 2003; Molly Moore, "Sharon Asks U.S. to Pressure Syria on Militants," *Washington Post*, April 17, 2003; Marc Perelman, "Behind Warnings to Damascus: Reassessment of Younger Assad," *Forward*, April 18, 2003; Ori Nir, "Sharon Aide Makes the Case for U.S. Action Against Syria," *Forward*, April 18, 2003; Shimon Peres, "We Must Unite to Prevent an Ayatollah Nuke," *Wall Street Journal*, June 25, 2003; "New U.S. Concerns on Iran's Pursuit of Nuclear Arms," *New York Times*, May 8, 2003; Marc Perelman, "Pentagon Team on Iran Comes Under Fire," *Forward*, June 6, 2003; Rachel Brownstein, "Those Who Sought War Are Now Pushing Peace," *Los Angeles Times*, April 17, 2003; William Kristol, "The End of the Beginning," *Weekly Standard*, May 12, 2003; Lawrence F. Kaplan, "Iranamok," *New Republic*, May 9, 2003; and Daniel Pipes and Patrick Clawson, "Turn Up the Pressure on Iran," *Jerusalem Post*, May 20, 2003.

65. For example, Syria was a useful partner in the U.S. campaign against al Qaeda after September 11, tipping off the United States regarding a possible attack in the Persian Gulf and giving the CIA access to a prominent al Qaeda recruiter (Mohammed Zammar), who was in Syrian custody. When the Bush administration tried to pressure Syria in the immediate aftermath of the Iraq invasion, however, Damascus promptly cut off these valuable contacts. See Hersh, "Syrian Bet."

66. Downloaded from the AIPAC website, www.aipac.org [emphasis added].

67. According to the 2000 census, for example, Indian Americans earned an average household income of roughly $68,000, compared to a national median income of roughly $41,000.

68. See Amy Waldman, "The Bond Between India and Israel Grows," *New York Times*, September 7, 2003.

69. See Amitabh Pal, "An Alliance of Insecurity," at www.alternet.org/story/17820.

70. He continues: "The Jewish–Indian alliance worked together to gain the Bush administration's approval for Israel's sale of four Phalcon early warning radar planes to India. Moreover, in July 2003 they were successful in getting added to a U.S. aid package for Pakistan an amendment calling on Islamabad to stop Islamic militants from crossing into India and to prevent the spread of WMD." See Efraim Inbar, "The Indian-Israeli Entente," *Orbis* 48, no. 1 (February 2004), p. 102.

71. See Waldman, "The Bond between India and Israel Grows."

72. See Aminah Mohammed-Arif, "The Lobbying Game of the Indian and Pakistani Diasporas in the US," Center for Indian and South Asian Studies, Paris, 2001; and Jill McGivering, "India Forges Closer Ties with Diaspora," *BBC News World Edition/South Asia,* January 9, 2003.

73. Prime Minister Atal Vajpayee, "Address to the Conference on the Contributions of Persons of Indian Origin," New Delhi, February 2000, available at http://www.indianembassy.org/special/cabinet/Primeminister/pm_feb_12_2000 .htm.

74. See Daniel Morrow and Michael Carriere, "The Economic Impacts of the 1998 Sanctions against India and Pakistan," *Non-Proliferation Review* 6, no. 4 (Fall 1999); and Robert M. Hathaway, "Confrontation and Retreat: The U.S. Congress and the South Asian Nuclear Tests," *Arms Control Today* 30, no. 1 (January/February 2000).

75. See Celia W. Dugger, "U.S. and India Map Path to Military Cooperation: More Arms Sales Are Seen," *New York Times*, November 6, 2001, p. B2.

76. *Report of the High Level Committee on the Indian Diaspora* (New Delhi: Government of India, January 2002), pp. xx–xxi [emphasis added].

77. During the 1990s, U.S. foreign aid to Armenia averaged $13.25 per capita, whereas the median level of aid to all Caspian Sea nations (Armenia, Georgia, Turkey, Kyrgyzstan, Turkmenistan, Tajikistan, Russia, and Kazakhstan) was only $1.56 per capita. Azerbaijan received an average of $1.18 per capita during this period. Based on data from *U.S. AID Loans and Grants* (Washington, DC: Agency for International Development, various years), cited in David King and Miles Pomper, "Congress and the Contingent Influence of Diaspora Lobbies: U.S. Foreign Policy Towards Armenia," *Journal of Armenian Studies,* forthcoming. See also Ekaterine Metreveli and Ester Hakobyan, "The Political Underpinnings of U.S. Bilateral Aid to the Countries of Transcaucasus," *Demokratizatsiya* 9, no. 3 (Summer 2001), pp. 367–81.

78. This section specifically states that U.S. foreign aid "may not be provided to the Government of Azerbaijan until the President determines, and so reports to the Congress, that the Government of Azerbaijan is taking demonstrable steps to cease all blockades and other offensive uses of forces against Armenia

and Nagorno-Karabakh." See *U.S. Public Law 102–511*. Section 907 does not ban Trade and Development Agency guarantees to U.S. firms investing in Azerbaijan, and does not prohibit other U.S. aid programs designed to foster commerce (such as Export-Import Bank and OPIC programs).

79. Quoted in Smith, *Foreign Attachments*, p. 14.

80. On this point, see Heather Gregg, "Divided They Conquer: The Success of Armenian Ethnic Lobbies in the United States," *Rosemary Rogers Working Paper Series No. 13* (Center for International Studies, Massachusetts Institute of Technology, August 2002).

81. According to former Senator Robert Torricelli (D-NJ), "As an organized community, the Armenians have few peers. As a source of campaign funding help, they are clearly one of the most prodigious." Quoted in Carroll J. Doherty, "Foreign Aid and Favored Nations," *CQ Weekly*, August 6, 1994; and see also Michael Dobbs, "Foreign Aid Shrinks, but Not for All: With Clout in Congress, Armenia's Share Grows," *Washington Post*, January 24, 2001, p. A1.

82. See Gregg, "Divided They Conquer," pp. 11–13.

83. As political scientists David King and Miles Pomper note, "Until U.S. petroleum companies rushed into the Caspian region . . . there were no effective groups lobbying Congress on behalf of anyone but the Armenians." See King and Pomper, "Congress and the Contingent Influence of Diaspora Lobbies."

84. Indeed, the FY2003 foreign-aid bill maintained the $90 million economic-aid allotment and added $4 million in military aid. See Gregg, "Divided They Conquer," pp. 23–24.

85. Gregg, "Divided They Conquer," p. 1.

Chapter 5

1. Advocates of this approach include Charles Krauthammer, "The Unipolar Moment," *Foreign Affairs* 70, no. 1 (1990–91); William Kristol and Robert Kagan, "Toward a Neo-Reaganite Foreign Policy," *Foreign Affairs* 75, no. 4 (July/August 1996); idem, eds., *Present Dangers: Crisis and Opportunity in American Foreign and Defense Policy* (San Francisco: Encounter Books, 2000); and the various individuals associated with the Project for a New American Century. Many of these ideas are implicit in the Bush administration's *National Security Strategy*, released in September 2002.

2. Thus, historian Niall Ferguson maintains that an American empire would be desirable, but he believes the United States lacks the institutions, domestic character, and will to achieve it. See his *Colossus: The Price of America's Empire* (New York: Penguin, 2004).

3. See Robert J. Art, *A Grand Strategy for America* (Ithaca: Cornell University Press, 2003); Henry Kissinger, *Does America Need a Foreign Policy? Toward a Diplomacy for the Twenty-first Century* (New York: Simon and Schuster, 2001); and Joseph S. Nye, *The Paradox of American Power: Why the World's Only Superpower Cannot Go It Alone* (New York: Oxford, 2001).

4. See John J. Mearsheimer, *The Tragedy of Great Power Politics* (New York: W. W. Norton, 2001), especially chap. 7; and Christopher Layne, "From Preponderance to Offshore Balancing: America's Future Grand Strategy," *International Security* 22, no. 1 (Summer 1997).

5. By limiting U.S. military commitments overseas, an offshore-balancing strategy might actually make it easier for the United States to intervene when mass murder or genocide seemed likely.

6. See *The Economist*, September 21, 1996; François Heisbourg, "American Hegemony? Perceptions of the U.S. Abroad," *Survival* 41, no. 4 (Winter 1999–2000), pp. 10–15; and Martin Walker, "What Europeans Think of America," *World Policy Journal* 17, no. 2 (Summer 2000), pp. 26–38.

7. Quoted in P. Edward Haley, *Revolution and Intervention: The Diplomacy of Taft and Wilson with Mexico, 1910–1917* (Cambridge: MIT Press, 1970), p. 100.

8. See David M. Edelstein, "Occupational Hazards: Why Military Occupations Succeed or Fail," *International Security* 29, no. 1 (Summer 2004). As of April 2005, the war in Iraq had cost over 1,500 American soldiers dead and more than 11,000 wounded, along with additional foreign and civilian deaths and tens of thousands of Iraqi casualties. The war had also cost approximately $160 billion as of that date, or nearly $500 per U.S. citizen.

9. It is worth noting that the publication of the *National Security Strategy* (2002) and its trumpeting by key administration spokesmen (including President Bush) did not convince Saddam Hussein to leave power voluntarily so as to avoid a U.S. attack.

10. See Stephen M. Walt, "Building Up New Bogeymen," *Foreign Policy* 106 (Spring 1997).

11. For a bipartisan proposal for a more nuanced U.S. policy toward Iran, see Zbigniew Brzezinski and Robert Gates, Co-Chairs, *Iran: Time for a New Approach*, Report of an Independent Task Force, Council on Foreign Relations (New York, 2004).

12. See Peter G. Peterson, Chair, *Finding America's Voice: A Strategy for Reinvigorating U.S. Public Diplomacy*, Report of an Independent Task Force (New York: Council on Foreign Relations, 2003); and David Hoffman, "Beyond Public Diplomacy," *Foreign Affairs* 81, no. 2 (March/April 2002).

13. When al Qaeda was created in the late 1980s, its leadership included a committee in charge of media affairs and propaganda. See *The 9/11 Commis-*

sion Report: The Final Report of the National Commission on Terrorist Attacks Upon the United States (New York: W. W. Norton, 2004), pp. 56, 362.

14. According to the State Department's Advisory Group on Public Diplomacy for the Arab and Muslim World: "Transformed public diplomacy can make America safer, but it must be sustained for decades, not stopped and started as moods change in the world." The Advisory Group also noted that only fifty-four State Department employees were fully fluent in Arabic, and that "only a handful can hold their own on television." See *Changing Minds, Winning Peace: A New Strategic Direction for U.S. Public Diplomacy in the Arab and Muslim World* (Washington, DC, 2003), pp. 17, 27.

15. There were nearly 600,000 foreign students studying in the United States in 2002, roughly double the number from two decades previously. See Institute of International Education, *Open Doors 2003*, summarized at www.opendoors.iienetwork.org.

16. This tendency is especially pronounced in U.S. law, business, and public-policy schools, which emphasize the virtues of competitive markets, democratic institutions, and the rule of law.

17. As the State Department's Advisory Commission on Public Diplomacy put it, " 'Spin' and manipulative public relations and propaganda are not the answer. Foreign policy counts. . . . [W]e were struck by the depth of opposition to many of our policies. Citizens in these countries are genuinely distressed at the plight of Palestinians and at the role they perceive the United States to be playing, and they are genuinely distressed by the situation in Iraq. Sugar-coating and fast-talking are no solutions, nor is absenting ourselves." See *Changing Minds, Winning Peace*, p. 18.

18. Israel is far more secure now than it was when it first occupied the West Bank and the Gaza Strip in June 1967. In 1967, Israel's defense spending was less than half the combined defense expenditures of Egypt, Iraq, Jordan, and Syria; today, Israel spends roughly 30 percent more than these four states combined (and Iraq is occupied by Israel's main ally). Israel's adversaries used to get substantial military aid from the Soviet Union; today, the Soviet Union is gone and Israel's ties to the United States have grown. Israel had no nuclear weapons back in 1967; today it has dozens. Within the 1967 borders, in short, Israel is more secure than it has ever been, and it is only the continued occupation of the West Bank and Gaza that creates a serious security problem for Israel, in the form of terrorist violence. Israel's supporters in the United States are doing it no favors by continuing to make the occupation possible.

19. Israel and the Palestinians will also have to reach agreement on the "right of return"—the right of displaced Palestinians to return to their homes. Allowing this "right" to be exercised in full would threaten Israel's identity and

is clearly infeasible, but the basic principle is both an essential issue of justice and an issue on which the Palestinians will not compromise save in the context of a final settlement. To resolve this dilemma, Israel should acknowledge a "right" of return, and the Palestinians must formally agree to give up this right in exchange for compensation. The United States and the European Union could organize and finance a generous program of reconstruction aid to compensate the Palestinians, which would be formally understood to end any and all claims for the physical return of Palestinians into what is now Israeli territory.

20. As President Bill Clinton told the Israel Policy Forum on January 7, 2001: "Both Prime Minister Barak and Chairman Arafat have now accepted these parameters as the basis for further efforts. Both have expressed some reservations." See www.ipforum.org/display.cfm?rid=544.

21. Opponents of this approach sometimes note that al Qaeda planned its attacks on the United States during the heyday of the post–Oslo peace process, thereby suggesting that a shift in U.S. Middle East policy would have no effect on Islamic hatred of the United States. Thus, Max Boot calls it a "fantasy to think that some change in Middle East policy would have an effect on the terrorists. For years, you had Bill Clinton focusing like a laser on an Israeli-Palestinian settlement, and did that discourage bin Laden from plotting to destroy us?" Quoted in Roger Cohen, "Israel, the U.S., and the Age of Terror," *New York Times*, November 7, 2004, p. 4:1. In fact, Clinton did not focus "laser-like" until very late in his second term and did not achieve an actual peace *agreement*. More important, the goal is not to win over Osama bin Laden; the goal is to reduce popular sympathy for Islamic radicalism and to marginalize these groups within Arab and Muslim societies. Given the overwhelming evidence that U.S. support for Israel's occupation fuels anti-Americanism in many parts of the world, pushing for a fair and just settlement is critical to addressing the terrorist problem.

22. See A. Shavit, "Weisglas: Disengagement is Formaldehyde for Peace Process," *Ha'aretz*, October 8, 2004.

23. See in particular Matthew Bunn, Anthony Weir, and John Holdren, *Controlling Nuclear Warheads and Materials: A Report Card and Action Plan* (Cambridge: Project on Managing the Atom, Belfer Center for Science and International Affairs, 2004); Matthew Bunn, *The Next Wave: Urgently Needed New Steps to Control Warheads and Fissile Material* (Cambridge: Project on Managing the Atom, Belfer Center for Science and International Affairs, 2000); and Graham T. Allison, *Nuclear Terrorism: The Ultimate Preventable Catastrophe* (New York: Henry Holt, 2004).

24. For a good summary of recent proposals, see George Perkovich et al.,

Universal Compliance: A Strategy for Nuclear Security (Washington, DC: Carnegie Endowment for International Peace, 2004), available at http://wmd.ceip .matrixgroup.net/UniversalCompliance.pdf.

25. On the Bush administration's nuclear-weapons proposals, see "The Nuclear Posture Review," *IISS Strategic Comments* 8, no. 3 (April 2002); Walter Pincus, "Nuclear Plans Go Beyond Cuts, Bush Seeks a New Generation of Weapons, Delivery Systems" *Washington Post*, February 19, 2002; "Faking Nuclear Restraint: The Bush Administration's Secret Plan for Strengthening U.S. Nuclear Forces," Washington, DC: National Resources Defense Council, at www.nrdc.org/media/pressreleases/020213a.asp. Excerpts from the 2002 Nuclear Posture Review can be found at www.globalsecurity.org/wmd/ library/policy/dod/npr.htm.

26. El-Baradei's statement is worth quoting at length: "Unless [the eight nuclear weapons states] send a strong message that they are really committed to move to a nuclear disarmament . . . nuclear weapons will continue to be very attractive for others, you know, as a sense of deterrent, as a sense of power, as a sense of prestige." See Mohamed El-Baradei, "Transcript of Remarks at the Council on Foreign Relations," May 14, 2004, downloaded from www.cfr.org on September 21, 2004.

27. In Article VI of the 1967 Nuclear Non-Proliferation Treaty, the signatories agreed "to pursue negotiations in good faith on effective measures relating to cessation of the nuclear arms race at an early date and to nuclear disarmament, and on a Treaty on general and complete disarmament under strict and effective international control." Although strategic nuclear arsenals have been reduced, a remaining arsenal of more than seven thousand weapons and plans for a new generation of weapons hardly constitutes "cessation of the nuclear arms race at an early date" or "general and complete disarmament."

28. See "2000 NPT Review Conference Final Document," at www.arms control.org/act/2000_06/docjun.asp. For a defense of the Bush administration's approach to proliferation, which also reveals a lack of enthusiasm for the thirteen steps, see "The Bush Administration's Nonproliferation Policy: An Interview with Assistant Secretary of State John S. Wolf," *Arms Control Today* 34, no. 5 (June 2004).

29. For an authoritative bipartisan statement on the feasibility of deep reductions, see Committee on International Security and Arms Control, National Academy of Sciences, *The Future of U.S. Nuclear Weapons Policy* (Washington, DC: National Academy Press, 1997).

30. See Mearsheimer, *The Tragedy of Great Power Politics*, chap. 10; and idem, "Better to Be Godzilla than Bambi," *Foreign Policy* 146 (January/February 2005).

31. See "Bush Tells Veterans of Plan to Redeploy G.I.'s Worldwide," *New York Times*, August 17, 2004; "The U.S. Global Posture Review," *IISS Strategic Comments* 10, no. 7 (September 2004), pp. 1–2, downloaded from www.iiss .org/stratcom.

32. For example, it is perfectly permissible to lobby on behalf of a foreign country, or to write articles favoring policies that would benefit a foreign country, but it is considered treason for someone to pass classified information to a foreign power, unless specifically authorized to do so.

33. By way of illustration, nonmilitary spending on international affairs (i.e., the State Department, foreign aid, United Nations dues, information programs, etc.) has declined 20 percent in real terms since 1986. The United States spent about 1.0 percent of its GDP on these programs in 1962—when it had a Cold War to win—but it spends only 0.2 percent of its GDP today. These are not the budgetary priorities of a Great Power that is really serious about using all the instruments of influence at its disposal.

ACKNOWLEDGMENTS

I have incurred many debts in writing this book, and it is a pleasure to acknowledge them now.

Research support from the Weatherhead Center for International Affairs, Harvard University, and the Dean's Research Fund at the John F. Kennedy School of Government was critical to completing this project. I am also grateful to the Ford Foundation for a travel grant that enabled me to conduct interviews in Japan and India. I would also like to thank the Belfer Center for Science and International Affairs and its director, Graham T. Allison, for providing office space for my research assistants during the final year of writing. I also thank then–U.S. ambassador to India, Robert Blackwill, and his senior adviser, Ashley Tellis, for facilitating my visit to New Delhi, and I offer similar thanks to Richard Samuels of MIT, who opened doors for me in Japan. I am especially grateful to the various individuals who shared their ideas about American power with me, including Deepanshu Bagchee, Kanti Bajpai, P. R. Chari, Pran Chopra, Brahma Chellaney, Arvind Gupta, Bharat Kharnad, Vijai Nair, Rajesh Rajagopalan, V. R. Raghavan, Masaru Honda, Hisao Mitsuyu,

Masashi Nishihara, Yukio Okamoto, Yushio Okawara, Hisahiko Okazaki, and Akihiko Tanaka.

Portions of this book were presented at seminars or lectures at the Belfer Center for Science and International Affairs, Harvard University; the Carnegie Endowment for International Peace; the Hamilton Hall Lecture Series in Salem, Massachusetts; the Program on International Security Policy at the University of Chicago; Boston University, the University of Missouri–St. Louis, the Mershon Center at Ohio State University; Ohio Wesleyan University; Purdue University, the Institute for Defence and Strategic Studies in Singapore, the National Defence College in New Delhi, Yale University; the International Institute of Strategic Studies, the Central Intelligence Agency; and the Naval War College. I am grateful to these institutions for allowing me to present this work "in progress," and I thank the participants in these sessions for their many helpful comments.

I am also grateful to the scholars who read and commented on some or all of the manuscript, including Robert Art, Matt Bunn, Seyom Brown, Jeff Frankel, Robert Lawrence, Steve Miller, Samantha Power, Fred Schauer, and Lawrence Summers. Each offered valuable suggestions (many of which I took) but I alone am responsible for any errors of fact or interpretation that remain. I also offer thanks to Jeff Kaplow, Stephen Smith, and Mark Haas for exemplary research assistance, and to the indispensable David Wright, who keeps the rest of my professional life in order.

A few passages in this book draw on some of my earlier writings, including "American Primacy: Its Prospects and Pitfalls," published in *Naval War College Review* 55, no. 2 (Spring 2002), and "Keeping the World 'Off-Balance': Self-Restraint and U.S. Foreign Policy," in G. John Ikenberry, ed., *America Unrivaled: The Future of the Balance of Power* (Cornell University Press, 2001). I thank both publishers for permitting me to use this material here

Three other individuals merit special thanks. My editor, Roby Harrington, was a genial scold when progress was slow and an astute critic once the book began to take shape. His friendship and encouragement are greatly appreciated. Some portions of chapter 4 draw on research conducted jointly with John Mearsheimer of the University of Chicago, and the arguments in that chapter owe much to his own efforts and insights. I also thank him for his suggestions on the rest of the manuscript and his friendship over many years. My wife, Rebecca Stone, was a valuable critic and an unfailing source of support. She also performed major reconstructive surgery on several portions of the manuscript, and what positive qualities these sections may now possess are due in large part to her own talents as writer, editor, and muse.

Finally, I dedicate this book to my children, Gabriel and Katherine. It's done. What would you like to do now?

INDEX